Contemporary Korean Political Thought and Park Chung-hee

East Asian Comparative Ethics, Politics and Philosophy of Law

Series Editors: Philip J. Ivanhoe, Chair Professor of East Asia Comparative Philosophy and Religion and Director of the Center for East Asian and Comparative Philosophy (CEACOP) at City University of Hong Kong; Sungmoon Kim, Associate Professor of Political Theory at City University of Hong Kong; Eirik Lang Harris, Assistant Professor of Philosophy at City University of Hong Kong

East Asian Comparative Ethics, Politics and Philosophy of Law series features path-breaking and field-defining works in East Asian comparative philosophy with a special interest in works of normative and applied ethics, political theory and philosophy of law.

Confucianism, Law, and Democracy in Contemporary Korea, edited by Sungmoon Kim.

Traditional Korean Philosophy: Problems and Debates edited by Youngsun Back and Philip J. Ivanhoe.

Contemporary Korean Political Thought and Park Chung-hee by Jung In Kang.

Contemporary Korean Political Thought and Park Chung-hee

Jung In Kang

ROWMAN &
LITTLEFIELD
——————INTERNATIONAL

London • New York

Published by Rowman & Littlefield International Ltd.
6 Tinworth Street, London SE11 5AL
www.rowmaninternational.com

Rowman & Littlefield International Ltd.is an affiliate of Rowman & Littlefield
4501 Forbes Boulevard, Suite 200, Lanham, Maryland 20706, USA
With additional offices in Boulder, New York, Toronto (Canada), and Plymouth (UK)
www.rowman.com

British Library Cataloguing in Publication Data
A catalogue record for this book is available from the British Library

ISBN: HB 978-1-78660-248-0
       PB 978-1-78660-249-7

Library of Congress Cataloging-in-Publication Data Available

Names: Kang, Jung In, 1952- author.
Title: Contemporary Korean political thought and Park Chung-hee / Jung In Kang.
Description: Lanham : Rowman & Littlefield International, 2017. | Series: East Asian
   comparative ethics, politics, and philosophy of law | Includes bibliographical
   references and index.
Identifiers: LCCN 2017007964 (print) | LCCN 2017024935 (ebook) | ISBN
   9781786602503 (Electronic) | ISBN 9781786602480 (cloth : alk. paper) | ISBN
   9781786602497 (paperback)
Subjects: LCSH: Park, Chung Hee, 1917-1979—Political and social views. | Park,
   Chung Hee, 1917-1979—Influence. | Korea (South)—Politics and government—
   1960-1988. | Political science—Korea (South)—History—20th century. |
   Authoritarianism—Korea (South)—History—20th century.
Classification: LCC DS922.42.P34 (ebook) | LCC DS922.42.P34 K35 2017 (print) |
   DDC 320.095195—dc23
LC record available at https://lccn.loc.gov/2017007964

♾™ The paper used in this publication meets the minimum requirements of American
National Standard for Information Sciences—Permanence of Paper for Printed Library
Materials, ANSI/NISO Z39.48-1992.

Printed in the United States of America

This book is dedicated to my family

Contents

Author's Note

In the main text and endnotes of this book all Korean, Chinese, and Japanese names appear in the text with the family name preceding the given name (the references follow the English-language practice of given name first). Also, the conventional transliterations for Korean, Chinese, and Japanese are used.

The source for the speeches and statements of Park Chung-hee that are quoted or otherwise cited herein is *Park Chung-hee Daetongnyeongyeonseol-munjip* [The Collected Speeches of President Park Chung-hee], published by Daetongnyeongbiseosil. It consists of six volumes and one *jip*—a booklet—covering the period from 1961 to 1979. When I quote or refer to one of Park's speeches or statements, its title and date are given, with the numbers of the volume (or *jip*) and pages added at the end for convenience: for example, "Air Force Academy Graduation Ceremony Address," February 22, 1963, 1:378.

Throughout the text, unless otherwise noted, translations into English of Korean texts are by me.

Preface

In order to understand the democratization of Korean politics and the "Koreanization" of democracy over the last seven decades since the establishment of South Korea in 1948, it is necessary to examine the ideological terrain of contemporary Korean politics, the characteristics of which have taken shape in the ongoing process of Korea's accommodation of four major ideologies of Western origin: liberalism (or liberal democracy), conservatism, nationalism, and socialism (or radicalism). These four ideologies have shaped democratization, competing with one another for political mastery and legitimacy, while they were in turn molded interactively to adapt themselves to democracy. I believe that such a task should be carried out with keen awareness and thorough clarification of the peripheral and belated nature of the Korean polity in modern world history. In other words, it requires macroscopic yet careful insight into the structural conditions that give Korea's contemporary ideological topography its own distinctive features in the context of world history shaped and dominated by Western civilization.

Focusing on these four ideologies, this book analyzes the ideological landscape of contemporary Korean politics while comparing it with that of European early comers such as England and France. This task is carried out by elucidating these ideologies in light of two concepts, the "simultaneity of the non-simultaneous" and the "sanctification of nationalism." These concepts are derived from my own reflection upon the characteristic experience that peripheral latecomer countries such as Korea had to undergo in accommodating political ideas and ideologies from the early-comer countries in the West. *Nonsimultaneity* is a structural property brewed from the clash between world historical time (a product of Western-centrism) and Korean national historical time and the resulting suppression, repulsion, mutation, and convergence, whereas *sanctification* can be seen as a substantive quality of the same terrain, formed by a combination of the defining influence of nonsimultaneity and Korea's own particular historical experiences since the late nineteenth century. The basic premise of this book, however, is that such differences from Western experience are not mere deviations from the "normal" or exceptions or derivatives; they must be interpreted as the outcome of the particular historical and political conditions in Korean society. Thus the two concepts work as a medium of interpretation for Western political theory.

After articulating these two most preeminent characteristics, I reconstruct and analyze the political ideology contained in the political discourses of President Park Chung-hee, the most revered, albeit the most controversial, president in the history of South Korea. The task assesses how nonsimultaneity and sanctification are interwoven with Park's thought, while reconstructing the political thought of former President Park in terms of four modern ideologies. I conclude by tracing the changes undergone by nonsimultaneity and sanctification in the three decades since democratization, with some speculation on their future, and by examining the ideological legacy and ramifications of Park Chung-hee's authoritarian politics in the twenty-first century.

In early December 2016, when the manuscript for this book was being finalized, the National Assembly of the Republic of Korea passed a resolution to impeach President Park Geun-hye by an overwhelming vote. There are many reasons for such an unusual political development: rampant widespread corruption and irregularities stemming from power abuse, chronic economic stagnation, diplomatic failures, and inveterate collusive links between business and politics. In addition, one of the immediate causes for triggering impeachment was that Choi Soon-sil, an old and close friend of the president's, wielded and abused enormous power without holding any official title, by usurping presidential power. Moreover, Park Geun-hye also appointed Kim Ki-chun, who had held a key position in the Korean Central Intelligence Agency during Park Chung-hee's notorious iron rule (Yusin regime), committing himself fully to sinister political maneuvers including red-baiting, as the current president's chief presidential secretary. Pulling strings behind the scenes, he launched public-security politics on a full scale, scrupulously placing under surveillance and suppressing any opinions and activities critical of the Park Geun-hye administration. This situation infuriated the general populace, driving millions of people to the streets where they staged nationwide candlelight demonstrations every weekend for a few months.

In his famous passage from *The Eighteenth Brumaire of Louis Bonaparte*, Karl Marx said "Men make their own history, but they do not make it just as they please; they do not make it under circumstances chosen by themselves, but under circumstances directly found, given and transmitted from the past. The tradition of all the dead generations weighs like a nightmare on the brain of the living." Koreans have now been engaging in a heroic struggle to fight against a "nightmare" weighing on their brain—that is, the evil legacy of Park Chung-hee's authoritarianism resurrected by his daughter. It depends on the outcome of this struggle whether Koreans are entitled to enjoy a more upgraded democracy by putting an end to the legacy of the Park Chung-hee paradigm once and for all.

Acknowledgments

Let me express my appreciation for the invaluable support and help I received in the process of publishing this volume in English. First of all, I must acknowledge that I was able to write and publish this book with the generous support of the National Research Foundation of Korea grant funded by the Korean Government (NRF-342-2009-1-B-00003). It was a great honor and pleasure to be nominated by the NRF for the five-year distinguished scholarship grant (2009–2014)—the first in the field of political science. I published the research outcome in 2014 as a monograph in Korean, titled *Hanguk Hyeondae Jeongchisasanggwa Park Chung-hee* (Contemporary Korean Political Thought and Park Chung-hee). The Terms of the grant required me to publish it in English as well, so I retained the right to publish the English translation of the book once my contract with my publisher, Acanet, expired. Still, I appreciate that Acanet granted this reservation from the beginning. Thus for the last several years I have been preoccupied with translating the Korean text into English, while also contacting overseas publishers. While translating, I have also made some minor changes and new adaptations to reflect the shifts and changes in my thinking and the Korean political situation.

Last June I was delighted to hear that Rowman & Littlefield International decided to publish my book as part of the CEACOP East Asian Comparative Ethics, Politics and Philosophy of Law series. I am so grateful to professors Philip Ivanhoe and Sungmoon Kim at the City University of Hong Kong for recommending my book proposal to such a renowned publisher as Rowman & Littlefield International. I was also fortunate enough to receive the 2016 Sogang University Research Grant (201610048.01), which has supported my research financially at the final stage of preparing the English manuscript as well as relieving my teaching burdens. Finally, I am glad to acknowledge that proofreading the manuscript at the final stage of publishing was partially supported by the National Research Foundation of Korea Grant funded by the Korean Government (NRF-2014S1A3A2043763).

Many people helped me with the task of English translation and other editorial works. First and foremost I must acknowledge, among others, Lynne Jensen Lampe's sincere and patient editorial work over the last two years. Lynne helped me complete the final version with her warm care and meticulous craft. Ben Jackson and Shannon Heit made great contributions to earlier drafts of the translation. Without their invaluable contributions, I could not have articulated my thinking in English so effectively. Isobel Cowper-Coles, assistant editor for philosophy at RLI, helped me greatly by supplying valuable information for publication and exchanging e-mails with me regarding my many publication queries, always with great encouragement and particular patience. I am also grateful to Han Yu-dong, my research assistant and PhD student. He examined the whole manuscript, particularly checking citations and the bibliography and filing index entries with great care. We worked closely together, and he has faithfully remained a best friend of mine for a long time, having meals and drinks with me and relieving my stress and solitude. I also appreciate Simon S. Hong for his long-lasting friendship and inexhaustible encouragement of my academic work.

Finally, my greatest thanks go to my entire family. First and foremost, my late parents, Kang Myung-shin and Kim Soon-ae, whose selfless Confucian sacrifices allowed their children to become good scholars. In particular, my father supported my study at Berkeley while he worked in Los Angeles, living apart from his family in Korea. I remember preparing dinner at his small apartment in LA, while staying there and waiting for him during my winter breaks and summer vacations. My wife, Yun-seon, and my two sons, Se-bin and Se-yun, have always been understanding of my long, frequent absences from home. They are the greatest sources of happiness and solace in my life. Without the patient support and understanding of my entire family I could not have come this far as a scholar.

Introduction

More than seventy years have passed since Korea's liberation from Japanese occupation in 1945 and almost that long since the establishment of separate governments in South and North Korea in 1948. In the aftermath of liberation, Korea faced adverse world historical conditions. The Korean Peninsula was divided and occupied by the United States and the Soviet Union immediately after liberation and was soon placed at the center of the Cold War that broke out between the two superpowers. Instead of carefully considering this adverse international situation, most Korean political leaders became embroiled in short-sighted ideological conflicts and power struggles, repeatedly dividing into rival factions and eventually making the tragedy of national division an inevitability.[1]

Considering the turbulent political scene confronting Korean political leaders at that time, it seems worthwhile to quote Machiavelli's penetrating insight presented in *Discourses* that points to the acute predicament political actors have to face in times of political crisis that demand complete reorganization of a polity. "To reorganize a city for living under good government assumes a good man," writes Machiavelli, "and to become prince of a state by violence assumes an evil man; therefore a good man will seldom attempt to become prince by evil methods, even though his purpose be good; on the other hand a wicked man, when he has become prince, will seldom try to do what is right, for it never will come into his mind to use rightly the authority he had gained wickedly" (Machiavelli 1965, 243).

In light of such an agonizing dilemma, the politicians who soon led the governments of South and North Korea came to power by plotting division through sinister means; furthermore, after taking power they did not make proper use of it to overcome national division or to implement good governance. It is possible that some other political leaders of the time, had they come to power, would have ruled more benevolently, but such figures either lacked the means to access the political resources necessary for taking power or did not attempt to take power using evil means when these were called for. Most of them had the misfortune to end up dead.

Looking back at the journey taken by South Korea (hereafter referred to primarily as "Korea") since the establishment of governments in each half of the peninsula, it is apparent just how turbulent this period of history and how dramatic its political vicissitudes have been. Key events immediately before and during this time include

- liberation from Japanese colonial rule
- reoccupation by the United States and the Soviet Union
- national division due to schisms among leading nation-building figures
- the Korean War (hereafter the "June 25 War")
- long-term authoritarian politics and rapid industrialization
- the Gwangju Democratization Movement of 1980 and its relentless suppression by the incoming military government headed by Chun Doo-hwan
- the June Struggle of 1987 and the beginning of democratic transition
- the financial crisis of 1997 and the ensuing rapid neoliberal restructuring of the national economy
- the first peaceful power transfer with the inauguration of the Kim Dae-jung government in 1998
- the first South-North Summit Talks of 2000
- the impeachment of then-president Roh Moo-hyun in 2004 and its dismissal at the Constitutional Court
- worsening social polarization due to neoliberal reforms
- the emergence of the Lee Myung-bak administration after ten years of so-called progressive governments
- the now-general recession that resulted from the global expansion of the US financial crisis in 2008
- the launch of the conservative Park Geun-hye administration, in 2013, with promises to introduce lifelong "customized welfare"

In the course of these events, Korea has experienced fierce ideological and practical conflict over the core processes of building a modern nation-state, the formation of democracy, and socioeconomic modernization (including industrialization). Compared with other non-Western latecomer countries, however, the industrialization and economic development led by conservative authoritarian governments until 1987 and the democratization led by democratic governments in the twenty years after 1987 were relatively successful. The task of building a unified nation-state, despite temporarily appearing more hopeful after the advent of democracy, remains as uncertain as ever.

Bearing these historical vicissitudes and ideological circumstances in mind, I use part 1 of this book to first provide an overview of ideological trends in contemporary Korean politics since national liberation and division, followed by an attempt to characterize the Korean ideological terrain using the concepts of *simultaneity of the nonsimultaneous* and the *sanctification of nationalism*. Part 2 contains an analysis and reconstruction of the political ideology contained in the political discourses of President Park Chung-hee and attempts to investigate and confirm the academic validity and relevance of the ideological characteristics articulated in part 1 in more specific terms. Part 3 concludes the book by tracing the changes undergone by nonsimultaneity and sanctification in the three decades since democratization, with some speculation on their future, and by examining the ideological legacy and ramifications of Park Chung-hee's authoritarian politics in the twenty-first century.

The aim of part 1, "Trends and Characteristics of Contemporary Korean Political Thought," is to provide an overview of the turbulent dynamic of Korea's contemporary ideological landscape. This is followed by an attempt to analyze and elaborate on the characteristics of this landscape by comparing the case of Korea with that of Western Europe in terms of the concepts of nonsimultaneity and sanctification. Chapter 1 paints a broad picture of trends and shifts in Korean political ideology since national liberation and division, whereas chapter 2 uses the concept of the dialectic of nonsimultaneity to examine the structural characteristics of Korea's ideological landscape. Chapter 3 uses the concept of the sanctification of nationalism to explore this same landscape in terms of actual content.

These aims make a discussion of the nature and status of four major ideologies—liberalism, conservatism, nationalism, and radicalism—an inevitable part of the analysis of both the nature of contemporary Korean ideology and the political thought of former president Park Chung-hee. These four ideologies have competed fiercely in Western democratization, at times promoting it and at times opposing it, yet ultimately converging toward democracy and forming the principal ideological framework of contemporary Western democratic politics. Accompanying the global expansion of Western civilization, they have now become universal categories, defining ideological terrains even in the non-Western world. The contemporary politics of Korea are no exception: These four major ideologies have proved deeply influential. At the same time, the ideologies have themselves been affected by the particular dynamics of Korean politics. Due to differences between political circumstances in the West, where these ideologies originated, and in Korea, where they were belatedly adopted, their development and transformation in Korea reflect local particularities as well as their general properties. This, in turn, offers a chance to examine their Western particularities from an outside perspective.

Of course, mutual understanding of such characteristics cannot be reached merely through simple comparative study. It is possible because the development of ideologies in each region embodies and shares a prima facie universality based on the framework of Western civilization. In other words, not only do Korea and the West share the material and spiritual foundations of modernity—capitalism, industrial society, enlightenment, rationalism, progressivism, democracy, and so on—but also Korea, as a latecomer country, took the four major ideologies as manifested in early-developing nations as its standards in the process of adopting and developing the same ideologies for itself, pursuing goal-oriented change (i.e., teleological change) while adding particular Korean qualities to an existing layer of universality. Given this, it is inevitable that, when describing contemporary Korean political thought, we seek to understand it through comparison with the Western version of the four major ideologies. I will therefore make a theoretical space for determining the compatibility of contemporary Korean and Western ideologies and for identifying the unique aspects of the former, while also describing trends in contemporary Korean political thought and the particular characteristics that have emerged in the development of those trends.

I also intend to present simultaneity of the nonsimultaneous and the sanctification of nationalism as defining characteristics of Korea's contemporary ideological terrain. When comparing the development of the four major ideologies in Korea and in Western Europe, the most striking differences are due to these two characteristics, which resulted from Korea's particular circumstances as a newly independent state that began facing the task of modernization only after World War II. Nonsimultaneity is a property that arises from a clash between world historical time (a product of Western-centrism) and Korean national historical time and the resulting suppression, repulsion, mutation, and convergence. If we regard this as a condition defining the structure of the contemporary Korean political terrain, then sanctification can be seen as a substantial property of the same terrain, formed by a combination of the defining influence of nonsimultaneity and the particular historical experiences of Korean politics such as the failure of autonomous attempts at modernization and nation-state building in the late nineteenth century, colonial rule by Japan in the early twentieth century, national division, the June 25 War, and problems with reunification since liberation. The basic premise of this book, however, is that such differences from Western experience are not mere deviations from the "normal" or exceptions or derivatives; they must be interpreted as reflections of the particular historical and political conditions in Korean society.

More than anything, the dialectic of nonsimultaneity has brought to contemporary Korean politics the conservative development of liberalism, the premature appearance of socialism, and the coexistence and overlapping of two political orders: authoritarianism and liberal democracy. It has also brought about phenomena such as liberalism without a bourgeoisie and socialism before the development of a proletariat, which are symptomatic of teleological change that may be conspicuous in other latecomer countries as well. As mentioned previously, the sanctification of nationalism was reinforced not only by Korea's particular historical experiences but also when nationalism came to function as an ideology of mobilization for "catch-up" modernization in Korea. As a result, anticommunism, national security, economic development, and modernization, as well as democracy and reunification, came to constitute a discourse on nationalism. At the same time, they enjoyed halo effects of their own, thanks to the sanctification and legitimation they gained by appealing to nationalism. Consequently, until the 1980s at least, dictatorship for the sake of anticommunism and modernization passed for liberal democracy in Korea. By the same token, socialism was isolated and suppressed by the invincible forces of anticommunism, failing from the start in the competitive struggle for legitimacy. But in the 1980s, when anticommunist taboos were mitigated due to anger at the Chun Doo-hwan regime, which came to power after bloodily suppressing a struggle for democracy in the city of Gwangju, radicalism attempted to acquire new legitimacy of its own among opposition activists by appealing to the populist values of *minjung*[2] (popular) liberation with strong class tendencies as well as national liberation. In this process, the types of nationalism promoted by conservatives and progressives acquired quite different undertones. The overall effect of the conflict between these two political forces, however, was to further reinforce nationalism and contribute to its sanctification.

Part 2, "The Political Thought of Park Chung-hee," examines the former president's ideology. Park, for better or worse, was one of the most influential contemporary Korean leaders in terms of both politics and ideology. His regime was the longest in postwar Korean history, dominating national politics for no less than eighteen years, from the day he seized power through a military coup on May 16, 1961, to the moment of his assassination in October 1979. During this time, the Park regime began Korea's modernization in earnest and achieved economic growth at a globally unprecedented speed. As a strongly authoritarian regime, however, it thoroughly demolished the institutional basis of liberal democracy and crippled its proper operation. Part 2 examines Park's political thought, focusing on the discourses he produced with regard to democracy, "modernizing conservatism," and nationalism. In the process, I consider how and to what extent Park's discourses reflected the ideological characteristics of nonsimultaneity and sanctification.

Among the Republic of Korea's past presidents, Rhee Syngman[3] and Park Chung-hee are subject to the most intense debate regarding their legacies. In the case of Rhee, in addition to criticism of his anticommunism and dictatorship, conflicting views exist over whether he, the republic's first president, is primarily to blame for national division or should be praised in South Korea as the founder of the state. Regarding Park, conservatives and progressives are vehemently at odds, one side emphasizing Park's achievements in the form of rapid economic development, the other his harsh authoritarian rule and human-rights abuses, the widened rich-poor divide, stunted economic structural development that included increased external dependence and the hypertrophy of the country's chaebols,[4] and the entrenchment of national division.[5] Consequently, a definitive assessment of Park has yet to be reached. With this controversy in mind, Im Hyeok-baek (2012) describes Park as "a man of many faces: Park the Japanese collaborator, Park the Communist Party member, Park the dissatisfied political soldier plotting a coup d'état, Park the president at odds with the United States, Park the father of Korean modernization, Park the destroyer of constitutional government, Park the 'prince' according to his own *Yusin* [Revitalizing Reform] Constitution, Park the leader of the *Saemaeul* Movement [New Village Movement], and so on. To standardize his image in accordance with just one of these faces, then, is unhelpful when it comes to revealing Park's true nature" (54).

In contrast to the fierce controversy that surrounds Park's legacy, public-opinion surveys conducted since democratization have overwhelmingly placed him in first place among past presidents in terms of qualifications, ability to govern, and leadership, beating the second-ranked president by a wide margin (Kim Kap-sik 2007, 82; *Segye Ilbo*, June 23, 2011).

Leaving assessments of Park Chung-hee aside, one thing that is hard to deny is the leap forward Korea has made to enjoy the fruits of both democratization and industrialization, a rare feat among latecomer countries. It is clear, too, that the rapid industrialization achieved under Park's regime has become an important basis for sustainable democracy. In 1997, in particular, when the Asian financial crisis wrought economic mayhem in Korea, the desire on the part of the panicking nation for a charismatic leader who could lead it back from the brink of disaster reached a peak. At this time, a mass nostalgia for Park Chung-hee, who could be called the flag-bearer of national regeneration, gripped conservatives and the rest of the public alike, leading to the emergence of what was termed *Park Chung-hee syndrome*. Even in the twenty-first century, as *seonjinhwa* (advancement to the leading nations) has emerged among conservatives as a new buzzword and successor to "modernization," several administrations have put forward a rosy vision of Korea soaring upward once again to reach a position of leadership in the world.

On the other hand, the shadow cast by Park's regime looms large. Ever since democratization, the chaebol-led economic structure cultivated by his regime—coupled with the neoliberal reforms demanded by globalization—can be identified as a contributing factor to the current phenomena of jobless growth and increased economic inequality. The extent of this is illustrated by the fact that in the 2012 presidential election even the leading conservative candidate, Park Chung-hee's own daughter Park Geun-hye (who went on to become Korea's eleventh president), made "economic democratization" one of the key pledges of her manifesto. Moreover, the anticommunist ideology that Park Chung-hee, like Rhee Syngman before him, developed systematically has remained—in the altered form of accusations of *jongbuk* (blindly following North Korea)—a key weapon in red-baiting attacks by conservatives today. Anticommunist ideology thus poses a powerful obstacle to further democratization as well as to inter-Korean peace, reconciliation, and reunification (though the responsibility borne here by the anachronistic and aggressive North Korean regime cannot, of course, be overlooked).

As a politician, then, Park Chung-hee laid the foundations for Korea as a modern state and left a political legacy in the light and shadows of which twenty-first-century Koreans continue to live. It therefore seems likely that Park's reputation will continue to fluctuate in the future as various positive and negative historical situations are attributed to him. This means that Koreans today, whether or not they care to admit it, are the descendants of the successes and failures of the Park Chung-hee regime. Thus Park's legacy remains a living presence in today's Korea. Just as Deng Xiaoping and Lee Kuan Yew have made postreform China and present-day Singapore, respectively, so has Park made modern Korea. It is regrettable, however, to find neither a full-length biography of Park nor a detailed examination of his political thought in academic works available in English, whereas there are some notable works available for Deng and Lee. This book intends to fill this academic gap by engaging intellectually with contemporary Korean political thought and Park's political ideology.

In contrast, the abundance of existing academic research on the Park Chung-hee regime by Korean political scientists has touched on various realms: leadership, ruling strategy, ruling ideology, and manner of authoritarian rule; constitutional reform to allow a third presidential term and the Yusin Constitution; the relationship between industrialization and democracy; the nature of the state; and opposition and student movements.[6] In terms of political history, too, research on the period from national liberation to the 1970s on topics such as "reassessing Korean political history" is flourishing. When the period being studied lies in the 1960s and 1970s, the overlap with the Park Chung-hee regime connects such research, be it directly or indirectly, to the regime. Even when the focus is narrowed to Park's personal political thought, the volume of existing work is considerable. Jeon In-gwon's 2006 book, *Park Chung-hee Pyeongjeon* (A Critical Biography of Park Chung-hee), is among the most outstanding and comprehensive studies of Park's political thought. When it comes to Park's stance on individual ideologies, there are occasional texts that focus on his view of democracy (Jeon In-gwon 2002; Park Hyeon-mo 2007; Kang Jung In 2011), but the greatest volume of research concerns controversies surrounding the nationalistic character of his regime.[7]

When it comes to researching Park Chung-hee's personal political thought, however, scholars have shown a considerable degree of reluctance. Most academics regard Park as a practical man with a personal focus on administration. In a study of Park's leadership, for example, Kim Young-su defines Park, even in his formative years during the Japanese colonial period, as "a realist devoid of ideology" who, in contrast to his comrades, had no "interest in ideology or nation" (2001, 183, 189). Im Hyeok-baek, too, likens Park to a "modern Machiavellian prince," branding him "the most strategic and rational of Korea's contemporary political leaders, and yet also a leader full of resolve who would use all possible means to galvanize support in order that his goals be reached" (2012, 55–56). Tracing the important political decisions made by Park throughout his life, Im asserts that Park was a "strategic leader" absorbed in making rational choices, not an "ideologue" making "ideological decisions," such as "deciding in advance which camp he should join according to his own beliefs and precommitment, before making choices" (56–57).

It appears persuasive to assert, as several scholars already have, that Park Chung-hee was not a man who acted on the basis of any particular passionately held ideology but, rather, was a practical and rational character. Nonetheless it cannot be said that he had no ideological stance whatsoever when it came to liberalism, conservatism, nationalism, and radicalism, all of which constitute important axes in contemporary Korean ideology; even those scholars who regard Park as a practical leader will accept this. At the very least it is hard to deny that Park consistently deployed a particular nationalist discourse in speeches after he took power, adhered to an anticommunist stance, mastered a form of authoritarian rule he justified in the name of political stability and economic development while maintaining a conservative attitude aimed at defending the existing political order, and asserted the "Koreanization of democracy" within the Korean political situation while adopting a reserved or negative attitude toward implementing Western-style democracy.

Of course, these ideological points of view were more an overall representation of those held by ruling right-wing conservatives than the fruits of Park's original thought. At the same time, however, they were systematically imposed on the general populace through organs of oppression such as the Korea Central Intelligence Agency, the prosecution service, and the police. These stances were also diffused among the populace via a large number of ideological mechanisms, including Park's own speeches and talks; various textbooks (e.g., history, social-studies education, national ethics) produced and distributed by educational bodies; mass media such as television and radio news, daily newspapers, and films; the proclamation and diffusion of the "Charter of National Education"; the management of cultural heritage such as national heritage for protecting the fatherland, as well as rediscovery and glorification of certain historical heroes; various national sporting events; the Saemaeul Movement; and national-security education delivered through both the regular army and police, the Homeland Reserve Forces, and student military training. It cannot be said, therefore, that even those in the prodemocracy movement who resisted Park's authoritarian regime so fiercely were entirely free from the ideological framework he had imposed on society. Consequently, today, more than twenty-five years after the advent of democracy in Korea, Park Chung-hee's ideology, the product of Japanese militarism, national division, and the Cold War era, continues to function as a source of sustainable ideological inspiration for Korean conservatism. The study of Park Chung-hee's political thought is, therefore, enormously helpful in understanding not just the ideological terrain of Korean politics while Park himself was in power but also that of postdemocratization Korea in the twenty-first century.

On the basis of this preliminary discussion, part 2 thoroughly examines the political ideology of Park Chung-hee. Before doing this, however, it is necessary to restate one point in order to avoid the reader's possible misunderstanding: The purpose of studying the political thought of Park Chung-hee in this book is to investigate the degree to which it embodied nonsimultaneity and sanctification. My aim is not to show whether Park's thought provides an unending source of inspiration for Korean conservatism. Chapter 4, first, analyzes Park's discourse on democracy. In the process of mediating the dual political order in which authoritarianism and liberal democracy coexisted as a consequence of nonsimultaneity, Park inevitably produced a variety of derivative discourses on democracy to justify his authoritarianism. Given that the democratization of Korean politics was a process of opposing and overcoming the democratic discourses put forward by Park Chung-hee, examining these discourses is critical to understanding both Park's authoritarianism and Korea's democratization. Chapter 5 illuminates Park's political thought from the angle of "antiliberal, modernizing conservatism." In the process of defending his authoritarian regime, Park completed the basic framework of Korean conservatism, centered around anticommunism (or national security) and modernization. His kind of conservative discourses have undergone partial continuity and partial change since democratization through themes such as "pro–North Korea left-wingers"; *jongbuk*; *segyehwa* (globalization); becoming a so-called advanced, first-rate, or central country; and "nation branding." Thus they continue to exert a powerful influence on Korean conservatives; as such, they are worth examining.

Chapter 6, the last in part 2, examines Park's discourses on nationalism. While in office Park put everything into modernizing Korea through industrialization and economic development. In order to get the entire nation behind his modernization agenda, he produced the most zealous nationalist discourse of any Korean president in history while appealing to top-down nationalism. But Park's nationalist discourses met with unending attacks from his opponents on the grounds that they ran counter to nationalism, which sought national independence, reunification, and development, by damaging democracy; openly violated popular sovereignty through ongoing coercive politics; perpetuated and reinforced national division by calling for (South Korean) nation building before reunification; and created an externally dependent economic structure in the process of development. In this respect, the emergence of reunification-oriented nationalism in the mid-1980s was partially based on attacking Park's division-maintaining nationalist discourse, particularly the argument that his doctrine of building up South Korea before reunification was one that perpetuated national division.

Part 3 (chapter 7) as the conclusion traces the trajectory that nonsimultaneity and sanctification have followed in the three decades since Korea's democratization and speculates as to their future. It also examines the changes undergone by political thought, represented by Park Chung-hee, over the same period and what we can expect of its legacy in the years to come.

NOTES

1. Of course, it might be unfair to blame politicians as a whole because there were some political leaders of integrity—such as Cho Man-sik, Kim Kyu-sik, and Yeo Un-hyeong, among others.

2. The Korean word *minjung* has traditionally and literally meant simply the people or multitude who were subject to rulers. With the emergence of *minjung* theology in the 1970s from the experience of South Korean Christians struggling for social justice, however, it has come to acquire strong ideological undertones, referring to the people who suffered from and were alienated by capitalist exploitation and political oppression by dictatorial regimes. Korean *minjung* theology may well be recognized as a significant attempt to "Koreanize" Christianity, similar to liberation theology in Latin America.

3. Rhee Syngman is internationally known and recognized by the name "Syngman Rhee," but for the sake of consistency in this book I will follow the Korean convention of placing the surname first.

4. *Chaebols* are South Korean business conglomerates. Since democratization, the debate over Park's legacy frequently boils down to how the relationship between industrialization and democratization is to be viewed.

5. For an overview of the heated academic debates over how to assess the legacy of the Park regime, see Lee Kwang-il 1997 and 1998 and Kim Kap-sik 2007.

6. For a review of research trends regarding the Park Chung-hee regime, see Lee Kwang-il 1998, Jeon In-gwon 2006, and Kim Kap-sik 2007.

7. For an introduction to and review of the research in this area, see Jeon Jae-ho 1997 and Kim Jeong-hun 2000.

Part I

TRENDS AND CHARACTERISTICS OF CONTEMPORARY KOREAN POLITICAL THOUGHT

Chapter 1

The Dynamic Evolution of Contemporary Korean Political Thought

An Overview

Since liberation in 1945, contemporary Korean political thought has comprised four major ideologies: liberalism (liberal democracy), conservatism, nationalism, and radicalism. This chapter presents their evolution and interaction in light of the democratic transition that began in 1987. Korean politics would follow a road to democracy whose path would be determined by the four ideologies competing to fulfill the task of modernization—that is, of building an industrial, democratic, and unified nation. In other words, Korean politics would be democratized, but only after fierce confrontations between authoritarian regimes and democratic forces, violent conflicts arising from different visions of nationalism, and turbulent accommodation of diverse, radical ideologies. In addition, as Korean politics have experienced democratic consolidation over the past three decades, the four major ideologies have undergone democratic transformation and convergence.

However, a somewhat unconventional periodization of contemporary Korean history will be adopted here, given that this chapter focuses more on the evolution of political ideologies than the actual flow of political events. Instead of dividing contemporary Korean history in two in the conventional way (i.e., predemocratization and postdemocratization eras with the year 1987 as the watershed), I will divide it into three eras, interposing "the great transformation era," which refers to the period from 1980 to 1992. This does not mean that we should ignore the historical significance of the year 1987 (when the military regime withdrew from politics and a full-fledged democratic transition, including revision of the constitution and the consequent founding election, began as a result of the 1987 June Struggle for democracy) as a decisive turning point for democratization.[1] The democratization that began in 1987, the last year of the Chun Doo-hwan authoritarian military regime, did indeed lead to the consolidation of democracy and provided the

3

basic framework to which diverse ideologies would have to adapt to survive. However, it should be noted that, seen in terms of the dynamic flow
of diverse political ideologies, democratization was not an abrupt event but
a product of cumulative change that had been proceeding for many years, I
suppose, beneath the surface of Chun's military government, which seized
power with a mini-coup in December 1979 immediately after Park Chung-
hee's assassination and the bloody suppression of the Gwangju Uprising in
May 1980; reached its critical turning point in 1987; and then crystallized in
1993 with the inauguration of the civilian democratic government headed by
Kim Young-sam.[2] Moreover, we cannot omit the short three-year period after
liberation that led to the eventual establishment of a government in the South
separate from that of the North, the fateful national division, which would
in turn decisively condition contemporary South Korean politics. Thus this
chapter examines the evolution of Korean political ideologies since liberation, dividing the whole period into four phases: the liberation phase (1945 to
1948), the long authoritarian rule (1948 to 1979), the great transformation era
(1980 to 1992), and posttransitional democracy (1993 to the present).

For the reader's convenience, I present the basic definitions of the four
ideologies, the core concepts of this book. First, *liberalism*, which originated in seventeenth-century England, is defined as "the creed, philosophy
and movement which is committed to freedom as a method and policy in
government, as an organizing principle in society and as a way of life for
the individual and community" (Lerner 1971, 1017). Liberalism is based
on Enlightenment philosophy—which supposes that a human being, as an
autonomous agent with the highest faculty of reason, can achieve his or her
ultimate end by using freedom—and on individualism—which holds that the
public good as well as the individual's interest can be realized best when the
individual is allowed to live according to his or her own freedom and thought.
Thus liberalism remains one of the most important sources of contemporary
democracy. Politically, liberalism demands that state interference with the
private realm be restricted and subjected to a set of regulations. Thus political liberalism has been enshrined in the modern constitution with principles
such as the guarantee of basic human rights, limited government, the separation of powers, the rule of law, and representative government. Likewise,
liberalism stipulates freedom of economic activity, whereby individuals are
able to pursue their interests freely without state interference. This concept,
of course, is based on individualism, which presupposes that the individual
is the best judge of his or her own interests; therefore, economic liberalism
functions as the strong ideational buttress for a capitalist economic order that
holds the guarantee of private property and a free-market economy as its core
principles. Thus liberalism consists of individualism, political liberalism, and
economic liberalism.

South Korea's 1948 Founding Constitution embodied liberal democracy, the final product of the democratization of liberalism.[3] However, this liberalism soon developed into a Korean variant that acquired a dualistic feature in that it functioned as an official ruling ideology bestowing legitimacy upon authoritarian regimes and, at the same time, functioned as an insurgent ideology opposing the authoritarian rule and institution that infringed upon (officially proclaimed) liberal democracy (Moon Ji-young 2009). Thus, bearing this dualistic feature in mind, I trace the historical trajectory of Korean liberalism in this chapter.

Conservatism refers to "an attitude, policy or set of values tending to accept authority, to prefer the known to the unknown, and to relate the present and future to the past" (Klemperer 1972, 164). Thus, *political conservatism* is usually defined as the political orientation of "parties and movements that celebrate inherited patterns of morality and tested institutions, that are skeptical about the efficacy of popular government, that can be counted upon to oppose both the reforming plans of the moderate Left and the deranging schemes of the extreme Left, and that draw their heaviest support from men who have a substantial material and psychological stake in the established order" (Rossiter 1968, 291). However, conservatism in predemocratic Korean politics played the role of defending the authoritarian regime and the capitalist order in the name of democracy while stressing the cause of political stability, which would be indispensable to anticommunism and economic development.[4]

Nationalism may be defined as an ideology and a movement seeking foremost to promote the independence, unification, and development of a nation (Cha Gi-byeok 1978, 13; Maruyama 1997, 323). As to what constitutes a nation, the primordial (objective) theory, which stresses the objective qualities of a nation such as a common history, language, ethnicity, and other cultural elements as well as its permanent nature, is in opposition to the instrumental (subjective) theory, which regards a nation as the product of modernization (Lim Ji-hyeon 1994). However, it is widely recognized that the concepts of *nation* and *nationalism* are ontologically different in Korea than in the West, given that Korea, together with China and Japan, has developed a historic state "composed of a population that is ethnically almost or entirely homogeneous" (Hobsbawm 1990, 66).

In Korea, *radicalism* basically refers to an "ideology and movement which seeks to transform the anticommunist, pro-American and capitalist social structure of Korea . . . in the direction of socialism" (Jeong Seung-hyeon 2009, 263).[5] The Namrodang (South Joseon Labor Party) in the liberation phase, the radical unification forces in the aftermath of the student-led April Revolution of 1960, the Tonghyeokdang (Revolutionary Party for Reunification) and Namminjeon (South Korean National Liberation Front Preparatory

Committee) in the 1960s,[6] diverse radical antigovernmental movements for the "nation, democracy and the *minjung*" in the 1980s and 1990s, and the Minjunodongdang (Democratic Labor Party) in the 2000s may well be classified as radical. The ruling conservative forces in pretransitional Korean politics had suppressed them relentlessly, condemning them as "reds," leftists, and/or communist sympathizers.

CONTENDING POLITICAL FORCES AND IDEOLOGIES IN THE "LIBERATED SPACE"

Korean liberation in 1945 emancipated the political space hitherto monopolized by the Japanese imperialists.[7] However, the political situation in Korea was decisively influenced by foreign powers, first by the joint US–Soviet occupation of South and North Korea and second by the decision to establish an interim unified government and four-power trusteeship (to last up to five years) at the Moscow Conference in December 1945. Diverse political forces with different conceptions of an "independent," "unified," and "democratic" state in the peninsula violently competed with one another for political mastery of the situation. Thus the task then facing Korean politics broke down into three elements: independence, unification, and democracy. Right-wing forces led by Rhee Syngman, Kim Gu, and the Hangukminjudang (the Korea Democratic Party; hereafter, KDP) and left-wing forces controlled by the Joseongongsandang (Communist Party of Korea) were violently opposed to each other over the issue of immediate independence versus independence after the trusteeship: the former were against the trusteeship, demanding immediate independence, and the latter supported it. As to establishing a coalition government to overcome the division between the left and the right, Kim Kyu-sik, Yeo Un-hyeong, and other middle-of-the-roaders who sought such a collaboration were confronted with strong opposition from both the leftists and the rightists. Moreover, most of the rightists insisted on instituting the government in the South first and then seeking unification with the incoming North Korean government. These two issues were vitally linked to the cause of nationalism, and those who were opposed to the trusteeship or insisted on a left-right collaboration would gain the upper hand in the cause of nationalism vis-à-vis those who supported the trusteeship or asserted the establishment of a separate government in the South.

Furthermore, diverse political elements advanced various conceptions of democracy, which would be divided roughly into two positions.[8] First, leftist political leaders promoted a "bourgeois democratic revolution," a "progressive democracy," "an associated front for new democracy," and so on, as a kind of people's democracy in the form of a united front that would constitute a transitional government leading to a proletarian dictatorship. Thus they were far from liberal democracy as we understand it now. In contrast, moderate leftists such as Yeo Un-hyeong, moderate rightists such as Kim Kyu-sik, and rightists such as the KDP, the Hangukdongnipdang (Korea Independence Party), and Rhee Syngman converged on liberal democracy as a basic political design, with various socioeconomic arrangements. If we ignore their divergent positions on such issues as land reform, nationalization of important natural resources and key industries, and the degree of central planning vis-à-vis the market economy, we see that a radical version of the people's democracy and a moderate liberal democracy were confronted with each other, insofar as political democracy was concerned.[9]

In the end, the establishment of a separate government in the South was to be orchestrated skillfully by Rhee Syngman and the KDP, both supporters of establishing a government in the South first and instituting liberal democracy as the form of government, being opposed to the trusteeship and radical people's democracy. In the process, those political elements that supported the trusteeship, the coalition government, and radical democracy were excluded or violently suppressed. Thus did the First Republic, headed by President Rhee Syngman and eagerly supported by the KDP, come into being. If we evaluate the First Republic according to the cause of nationalism, it began with a nationalist surplus for opposing the trusteeship and a nationalist deficit for initiating a separate regime for the South. The Founding Constitution adopted a liberal democracy that combined a presidential system with some elements of a parliamentary government. The constitution, however, incorporated strong socialist elements to manage the economy, declaring the role of the state as coordinator of the economy and proclaiming the realization of social justice, including some progressive provisions that stipulated the nationalization of important natural resources and key industries, land reform for distributing farmlands to tillers, and even profit sharing for workers.

Contemporary South Korean ideologies have focused on three kinds of contradictions: national division, various antidemocratic authoritarian regimes, and rapid capitalist industrialization until 1993 when the democratic transition was completed. Meanwhile, liberalism was differentiated into an official ideology that would justify authoritarianism and an insurgent ideology that would challenge it. Nationalism, in turn, was split into "nationalism-from-above" justifying the national division and "nationalism-from-below" actively seeking national reunification.[10] To justify authoritarian governments controlled by the ruling elite and their vested interests, conservatism emphasized anticommunism, national security, and economic development in the name of defending liberal democracy, urging political stability. Radicalism has emerged intermittently as a revolutionary ideology that launched a sweeping critique of authoritarian governments, division-maintaining nationalism, and the capitalist system, aspiring to a revolutionary transformation of South Korea. However, after a three-decade experiment with democracy, the four ideologies seem to be converging steadily but irreversibly on liberal democracy and unification-oriented nationalism.

LONG AUTHORITARIAN RULE, 1948 TO 1979: UNFOLDING AND REFRACTION OF THE FOUR IDEOLOGIES

The Rhee Syngman Regime: The First Republic, 1948 to 1960

Liberal democracy was first institutionalized as the ruling ideology with the establishment of the Founding Constitution and the government in 1948, made possible by not only pressure from world historical time but also the demands of the Korean people. But presidents Rhee Syngman, Park Chung-hee, and Chun Doo-hwan were persistent in their authoritarian rule, arbitrarily impairing and openly violating the principles of liberal democracy stipulated in the constitution, sometimes even illegally revising the constitution for the worse.

Rhee Syngman, in his capacity as speaker of the National Assembly, proclaimed in a congratulatory speech to the opening session of that body on May 31, 1948, that the First Republic had secured national legitimacy and democracy, for it was the successor to the spirit of 1919's March First Movement, which had heralded the "Great Korean Independent Democratic Nation" all over the world, and the provisional government, which had been set up as a centripetal point for the overseas independence movement in Seoul just after the March First Movement and had laid the foundation for democracy (Gongbocheo 1953, 1). To Rhee, the communist North was antinational and antidemocratic, for it "abandoned national independence and people's freedom, by being subservient to a foreign power [the Soviet Union] and living like a slave" (35). Thus anticommunism against the North was identified with democracy. Democratic institutions in the South were regarded as preserving national independence and people's freedom. In this way, liberalism (i.e., liberal democracy) was able to reign as a dominant ideology from the beginning, upholding anticommunism.

Yet the ruling elite, headed by Rhee Syngman, systematically violated the principles of liberal democracy in a series of events that included the incapacitation of the Special Committee for Investigation of Antinational Activities during Japanese colonial rule that was installed in the National Assembly; the North Korean spy case, also in the National Assembly; the enactment and revision of the National Security Act; the suppression of Cho Bong-am and his Jinbodang (Progressive Party); the twice-committed illegal revision of the constitution; and illegal management of elections via governmental interference. The ruling Jayudang (Liberal Party) was also Rhee's faithful pawn, aiding and abetting his authoritarian and corrupt rule.

This in turn provoked oppositional struggles to defend liberal democracy. Opposition parties—in particular the Minjudang (Democratic Party), which was founded in 1955 as an alliance of various opposition parties and politicians to check the permanent rule of President Rhee—called for democracy and guarding the constitution, confronting the illegal revision of the constitution. Although they were sufficiently anticommunist to acquiesce in the execution of Cho Bong-am and the suppression of the Progressive Party, they still rallied to protect the constitution, the rule of law, the guarantee of people's basic human rights—especially freedoms of the press, publication, association, and assembly—and free and fair elections without government interference, which were necessary to protect liberal democracy (Kim Sam-ung 1997, 224–26). Thus they displayed what might be termed *insurgent liberalism.*

In discussing the Rhee period, I must mention *Sasanggye* (World of Ideas)—the famous and widely read monthly current-affairs magazine published by such critical intellectuals as Chang Chun-ha—as a notable example of insurgent liberalism. This was well manifested in the magazine's editorials. Anticipating the presidential election in 1956 and the general election in 1958, *Sasanggye*'s editor criticized government interference in elections, urging citizens to exercise their democratic right to vote properly as sovereign entities.[11] Furthermore, the essence of insurgent liberalism was well expressed and confirmed in many manifestos and declarations issued to condemn the rigged presidential election of March 1960. These announcements, laden with terms such as *freedom, popular sovereignty,* and *democracy,* were made by students, professors, and other intellectuals before and after the April Revolution in 1960, which led to the ultimate overthrow of the Rhee government.

To compensate for the deficit in nationalism caused by the preemptive establishment of a separate government in the South, President Rhee promoted anticommunism and "unification by marching forward to the North" throughout his rule, and the assertion gained more strength and support due to the June 25 War. Here it should be noted that the anticommunism of President Rhee was justified within the context of the nationalist discourse. Because the regime that occupied the North "illegally" was a puppet following slavishly in the Soviet footsteps, so the thinking went, it was "antinational"; therefore, opposing the communist North would be regarded as nationalist. However, Rhee's position was at best a nationalism supporting the status quo, merely paying lip service to the call to overcome the division without making any substantial and peaceful initiative to transform the divided Korean Peninsula (Choi Jang-jip 1996, 201).[12]

Rhee also felt the need to stress nationalism more actively and thus advocated *ilminjui* (the doctrine of the unitary nation). Given that Koreans represented a homogeneous nation, ilminjui asserted the repeal of the distinction between nobles and the ordinary people, the removal of the distinction between the rich and the poor, the abolition of factionalism and regionalism, and the equality of men and women. Ilminjui retained the dual nature of nationalism and conservatism. It was nationalistic in the sense that it stressed the blood lineage of a unitary nation and conservative in the sense that it sought to mitigate opposition to the Rhee government, asserting that "united we live, and divided we perish" (Kim Hye-su 1995, 338). The doctrine was elaborated by Ahn Ho-sang, the ultranationalist minister of education who once studied at Jena University in the late 1920s and was sympathetic to Nazism. Rhee sought to organize his supporters by encouraging them to form political parties with ilminjui as their platform, such as the Daehangukmin-dang (Great Korean People's Party), the Ilmin Group, and the Liberal Party. He also sought to propagate ilminjui to the general populace by making it part of school education and organizing Councils for Ilminjui Dissemination all over the country (Kim Hye-su 1995; Yeon Jeong-eun 2003). It should be noted, however, that during Rhee's rule there was no substantial challenge to his anticommunist division-maintaining nationalism due to his charisma, formed by his lifelong devotion to national independence movements during the Japanese colonial period and the attitude of anticommunism strengthened among the populace by the June 25 War, except the challenge from Cho Bong-am and his Progressive Party, as I will discuss later.

In addition to ilminjui as a conservative ideology, one should note the political creed of the KDP, which took the lead in establishing the separate government in the South in collaboration with Rhee Syngman, fighting against leftists and moderates. Kim Seong-su, Song Jin-wu, and other politicians who took the initiative in organizing the KDP were right-wing conservatives with backgrounds as landlords, businessmen, financiers, intellectuals studying abroad, and government officials working for the Japanese colonial authority, along with some notable Christians. Thus they had internalized strong anticommunism even before liberation and had some experience cooperating with the colonial government. Most lower-echelon administrative officials also retained a strong sense of anticommunism inculcated during Japanese colonial rule, thus providing a solid base for conservative right-wing political parties (Seo Hui-kyeong 2005). The KDP also had a strong pro-American leaning, cooperating with the United States Army Military Government during its occupation of South Korea and filling key positions therein. Although professing to espouse revised capitalism, the party had no strong will for economic reform, revealing an ambiguous attitude toward land reform, which was supported by an overwhelming majority of the population

(Shim Ji-yeon 1982). The reason they supported liberal democracy with a capitalist economic order was the belief that it would protect their political and economic interests better than the radical democracy communists and socialists advocated (Kang Jung In and Seo Hui-kyeong 2013). However, their creed of liberal democracy turned out to be rather fragile and unreliable, for they were willing to make compromises with Rhee's dictatorial rule, presenting lukewarm opposition at best.

There was hardly any radicalism visible during Rhee's rule because it was almost eradicated in the turbulent process of establishing an anticommunist government in the South and the ensuing June 25 War, which wiped out many suspected communists. Yet Cho Bong-am, who later founded the Progressive Party, succeeded in mobilizing considerable electoral support as an independent in the 1956 presidential election, actively campaigning against Rhee's doctrine of "unification by marching forward to the North" with appealing slogans such as "unification by peaceful means" and "Unite the persecuted masses!" Cho, who had originally been a revolutionary communist engaged in the independence movement during Japanese colonial rule but converted to moderate social democracy after liberation, advocated anticommunism and did not reject capitalism and liberal democracy in principle; however, his slogans were threatening to Rhee's brand of anticommunism. Cho and his Progressive Party asserted social democracy and stressed national autonomy, criticizing those far left and far right for "slavishly following foreign powers and thereby being *sadaejuuija* [the person slavishly serving the great]" (Seo Jung-seok 2009, 306). However, Rhee's unification doctrine was one of the major ideological "weapons that strengthened the ultra right-wing anticommunist regime in the 1950s" by ruling out any kind of genuine talks about unification, "creating and perpetuating warlike tensions" in South Korean politics, and incapacitating any kind of opposition to the regime (Seo Jung-seok 1992, 26). In that context, Cho's unification-oriented nationalism—"unification by peaceful means"—was indeed a serious threat to Rhee's ultra-right-wing anticommunist dictatorship, and the regime eventually sent Cho to the scaffold.

The Park Chung-hee Regime: The Third and Fourth Republics, 1961 to 1979

The Chang Myon government in the Second Republic, established as a result of the April Revolution in 1960, announced an "economy-first policy." It placed highest priority on the stability and development of the national economy in order to cope with both the chronic economic stagnation that had begun in the late 1950s and the shift in US foreign-aid policy from grants to loans. By taking advantage of the free, democratic atmosphere of the time, radical talks about unification like the South-North talks and the South-North Exchange came pouring out from progressive parties and college students, but the Chang government adhered to an anticommunist stance, advocating "construction first, then unification." However, the government did not seriously impede liberal democracy in the sense that it did not undemocratically derail radical talks about unification by mobilizing anticommunist ideology and violently suppressing progressives, though it did prioritize economic development and anticommunism.[13] Yet the military, the last bastion of anticommunism, which felt most threatened by such radical movements, staged a coup d'état on May 16, 1961, with Major General Park Chung-hee as leader. The Chang government's democratic experiment turned out to be short-lived.

The constitution of the Third Republic, introduced during Park's military regime, adopted liberal democracy as the ruling ideology and was actually democratic, stipulating direct election of the president, strong protection of basic human rights, a strengthened party system, strict separation of powers, and the restriction of the president to two terms. However, the antidemocratic nature of the Park regime would later be revealed by three crucial political events designed to allow him permanent rule eventually. First, the general election of June 1967, which was held after Park's successful reelection, was managed illegally, with the government's deliberate interference to secure a sufficient number of seats in the National Assembly to pass a constitutional amendment allowing President Park's reelection to a third term. Second, the so-called Third-Term Constitutional Amendment dealt a serious blow to liberal democracy by legitimizing Park's third term. Third, Park declared a national state of emergency in December 1971 and framed the Yusin (Revitalizing Reform) Constitution by emergency decree, passing the constitution in 1972 by national referendum. The inauguration of the Yusin regime[14] at the end of 1972 represented a frontal attack on liberal democracy, for the new constitution stipulated both the indirect election of president by a rubber-stamp electoral college called the National Conference for Unification, which would allow Park permanent rule, and the election of one-third of National Assembly seats by the conference, which meant virtual appointment by the president. It was an antidemocratic constitution that seriously violated the principle of separation of powers and restricted basic human rights. The Yusin Constitution was no less than the official abrogation of liberal democracy as the ruling ideology.

President Park gained confidence by successfully concluding the Korea-Japan Normalization Treaty despite vehement resistance from opposition parties and violent student demonstrations. Then Park overpowered the opposition parties and other critical elements on various political occasions to perpetuate his rule, frequently resorting to emergency decrees, martial law, and other compulsory measures. As time went on, therefore, political power became concentrated in the office of president. The power of the Blue House, the Korean Central Intelligence Agency (hereafter, KCIA), and governmental bureaucrats, including notably coercive apparatus such as the police and the prosecution office, was to be expanded as well. In turn, the power of political parties—even the ruling party and the National Assembly—was diminished. The KCIA wielded enormous power, keeping even Park's close entourage as well as opposition politicians under close surveillance, so that such phrases as "intelligence politics" became popular (Han Bae-ho 1994, 241).

Oppositional democratic forces staged insurgent liberalism by exposing and criticizing the antiliberal and antidemocratic features of the Park regime. Their advocacy may be summarized with three points: First, they were distinguished from the later opposition forces that would fight against the Chun regime in the 1980s in that the former advocated the protection or restoration of liberal democracy whereas the latter professed a radical people's democracy or revolutionary socialist democracy. Thus, their ideological horizon did not go beyond the scope of liberal democracy. Second, they paid attention to the unequal economic reality and distorted economic structure that Park's developmental dictatorship brought about with its rapid economic development. Therefore, they began to explicitly include "distributive justice, welfare, and egalitarian development" in their claims for democracy (Moon Ji-young 2009, 149). Third, to confront the governmental position, which equated liberal democracy with anticommunism, they refined the previous argument that freedom or liberal democracy had greater value than anticommunism or that liberal democracy was a necessary condition for anticommunism, even if the latter should be valued more highly than the former (150–51).[15]

The Park regime's nationalist discourse was basically in line with division-maintaining status quo nationalism that was based on anticommunism and national security. In his "Pledge of the Revolution," which Park issued immediately after the military coup, he declared anticommunism as the first article in the state doctrine (Kim Sam-ung 1997, 256). He condemned *bukgoe* (Northern puppets), the North Korean communists, for being antinational. Thus the anticommunism opposing them was automatically translated into nationalism. Simply put, the logic was "communism equals to antinationalism, and thus anticommunism equals to nationalism" (Jeon Jae-ho 1997, 61).

The Park regime announced economic development as the core of "modernization of the fatherland." Stressing economic self-reliance and national prosperity through economic development, Park added economic nationalism to Rhee's nationalist discourse and pursued it ardently. Park advocated overcoming "chronic poverty of the people facing despair and starvation" in the "Pledge of the Revolution" (Kim Sam-ung 1997, 256). Thus he criticized the economic failures of the preceding regimes as resulting from their "subordinate economy" and "aid-dependent economy" and promised to build

a self-reliant economy. In a campaign speech for the 1967 presidential election, he set the building of economic self-reliance as the primary goal of his
"national democracy" and stressed a self-reliant economy as the foundation
of democracy (April 15, 1967, 2:1005). He also asserted that the "unification by defeating communism" he proposed was dependent on the success of
economic development, and he stated that such development was a necessary
condition for anticommunism and unification (August 15, 1964, 2:162). Park
also pursued cultural nationalism by advocating national subjectivity, which
stressed the excellence of Korean history and tradition.

Of course, Park's division-maintaining nationalism was not free from
critical reaction. His political opponents attacked the Park regime for being
antinational as well as antidemocratic. First, the famous manifesto "Holding a Funeral Ceremony for National Democracy," issued in a demonstration opposing the impending Korea-Japan Normalization Treaty, declared
Park's May coup d'état as a "frontal attack upon nationalism and democracy" and criticized Park's slogan of "national democracy" as being not
only antinational but also antidemocratic. It also criticized Park's economic
nationalism, espoused in the phrase "modernization of the fatherland," for
being an "antinational conspiracy" because the treaty would put the Korean
economy into double bondage: being yoked to the Japanese as well as to the
Americans. They also accused big Korean corporations of being "comprador
capital" and the government that nourished them of "selling out the fatherland" (Kim Sam-ung 1984, 41).

Likewise, the "Declaration against the Third-Term Constitutional
Amendment" issued in 1969 by Korean students overseas condemned Park's
amendment for being an antidemocratic, antinational maneuver for his
permanent rule. This statement merits our attention, for its critique of the
Park regime relied on an anticommunist logic and argument: "We should
reach the destination of 'unification by defeating communism' only by way
of genuine democracy" (Kim Sam-ung 1984, 77). If we follow this logic,
neither the amendment nor Park's Yusin regime could sidestep the charge
of being antinational. The opposing forces criticized the regime not only
for being antidemocratic by oppressing people's freedom but also for being
antinational because such an antidemocratic system was a stumbling block
to the genuine unification of the fatherland. During the Yusin period, various
antigovernmental manifestos and declarations were deliberately issued on
the national anniversary of the 1919 March First Movement, the time when
the Korean people staged nationwide demonstrations and rallies demanding
(and declaring) national independence from Japanese colonial rule. Taking
advantage of the occasion, opposition forces condemned the Yusin regime
for oppressing basic freedoms more harshly than had the Japanese imperialists, thus being more antinationalistic than the Japanese. For example, in a

manifesto issued on March 1, 1975, they declared, "Basic freedoms of the people our ancestors shouted for so desperately [against the Japanese] are [now] trampled down relentlessly not by a dictatorship of a foreign nation, but by that of the same nation" (257).

Park's discourses on nationalism and statism also functioned as the regime's expression of conservatism, for he stressed anticommunism, division-maintaining nationalism, economic development, and national security during his rule to compensate for the obstruction and abrogation of liberal democracy. First, according to a study that analyzed Park's speeches at his inauguration and at the New Year's press conferences, phrases pertaining to economic development—such as "self-reliant economy," "building an economy," and "modernization"—and a stress on "production, export and construction" were prevalent from 1963 to 1967. However, expressions stressing statism and militarism—such as "self-reliant national defense" and "strengthening national defense"—appeared in parallel with those on economic development from 1968 on. After imposing the Yusin system in 1972, however, Park began to emphasize national security and anticommunism more strongly than before, as evidenced by such phrases as "all-out security," "all-out national unity," and "security-first principle." In this way, economic stability and growth were relegated to second place while democracy was hardly mentioned (Jeon Jae-ho 1997, 55–58).

Immediately after establishing the Yusin Constitution, Park advanced "Korean-style democracy," citing specifics like Korea's unique traditions and culture and the direct threat from the North Korean communists. However, it was not a genuine democracy, insofar as it only aimed for the "acceleration and organization of the cultivation of the state's capacity" for the sake of constructing "all-out national unity" (July 17, 1974, 5:299). He used conservative rhetoric to criticize university students opposing the regime, stating, for instance, that "individual freedom can never take precedence over public peace and order" at the New Year's press conference of 1974 (5:238).

To conclude this examination of the Park regime, let us address the radicalism of the period. The student-led April Revolution—which overthrew the Rhee regime and gave birth to the short-lived Second Republic (1960–1961)—did provide an opportunity for radical elements to raise their political voices, however briefly. The moderate Tongilsahoedang (Unification Socialist Party), the centrist Hyuksindang (Innovative Party) and Sahoedaejungdang (Socialist Mass Party), the radical Sahoedang (Socialist Party), and so on, represented the progressive forces yet had to confine their ideological spectrum to moderate social democracy, declaring their commitment to anticommunism to avoid governmental oppression. For that reason there were no substantial differences among these parties in terms of ideology and policy orientation. They advocated invariably moderate slogans such as "anticommunism, rapid economic development by economic planning, the maintenance of friendly relations with the US, overcoming backwardness, the realization of democracy, the accomplishment of autonomous, self-reliant national economy, the electoral road to social democracy" (Jeong Seung-hyeon 2009, 283). Yet even such moderate assertions were so radical they led to the persecution of those parties and their members immediately after Park's military coup in 1961, when the regime branded them as communist sympathizers. Incidentally, the case of the Unification Revolutionary Party (Tongilhyeokmyengdang)—in which some radicals advocating strong nationalist aspirations and communist ideology went to North Korea and joined the Joseonnodongdang (Workers' Party of Korea) in Pyongyang—created a temporary sensation during Park's reign but did not have a substantial impact on South Korean politics.

THE GREAT TRANSFORMATION ERA, 1980 TO 1992: THE VICISSITUDES OF THE FOUR IDEOLOGIES

The Historical Significance of the Gwangju Democratization Movement of 1980

Here it seems necessary to highlight the Gwangju Democratization Movement as the point of departure for a great transformation in the direction of democratization. Chun Doo-hwan and his military cliques violently suppressed the Gwangju Democratization Movement in May 1980. Many Koreans had hoped to restore democracy in the aftermath of President Park Chung-hee's sudden assassination in October 1979, but Chun and his clique seized political power, eventually founding the Fifth Republic with Chun as president. But the Chun regime was not able to address the inherent lack of legitimacy resulting from its violent suppression of residents of the city of Gwangju who were demanding democracy and from its illegal seizure of power, and thus it had to resort to physical coercion throughout its reign. There had risen intense ideological polemics among opposing democratic activists over the proper interpretation of the Gwangju struggle, the clarification of the true nature of the Chun regime, and the corresponding strategy to overcome it; these contentious arguments resulted in profound shifts in the ideological terrain in which liberalism, nationalism, conservatism, and radicalism would unfold in the future.

First, liberalism as an insurgent ideology revealed its limits and underwent a decline in influence, experiencing relative isolation in democratic struggles, which grew more violent and more radical in reaction to Chun's iron rule. In contrast, radicalism became more revolutionary and extended its influence, reacting violently to the physical oppression of the regime and the US patronage of it. Conservatism, which had emphasized economic development and anticommunism to justify the authoritarian rule of the Park regime, began to rapidly lose its popular appeal. Anticommunist, division-maintaining nationalism, which had retained a certain degree of legitimacy and persuasiveness, now began to recede steadily. It did so all the more because the antinational nature of the regime had been starkly exposed when it had massacred the innocent Gwangju residents, citizens of the same nation, painting them as a "mob" abetted and incited by the North Korean communists. Furthermore, as many people, including young radical student activists, came to realize that Korea's dictatorship was deeply rooted in the national division and the American imperialist patronage of the Chun regime, unification-oriented nationalism began to take on an anti-American and pro-North inclination. Thus the Gwangju Democratization Movement would constitute an ideological turning point that brought about a drastic decline of liberalism, division-maintaining nationalism, and conservatism as ruling ideologies that had contributed significantly to the stability of authoritarian regimes, while leading to the rapid diffusion of radicalism and unification-oriented nationalism as opposing ideologies. Thus events in Gwangju would provide an enduring driving force for the democratization movement throughout the 1980s, which culminated in the June Struggle of 1987. Given that this chapter focuses on ideological vicissitudes more than the flow of actual political events, it naturally sets the Gwangju Democratization Movement in 1980 as the point of departure for the great ideological transformation toward democratization and the Roh Tae-woo government (1988–1992), in which the decisive decline of authoritarian conservatism and division-maintaining nationalism was to be confirmed, as the close of the transformational period.

Political Isolation and the Decline of Liberalism

During Chun Doo-hwan's Fifth Republic, liberalism had completely lost its legitimacy as the official ruling ideology in Korea. The process of constitutional revision was completely undemocratic, and some of the new content included antidemocratic provisions. First, the revision was drafted by the Emergency Measures Council for Guarding and Defending the State without a popular mandate, and it was passed without being submitted to a national referendum.[16] Second, the constitution of the Fifth Republic retained the antidemocratic provisions of the Yusin Constitution, specifically those regarding presidential election and power, although it removed or moderated other undemocratic stipulations to a considerable degree. To prevent a prolonged one-person rule, the constitution restricted the office of president to a single seven-year term and explicitly prohibited a constitutional amendment that would allow an incumbent president to prolong his or her rule. That was definitely an advance over the Yusin Constitution. It retained, though, the method of indirect election of president via the electoral college. This violated not only the principle of popular sovereignty but also opened the door to a kind of electoral oligarchy. The incumbent president could recommend a candidate to the rubber-stamp electoral college and thereby determine his or her successor; therefore, military rule (as in Latin America) or the permanent rule of oligarchs could be secured institutionally. In addition, the presidential power established in the constitution was so strong as to overwhelm the principle of the separation of powers, such that a lawful or institutionalized dictatorship was still possible. Thus the constitution of the Fifth Republic was less democratic than those of the Second and Third Republics, and the status of liberal democracy as the ruling ideology fell into sharp decline.

In these political circumstances, three ideological movements searched for antidictatorial democratic alternatives: "civic democracy as a variant of liberal democracy," succeeding the liberal democratic movements of the 1970s; "people's democracy focusing upon the contradictions of capitalism"; and "revolutionary nationalism stressing liberation from the imperialist yoke" (Kim Dong-taek 1992, 492). However, civic democracy (or liberalism) as an insurgent ideology underwent political isolation and decline, losing its influence as a viable alternative, criticized by the Marxist-oriented revolutionaries for being abstract and romantic. This meant that the goal of radicalized democratic movements in the 1980s was not confined to overthrowing the dictatorial military government and replacing it with a civilian one that had democratic legitimacy. Rather, it extended to demolishing and transforming in a revolutionary way the contradictory structures engendered by the dictatorial regime and capitalist development. Thus the opposition's radicalism in the 1980s grew into sweeping revolutionary ideologies, increasingly relying on Marxist scientific method and class-oriented epistemology, and thus it critically rejected the liberalism that had led the earlier democratic movements in the 1970s (Moon Ji-young 2009, 151–54).

It would be rash, however, to conclude that liberalism had lost its influence completely as an oppositional ideology, though this appeared to be the case because the violent, oppressive rule almost stifled institutional politics at the beginning of the Fifth Republic. However, when the regime adopted an appeasement policy toward political opposition and opened the tightly controlled political space in 1983 in advance of the general election scheduled for 1985, the insurgent liberal forces began to recover their influence. Thus the former politicians from whom the ban on political activities was lifted took the initiative to create the Sinhanminjudang (New Korea Democratic Party; hereafter, NKDP) only two months before the impending general election in February 1985. They participated in the election with the slogan "Winning

Direct Election of the President" and recorded a stunning success, rising to the largest opposition party. It was an occasion to remind the ruling elite as well as the general electorate of the unmitigated influence of insurgent liberalism.

Taking advantage of this momentum, the NKDP launched a nationwide campaign, "Movement to Attain Ten Million Signatures for Winning Direct Election of the President," to demand constitutional revision to enable a direct popular election. Liberal and radical democratic activists joined hands to organize the National Headquarters of the Movement for Winning a Democratic Constitution during the historic June Struggle for democracy in 1987. In order to maximize the number of participants and supporters, they restricted their democratic agenda to winning direct election of the president. Considering these together, it should be noted that at a crucial juncture for democratization, insurgent liberalism provided a rallying point for which all the people united to fight.

Revolutionary Radicalism for the Liberation of the Working Class and the Nation

Revolutionary radicalism had grown rapidly in the 1980s through radical interpretation of and critical reflection on the relentless suppression of the Gwangju Democratization Movement and the unprecedentedly coercive dictatorship of Chun's military government. Thus those seven years of oppressive domination constitute the period in contemporary Korean politics when antigovernmental movements by activists and students were the most radicalized and intense—excepting only the tumultuous period in the aftermath of liberation. The movement sphere thus radicalized began to passionately absorb revolutionary socialism, which had been banned since the June 25 War. Therefore the radicalized movements in the 1980s were characterized by militant activism and revolutionary ideology.

Ideological polemics such as social-formation controversies and revolutionary-strategy debates, which went beyond the ideological terrain of capitalism and liberal democracy, had been heatedly launched and deepened in the radical activist camp of the 1980s. First, they questioned whether it would be desirable to seek partial release or moderation of the oppressive military dictatorship without asking what a proper democracy would look like. Second, they came to stress the initiative and leadership of the working class in the impending revolutionary struggles, judging that the working class now constituted the majority in Korean society and that the class contradiction between workers and capitalists was the basic conflict in Korean society. Third, they posited the task of overcoming the capitalist system as the goal of their social movement and then exchanged heated polemics over proper strategies and tactics.

In that process, the revolutionary activists went through bifurcated differentiation according to the priorities they set in their revolutionary tasks.
The National Liberation First activists gave priority to overcoming the
national contradiction resulting from the division of South and North Korea,
whereas the People's Liberation First activists prioritized overcoming the
class contradiction brought about by a capitalist social structure. Then
they were subsequently subdivided into various factions over the question
of how to resolve the overlapping, dualistic contradictions (Cho Hui-yeon
1992). Nevertheless, the basic position of radical revolutionaries was rather
consistent: they stressed socialist over capitalist industrialization, "socialist
proletarian democracy" over liberal democracy, and "anti-American, North
Korea–allied unification or coexistence" over "pro-American, anticommunist
unification" (257).

After all, the June Struggle gave birth to a democratic revision of the
constitution in October 1987 by way of political negotiations concluded by
ruling and opposition party politicians. Roh Tae-woo, official successor to the
Chun regime, was elected president by winning the founding election held in
December 1987. His victory was made possible only because of the division
between Kim Young-sam and Kim Dae-jung, the two most prominent opposition democratic leaders, who ran separately for president in the election. The
revolutionary radicals were, however, vehemently opposed to the Roh Tae-
woo government, refusing to grant it any legitimacy. Although they staged
an all-out struggle in May 1991 by taking advantage of an incident in which
a college student was beaten to death by a riot squad at an antigovernment
rally, they failed to receive sympathetic public attention sufficient to support
their goal of overthrowing the Roh government. Finally, their revolutionary
ideology fell into rapid decline as socialist regimes in the Soviet Union and
Eastern Europe collapsed successively after 1989, and the Kim Young-sam
government, which succeeded the Roh government in 1993, carried out more
drastic democratic reform.

The Debilitation of the Conservative Hegemony: Propped Up
by Physical Coercion

The Chun regime was quite successful in securing a foothold for resuming
rapid economic development but was unable to relate such an achievement to
conservatism by stressing political stability. Its emphasis on national security
by reminding the electorate of the North Korean threat did not persuade the
populace, due to the antinational violence the regime had committed against
the residents of Gwangju. Thus the regime sought only to appeal to people's
patience by stressing the limited duration of the single seven-year term in
order to placate the people's repulsion to a prolonged one-person rule, such

as Park's. Yet it is clear that the appeal fell far short of the positive legitimation of authoritarian conservatism. In this way the hitherto solid bond joining
economic development, anticommunism, and national security to liberal
democracy, which together constituted conservatism, dissolved, such that the
decline and disintegration of conservatism proceeded rather rapidly.

In order to appease democratic demands, which had culminated dramatically in the June Struggle of 1987, Roh Tae-woo, then presidential candidate
of the ruling Minjujeonguidang (Democratic Justice Party), issued the June
29 Declaration that year. In the declaration he promised to revise the constitution to include direct election of the president, to release and offer amnesty
to political prisoners—notably Kim Dae-jung—and to guarantee basic human
rights, including freedom of the press. But it was nothing more than the official acknowledgment of the breakdown of authoritarian conservatism barely
propped up by physical coercion. Taking advantage of the division between
the two prominent opposition leaders, Kim Young-sam and Kim Dae-jung,
as mentioned earlier, Roh won the presidential election, beginning the Sixth
Republic.

Although during the campaign Roh committed himself to carrying out
democratic reform, his government was not genuinely democratic. It retained
the power base and important political apparatus inherited from the preceding
military regime. However, Roh felt threatened by the new political situation
resulting from the emergence of a divided government after the opposition
parties won the general election in the spring of 1988 and gained the majority. Thus he was barely able to manage political power, and politics fell into
an *immobilisme*. To overcome this, he created the huge ruling Minjujayudang
(Democratic Liberty Party) in early 1990 by forging a surprising three-party
merger through a series of secret negotiations. The party embraced the liberal
forces of Kim Young-sam and his Tongilminjudang (Unification Democratic
Party) to arrange a succession scheme in which Kim was secretly promised
that he would represent the party in the coming election. This demonstrates
that Korea's conservative forces were now unable to reproduce themselves
to stay in power and had to receive a transfusion from liberal forces to perpetuate their rule—the final public acknowledgement of the bankruptcy of
authoritarian conservatism in Korea.

Division-Maintaining Nationalism Declines and Unification-Oriented Nationalism Rises

With regard to the nationalist discourse, notably during the Chun regime,
a situation unfolded that was the reverse of that in the 1970s. In other
words, unification-oriented nationalism combined with anti-Americanism
was widely diffused, whereas division-maintaining nationalism had fallen

into rapid decline. The disclosure that the United States had supported Chun's seizure of power by endorsing the dispatch of Korean troops to suppress the Gwangju Democratization Movement led to criticisms of the United States for perpetuating the dictatorial regimes in South Korea as well as the division between South and North Korea; these criticisms were widely circulated among the general populace as well as among radical groups. As a result, radical democratic movements and national-unification movements jointly staged revolutionary activities against their common enemies, the Chun dictatorial regime and US imperialism. Thus democratic movements were perceived as the extension of the national liberation struggle against imperialism, such that democratic discourse naturally merged with nationalist discourse in revolutionary activism. At this stage the division-maintaining nationalism that had been imposed and propagated from above since the Rhee regime underwent rapid disintegration in the ideological terrain, although it still maintained its influence in actual politics backed by physical coercion.

Such a shift in nationalism had been hinted at as early as 1981 in Chun's inaugural address. He had opened his address with some perfunctory remarks about the cultural excellence of the Korean nation, one hundred years of national humiliation, and the need to achieve peace and to build mutual trust between the South and the North. Then he suggested as objectives of his government the "indigenization of democracy," "building a welfare society," "the realization of a just society," and "educational reform and cultural renewal" (Chun Doo-hwan 1981). However, such goals were not strongly related to nationalism. Instead, in order to secure comparative superiority to the preceding Park regime, Chun stressed that he would never fail to establish the tradition of peaceful transfer of power in Korean politics (ibid.).

Nevertheless, radical activists pressed the Chun regime, denouncing it as a dictatorship subordinate to US imperialism and accusing it as being antinational, antipeople, and antidemocratic. For instance, when in March 1982 students set fire to the United States Information Service in Busan, they issued a statement denouncing the United States as the imperialist that "supported the fascist military regime—which refused democratization, social reform and national unification as a matter of fact—to perpetuate the national division" and condemned the Chun regime for being slavishly subservient to US imperialism (Kim Sam-ung 1997, 367). Such perception was not confined to radical activists but was also shared by moderate opposition leaders such as Kim Dae-jung and Kim Young-sam, who issued the "August 15 [Liberation Day] Joint Statement of Kim Dae-Jung and Kim Young-Sam" during the heyday of the Chun regime in 1983. The two Kims declared that the "democratic struggle is the struggle for the independence and emancipation of the nation," comparing it with the independence movements during Japanese colonial rule (369).

Another point to note with regard to the shift in the nationalist discourse is that the Roh Tae-woo government actively co-opted unification-oriented nationalist discourses that had been originally developed by opposition movements, put them into concrete policies, and attained considerable success. The Roh government claimed to be a democratic government established by a democratic election yet felt the need to enhance its legitimacy to compensate for its implication in the preceding dictatorial Chun regime. Thus, taking advantage of the end of the Cold War and the nationalist zeal for unification in the 1980s, Roh concluded normalization treaties with Russia, China, and former socialist countries in Eastern Europe and initiated a series of peaceful gestures to improve South-North relations. In particular, President Roh announced that North Korea was not "our enemy" but "our brethren" and "our partner" in his "July 7 Special Declaration" in 1988 and in his subsequent proposal for "The Korean National Community Unification Plan" in September 1989. He then presented a drastically altered North Korean policy that included a gradual unification plan, the promotion of a South-North exchange, and other elements (Ha Sang-bok and Kim Su-ja 2009, 240). Consequent to the development of that policy, there occurred a series of positive political developments between South and North Korea, including the simultaneous admission of South and North Korea to the United Nations and the conclusion of the "Agreement for Reconciliation, Non-Aggression, Exchange, and Cooperation between South and North Korea." Such political developments that took place at the end of the great transformation era would presage the impending transition from division-maintaining to unification-oriented nationalism in the 1990s, although anticommunism would continue to trigger a backlash for the time being in Korean politics.

IDEOLOGICAL CONVERGENCE AND NORMALIZATION IN POSTTRANSITIONAL DEMOCRACY, 1993 TO 2007

Democratization of Korean Politics

Democratization entered the stage of stable consolidation with the Kim Young-sam government, which took power in 1993. The revised constitution of the Sixth Republic had been characterized as securing democratic legitimacy, including direct popular election of the president, prevention of power concentration in the office of president and strict separation of powers, strong protection of basic human rights, an emphasis on balanced economic growth, and strengthened social-welfare programs. However, the Roh government's will and motivation for democratic reform was lukewarm and uncertain, and it might well be interpreted as the government that sought to protect the final path of retreat for the safe withdrawal of the military from politics. Thus there was no optimism regarding prospects for sustainable democratization in the Roh government. In contrast, the subsequent Kim Young-sam government carried out a series of drastic democratic reform and measures that were long overdue, eradicating lingering authoritarian elements, establishing a fair electoral system through amending such laws as the Political Funding Law, the Electoral Law, and the Political Party Law, and holding a large-unit local election for choosing metropolitan mayors and provincial governors, thus placing democracy on a firm and stable base. However, the financial crisis that befell the Kim Young-sam government at the end of its term and the drastic neoliberal reform subsequently imposed by the International Monetary Fund would become a decisive stumbling block to Korea's transition to socioeconomic democracy.[17] Thus the Kim Young-sam government would cast both light and shadow upon prospects for Korean democracy.

The arrival of the Kim Dae-jung government indicated an irreversible signal for the consolidation of democracy in Korean politics by recording a peaceful transfer of power by election for the first time in Korean history. The Kim Dae-jung government settled the unprecedented economic crisis inherited from the preceding administration with relative success. It also provided a decisive framework for converting the hostile relationship between South and North to a peaceful one by implementing the so-called Sunshine Policy and achieving the historic June 15 South-North Summit Talks in 2000. The Kim Dae-jung government also created the National Human Rights Commission and the Ministry of Gender Equality, systematically introduced welfare policies, and coped with evils committed during preceding authoritarian regimes, thereby further deepening political democracy. However, because the Kim administration introduced and adopted neoliberal reformist policies indiscriminately as a rather hasty solution to the economic crisis, impoverishment of the middle and lower classes increased social polarity so that the transition to socioeconomic democracy was made more difficult.

The successive Roh Moo-hyun government claimed to be a "clean government" and made systematic efforts to eliminate political corruption, thereby enhancing the transparency of politics. It also continued to follow the basic framework of Kim Dae-jung's engagement policy and thus consolidated South-North relations on the basis of reconciliation and peace. Notable during Roh's rule was the entry of the Minjunodongdang (Democratic Labor Party), a moderate social-democratic party, into the National Assembly for the first time after the party won a considerable number of popular votes in the 2004 general election, becoming Korea's third-largest party. Thus the twenty-year experiment with democracy in Korean politics, which had started in 1987, can be summarized as the decline of authoritarian conservatism, the growth of liberal democratic forces, and a considerable advance of social democratic elements.

Of course the democratization of Korean politics was not carried out in isolation from world historical change but, rather, in conformity to it. First of all, it proceeded, taking advantage of the so-called third wave of democratization launched in the 1970s, from the Portuguese democratization and the later liberalization and democratization of postcommunist regimes in Eastern Europe and Russia. Furthermore, the liberalization of the economy and democratization of politics, which had been proceeding in countries worldwide, were also facilitated by the de-territorial transformation of informationization and globalization that had begun at the end of the 1970s and had pulled down temporal and spatial barriers. On the other hand, the forceful diffusion of neoliberalism, which took advantage of economic globalization and expanded its influence unchecked at the end of the last century, has reshaped the world economy according to the design of market fundamentalism. Confronted with this flow of world history, social democracy has experienced decline and reversal in Western countries, and newly democratized countries such as Korea have been suffering from accelerated social polarity, not to mention a delay in progress toward socioeconomic democracy.

Bearing this democratized Korean politics in mind, I will present an overview of the transformation the four major political ideologies have been undergoing. Because the simultaneity of the nonsimultaneous has been weakened considerably since democratization, the overall transformation demonstrates that the four ideologies have been converging on and adapting to democracy, although temporary backlash and reversal are to be anticipated as a matter of course.

Internal Differentiation of Liberalism and Conservatism and Their Partial Convergence

In posttransitional Korean politics, liberal democracy has now solidly secured its status as ruling ideology in practice as well as in norm. Liberalism has been appealed to in the struggle for the human rights of minorities—such as homosexuals, conscientious objectors, people with handicaps, migrant workers, and others. Along with the creation of the Ministry of Gender Equality and other progressive measures, the status of women has been improved within the framework of liberal feminism as well. Conservative politicians, transformed into the opposition, resorted to the rule of law and constitutionalism to oppose policies of reformist democratic governments headed by Kim Dae-jung and Roh Moo-hyun, so that they, too, jumped on the bandwagon of democracy, sharing its fruits. Thus the base for liberal democracy has been broadened and consolidated.

However, democratization has also led Korean liberalism to internal differentiation, due to two new developments: the diffusion of neoliberalism and a new situation between South and North Korea. The first change was brought about by the aggressive global diffusion of neoliberalism. In the case of Korea, neoliberal reform was carried out more forcefully and drastically to settle the 1997 financial crisis. Thus market liberalists who enthusiastically supported deregulation, the privatization of public corporations, a more flexible labor market, the minimization of governmental interference in the economy, and the liberalization of the transnational flow of capital and finance began to gather forces and clamored more than ever for neoliberal reformist policies. In this way neoliberalism has emerged as a dominant discourse. It is regarded as an element of conservatism in the West. In Korea, too, old and new conservatives, including big corporations, conservative politicians, some bureaucrats, economists and scholars, and the mass media, began to assert neoliberalism, which in turn constituted the new version of Korean conservatism.

In contrast, the previously insurgent liberals and some radicals have now begun to assert the "democratic coordination and control of market order distorted by the developmental dictatorship, and the rectification and mitigation of contradictions inherent in capitalism by the extension of welfare policies and the realization of distributive justice and balanced development," thereby transforming themselves into advocates of social liberalism (Moon Ji-young 2009, 171). In this way they continued to stress the social justice claim they had advanced previously under authoritarian regimes and sought to check or remove evils brought about by neoliberal reforms.

The second change brought about by democratization refers to the peaceful coexistence of South and North, which ensued from Kim Dae-jung's engagement policy. Feeling considerable uneasiness in reaction to this new situation, conservative liberals still maintained an anticommunist position with strong distrust of the Pyongyang regime and cautioned against reckless reconciliation with the North. But progressive liberals supported the peaceful coexistence, pointing to the harm caused by anticommunism. Therefore we have been witnessing the differentiation of liberalism: the conservative version supported neoliberal economic reform and maintained an anticommunist attitude toward the North, whereas the progressive version espoused a kind of social liberalism and more tolerant approach to the North (Moon Ji-young 2009, 168). The reason we should define the former as liberal is that it does not defend or assert authoritarian rule, at least explicitly, in contrast to the previous authoritarian conservatism. That leads us to an examination of how the authoritarian conservatives transformed themselves into liberal conservatives.

The ruling authoritarian conservatives lost control of Korean politics for the first time in contemporary history with the advent of the Kim Dae-jung and Roh Moo-hyun governments. In particular, as the professedly "progressive"

Roh government pursued drastic reformist measures in such areas as external policies toward North Korea and the United States and internal policies pertaining to media, welfare, economics, and education, conservatives began to experience feelings of political deprivation and crisis, more so than ever before. They had been deprived of political power as the ruling stratum, thus experiencing status reversal, and their conservative ideology had been forced to shift from a dominant to an oppositional ideology. In this way they came to face a situation in which they had to oppose radical or drastic measures of the reformist democratic governments and at the same time innovate their conservatism while adapting to the democratic rules of the game. That is, political reversals had forced them to undertake democratic self-renovation (Kang Jung In 2009b, 94).

Such self-renovation was expressed publicly by some conservatives who actively adapted themselves to pluralism and liberalism and then forged an alliance with moderate liberals that would culminate in the organization of the New Right in 2004.[18] Then, in alliance with the opposition Hannaradang (Grand National Party), they began to raise strong opposition to the reform policies and measures of the progressive Roh government by appealing to the rule of law and the Constitutional Court for judicial review to check the rule of the majority. In particular, deprived of active control over politics, as the opposition camp they utilized such appeals as political weapons to contain democratic reforms and met with considerable success. In this respect they also became beneficiaries of the democratic reforms. For example, they criticized President Kim Dae-jung for having issued a statement in support of the Citizen Alliance for the General Election, accusing him of having interfered unlawfully in the election. The alliance had disclosed a list of politicians who were corrupt and had been previously convicted and disqualified for various reasons, demanded publicly that their nominations from political parties be revoked in the impending 2000 general election, and requested that the electorate not vote for those who were nominated despite their opposition. Furthermore, the Grand National Party, then holding the majority of seats in the National Assembly, also allied with another opposition party to pass a resolution to impeach President Roh for his statement about the impending 2004 general election, asserting that not only did his statement violate electoral law but that he had also intended to interfere illegally with the management of a fair election; however, they lost their case at the Constitutional Court. They also attained the verdict of the Constitutional Court in 2004, which declared that the decision of the Roh government to build an administrative capital in Chungcheong Province was unconstitutional. In addition, conservatives in civil society, including conservative Christians, staged conservative activism with mass demonstrations and rallies, declaring their opposition to external policies toward North Korea and the United States as well as to the

educational policy and other reformist policies of the democratic governments (Kang Jung In 2009b, 96–100).

Seen from this perspective, Korean conservatives seemed to undergo some
differentiation. They all advocated for market liberalism and a pro-American
stance as well as opposition to the expansion of social-welfare programs
that aimed for equitable distribution. But with regard to policies concerning
North Korea, they were divided into hard-line and moderate positions. Like
American neoconservatives, the hard-liners actually designated North Korea
the "axis of evil" and preferred a regime change or collapse to dialogue or
negotiation with the current leadership. But the moderate conservatives were
passive rather than active in the dialogue with the North Koreans (although
not rejecting them) and opposed one-sided economic aid to the North, prefer-
ring give-and-take economic cooperation. This position showed some ideological affinity with conservative liberals who defended market liberalism
and respected the rule of law and constitutionalism, so the two forces tended
to converge.

Conversion to and Challenge from Open Nationalism

Unification-oriented nationalism was not able to make any substantial progress due to the abrupt death of North Korean leader Kim Il-sung in 1994
and other unexpected contingencies in the Kim Young-sam government.
However, the following Kim Dae-jung government decisively weakened
division-maintaining nationalism with its patient and consistent engagement
policy and the South-North Summit Talks in 2000. Thus, despite the outbreak
of the second North Korean nuclear crisis, friendly and peaceful relations
with the North were maintained, and economic cooperation—notably, the
opening of Mount Kumgang to tourism in 1998 and the development of the
Kaesong Industrial Region in the early 2000s—was expanded until the Roh
Moo-hyun government. The Roh government, which succeeded Kim's government in the engagement policy, "tried to manage the relations with North
Korea peacefully despite the Bush administration's heavy pressure upon
North Korea and succeeded in holding the second South-North Summit Talks
in October 2007" (Jeon Jae-ho 2012, 99).

As a result, unification-oriented nationalists seeking peace and reconciliation seemed, more than ever, to be making steady and solid progress
at all levels of government and within civil society. Thus the discourse to
emphasize the threat from North Korea and refuse mutual reconciliation
and cooperation seemed to have been driven into the corner. The perennial
perception of North Korea as enemy was then eclipsed by the slogan of
minjokgongjo (intranational partnership). Thus political forces and citizen
groups once opposed to one-sided economic aid shifted their position from

unilateral opposition to conditional cooperation and support and their slogans from general phrases such as "anticommunism" and "anti-North" to selective wordings such as "antinuclear missiles" and "anti-Kim" (the dictator Kim Jong-il). This would indicate a subtle change in the conditions for anticommunist discourses.[19]

In addition, Korean nationalism is now facing multidimensional challenges not only from South-North relations but also from global and domestic sources. It has to cope with forging an economic region among Korea, China, and Japan in Northeast Asia to meet the global trend of regionalization in Europe, North America, Latin America, and Southeast Asia. It also has to shift from stubborn ethnic nationalism to open nationalism to deal with the increasing presence of migrant workers from other Asian countries as well as Korean-Chinese workers, North Korean refugees, and naturalized spouses of foreign origin. In sum, the conversion to open nationalism, which attempts to meet the open expression and recognition of unification-oriented nationalism and the challenge of a multicultural society stemming from the inflow of diverse immigrants, seems to be the natural outcome of democratization in Korea gearing to the global transformation of informationization and globalization, a change that opens the ideational and cultural space in Korean society.

The Acquisition of Political Citizenship for Moderate Radicalism

As mentioned earlier, the Democratic Labor Party (hereafter, DLP) secured quite a considerable number of seats in the general election held during the impeachment crisis of April 2004 and entered the National Assembly. This event had historical significance in the sense that radical elements were finally admitted into the institutionalized political sphere long monopolized by conservatives and liberals.

However, the fact that the creation and activity of the DLP had to go through intense ideological polemics and struggles among radical activists indicates that they had their own share of anguish in adapting to democratized political situations. An examination of ideological debates within the DLP shows that some significant hard-liners sought to maintain their party identity with the inertia of revolutionary ideologies and struggles, whereas their actual practice is oriented to social democracy based on parliamentary politics (Jeong Seung-hyeon 2009, 328–32). As a matter of fact, this represents a Korean version of perennial tension among revolutionary radicals between "ideological radicalness" and "mass appeal" reminiscent of the predicament of radicals in nineteenth-century Europe. At the same time, the division and tension between the Independent and Egalitarian factions in the party,[20] a legacy from the revolutionary movements in the 1980s, developed to a serious level, and the latter broke away from the DLP and set up the Jinbosindang (New Progressive Party) before the general election in 2008.[21]

Nevertheless, considering the DLP's central role in the ideological debates among radicals and the familiar history of social democrats in the West who had to adapt themselves to parliamentarism, at the end abandoning revolutionary activism, radical activists in Korea will have to search for an alternative strategy for transformation. In that process they may well have to accept coexistence with the constitutional order of liberal democracy rather than seek to overthrow it by revolutionary actions. This prospect also presupposes that political alternatives and discretionary strategies available to them are now rather narrow, considering the collapse of former socialist regimes and the global prevalence of neoliberalism.

CONCLUDING REMARKS

Thus far the flow and shift of contemporary Korean political thought has been surveyed from liberation to the Roh Moo-hyun government, focusing on the four ideologies of liberalism, conservatism, nationalism, and radicalism and dividing the period into four parts—the liberation phase (1945–1948), the long authoritarian rule (1948–1979), the great transformation era (1980–1992), and the posttransitional democracy (1993–2007). Chapter 7 presents prospects for Korean political thought, examining the shift in the characteristics of the ideological terrain and the legacy of Park Chung-hee's political thought. To prepare for this, political development following the Roh government merits a brief introduction.

Liberal-reformist political forces represented by the Kim Dae-jung and Roh Moo-hyun governments lost their power in the 2007 presidential election and in the 2008 general election due to economic failures like worsening social polarity, increasing unemployment, and Roh's self-righteous leadership. Lee Myung-bak, a former businessman, who was a pragmatic and moderate conservative, was elected president by effectively forging an alliance of moderate conservatives and market liberals and taking advantage of widespread popular discontent with the Roh government. The opposition Grand National Party also regained the place of the ruling party with a secure majority of seats after a ten-year loss of power. However, the Lee government was not able to competently manage the global financial crisis that issued from the United States in 2008. Korea's economic performance was rather poor in comparison with that of similar countries such as Taiwan and Singapore, and socioeconomic polarization worsened (Lee Jun-gu 2013). The Lee government refused to maintain and/or further the basic framework for peace and reconciliation between South and North that had been forged by the preceding governments, instead taking a hard-line policy toward North Korea, straining relations. South-North relations reached their worst point in 2010 with the alleged North Korean sinking of the Cheonan, a South Korean naval warship, near the Northern Limit Line and the North Korean bombing of Yeonpyeong Island later that year. As a consequence, unification-oriented nationalism cooled rapidly (Jeon Jae-ho 2012).

Meanwhile, the reformist liberal party was defeated in the 2007 presidential election and in the 2008 general election, becoming the opposition party once again. Because they seemed lethargic throughout the Lee government without strong party leadership, Korean democracy, which seemed to have been well consolidated since 1994, showed noticeably conservative leanings in which authoritarian elements became pronounced and democratic elements weakened. This was to be confirmed with ease by the political situation in the Lee government, which witnessed the crippled operation of the National Commission for Human Rights, the infringement of the political neutrality of the public broadcasting service, and frequent suppression of basic human rights such as freedoms of expression, assembly, and association.

The year 2012 was a critical political turning point, given that the presidential and general elections were held in the same year, because the outcome of elections would determine the future direction of Korean politics. Public opinion about the management of state affairs and the economic performance of the Lee government was so negative, the ruling Saenuri Party (Saenuridang, New World Party; formerly the Grand National Party) was at a disadvantage in the general election. In contrast, the opposition camp regrouped their forces with the Tonghapminjudang (United Democratic Party, a reformist liberal group) and the Tonghapjinbodang (United Progressive Party, social democratic elements) as centripetal points and aimed to win the election through an electoral alliance of opposition parties and a joint nomination. The overall prediction favored the victory of the opposition forces right up to election day. To the surprise of the public, however, the ruling Saenuri Party won the election. Whereas the Saenuri Party regained popular trust despite the party's initial crisis because Park Geun-hye, a strong presidential candidate, led the campaign effectively as chair of the Emergency Measures Committee of the Saenuri Party, the opposition parties fought for hegemony in their alliance and failed to establish and exert consistent leadership due to its hasty formation; thus they were defeated in the election. They failed to satisfy the people's aspiration for "new figures and new politics" by clinging to the nomination of candidates in the same old way and allocating factional shares to preserve their vested interests. They also failed to present a new, appealing vision that went beyond the punishment of the Lee government and to outdo the ruling party in agenda setting in the election. The general election ended with the victory of the ruling Saenuri Party winning a majority of seats. In the following presidential election, Park Geun-hye, presidential candidate of the Saenuri Party, was victorious over Moon Jae-in, the united opposition candidate.

Consecutive installation of conservative governments since 2008 (i.e., the Lee Myung-bak and Park Geun-hye governments) may cast a short-term prospect that the political democratization carried out consistently since 1993 will undergo stagnation or even reversal. But it may also provide the momentum whereby the lower limit of Korean democracy is confirmed and solidified, awakening the Korean people to the simple insight that history does not move in a unilinear fashion.

NOTES

1. It is important to note, however, that it was not until the inauguration of the Kim Young-sam government in 1993 that it became possible to retrospectively designate 1987 as the beginning of sustainable democratization. As will be shown later in the chapter, the Roh Tae-woo government (which assumed power in 1988 after the 1987 June Struggle and the democratic constitutional revision in 1987 that included the direct election of the president) was quite uncertain in democratic prospects, given that Roh himself was the direct inheritor of the preceding military regime, the target of the democratic opposition movement. Besides, the later three-party merger forming the conservative grand coalition in 1990 further darkened prospects for democracy. When our examination focuses on the flow of actual political events, however, the year 1987, rather than the inauguration of the Kim Young-sam government, will be treated as the beginning of democratization.

2. The validity of such periodization will be confirmed later in light of the overall summary of the flow of contemporary Korean political thought.

3. The Founding Constitution, however, did not stipulate a laissez-faire capitalist order, as will be discussed later.

4. Here the phrase "in the name of democracy" is important, as will be discussed in chapter 3.

5. Due to the strong influence of anticommunism ("red complex") and the long history of severe persecution of socialists and communists before democratization in Korean politics, these words have been long avoided by activists and thinkers espousing them, and radicalism has been used instead. This book follows the general Korean convention.

6. In the 1970s, due to the severe oppression, there were no radical movements except those fabricated by the regime, as I will explain later.

7. In Korean history, the three-year period from liberation in 1945 to the establishment of the South and North Korean governments in 1948 is frequently referred to as the history in the *haebanggonggan* (liberated space).

8. See Yeo Hyeon-deok 1987 for a detailed analysis of various democracies advanced by diverse political forces in the aftermath of liberation.

9. Here I do not attach great importance to the distinction between liberal and social democracy as far as the attributes of political constitution are concerned.

10. Hereafter I will often call the former "division-maintaining nationalism" and the latter "unification-oriented nationalism" for convenience. This distinction will be elaborated in chapter 3, when the sanctification of nationalism is addressed.

11. With regard to this, for example, see Chang Chun-ha's editorials (1956a, 1956b, 1958).

12. Unification slogans and plans—such as "unification by marching forward to the North," "unification by exterminating communists," unification by holding a free general election in the North after the withdrawal of the communist army, and unification by holding a free general election both in the South and the North with UN monitoring, which were all proposed by Rhee Syngman, Park Chung-hee, and other ruling elite—may well be criticized for the following reasons: First, they were unrealistic because there was hardly any possibility for North Korean communists to approve or accept them. Second, they were used to relentlessly suppress politicians and intellectuals who advocated more progressive and active unification proposals. Third, as a consequence, conservative plans for unification contributed to the perpetuation of the division by ruling out (in advance) the progressive proposals, which might have been more plausible. Yet it would be going too far to assert that because their anticommunist unification plans were "antiunificational" they were also "antinational." Although it would be unfair to compare the 1960s and 1970s with the 1990s and 2000s on an equal basis, given that a sea change has occurred in the meantime in South-North relations as well as international politics, it is still important to be reminded that advocacy of the absorptive unification of the North by the South—a virtually anticommunist unification by the South—would not now be criticized for being antiunificational in its realistic assessment and ideological preference.

13. The Chang government once sought to regulate demonstrations and to pass a special provisional law for anticommunism, but the legislation was not realized.

14. The Park government before and after the Yusin Constitution is called, respectively, "the Third Republic" and "the Fourth Republic."

15. Of course, they did not deny the necessary link between anticommunism and liberal democracy, considering the security problems confronting North Korean communists.

16. The Supreme Court of Korea officially confirmed this in 1997 by passing a sentence on the so-called May 18 Case, in which General Chun Doo-hwan and his military clique seized power illegally in 1980, violently suppressed the Gwangju Democratization Movement, and took various political measures thereafter, including revision of the constitution. They were charged with the crimes of rebellion, the purposive murder for rebellion, and mutiny.

17. Here *socioeconomic democracy* means the strengthening of social welfare and distribution by enhancing social citizenship.

18. The New Right was organized initially with the founding of the "Alliance for Liberalism" (Jayujuuiyeondae) in November 2004, which some right-wing intellectuals and activists participated in, distinguishing themselves from the so-called Old Right. The Alliance for Liberalism was joined immediately by intellectual groups and organizations in civil society and expanded its influence with the support of major conservative newspapers. They criticized the Old Right for sticking to outdated authoritarianism and anticommunism despite democratization and ostensibly upheld

liberal democracy and a market economy as their slogan. Furthermore, they spoke for conservatives' feelings of crisis after the successive installations of the progressive Kim Dae-jung and Roh Moo-hyun governments, declaring that the ideological legitimacy of liberal democracy and a market economy and the historical orthodoxy of the foundation of Korea had been seriously cast into doubt by the current "left-wing" governments so that state identity had been severely impaired (Kang Jung In 2009b, 102–3). For a more detailed analysis of the New Right, see Kang Jung In 2009b, 102–9.

19. However, the so-called Sunshine (engagement) Policy of the Kim Dae-jung government—seeking to shift the political situation on the Korean Peninsula in a post–Cold War direction—triggered an intense backlash called the "South-South Conflict," a phenomenon in which public opinion was severely divided into pros and cons over the government's policy toward the North, due to strong conservative reactions (Kyungnamdaehakkyo Geukdongmunjeyeonguso 2004).

20. Here the Independent faction refers to an ideological group that prioritizes the independence (national autonomy) of Korea—that is, overcoming Korea's dependence on strong powers like the United States and Japan—and the Egalitarian faction to a group that prioritizes socialist revolution to remove class inequality. This division is the legacy of the earlier distinction between the National Liberation First and People's Liberation First groups among radical activists in the 1980s.

21. The two parties merged into the Tonghapjinbodang (the United Progressive Party) before the general election in 2012 and then divided again later.

Chapter 2

The Dialectic of Nonsimultaneity

This chapter examines the ideological terrain of contemporary Korean politics in terms of four major ideologies—liberalism, conservatism, nationalism, and radicalism—focusing primarily on the period from liberation until 1993, when democratization had been almost completed with the inauguration of the Kim Young-sam government, and compares it with that of European early comers, such as England and France.[1] This task is carried out by illuminating the characteristic experience that peripheral latecomer countries such as Korea had to undergo in accommodating political ideas and ideologies from the early-comer countries in the center, in light of the concept of the simultaneity of the nonsimultaneous, which was introduced by German Marxist philosopher Ernst Bloch. This is expanded upon in chapter 3, which addresses the sanctification of nationalism as the substantial characteristic of Korean politics. The two concepts—nonsimultaneity and sanctification—are to be applied with great utility when the political thought of Park Chung-hee is analyzed in part 2. It should be noted, however, that the examination of the Korean ideological terrain in this chapter remains on a very abstract level without going into concrete details, because here I intend to present only a broad outline.

This chapter first briefly reviews Bloch's concept of nonsimultaneity and the ways in which Korean scholars have used it, then distinguishes between Bloch's intention and my use of the concept. Thereafter it suggests and elaborates on the dual political order of authoritarianism and liberal democracy as well as an ideological ambiguity in Korean conservatism. This duality is dictated by the dialectic of nonsimultaneity, which the chapter addresses as the most striking characteristic of the ideological terrain in Korean politics. Subsequently, various features of the Korean ideological terrain derived from the dialectic are elaborated in subthemes, such as the importation of various ideologies as finished products, the premature clash of divergent ideologies, the precocious "conservatization" of liberal democracy, transcontextual confrontation among ideologies, and the authenticity controversy. The chapter ends with brief suggestions that nonsimultaneity was observed even during Japanese colonial rule as well as in the postliberation period and that its legacy persists to a certain extent, even after democratization.

SIMULTANEITY OF THE NONSIMULTANEOUS

In order to understand the democratization of Korean politics and the "Koreanization" of democracy since the establishment of South Korea in 1948, it is necessary to examine the ideological terrain of contemporary Korean politics, the characteristics of which have been shaped during the continuing process of Korea's adoption of four major ideologies of Western origin. I believe that such a task should be carried out with keen awareness and thorough clarification of the peripheral and belated nature of the Korean polity in modern world history. In other words, it requires macroscopic yet careful investigation into the structural conditions that give Korea's contemporary ideological terrain both universal and its own particular attributes in the context of world history as shaped and dominated by Western civilization. Thus the ideological terrain in contemporary South Korea is here explored through the application of Bloch's concept of nonsimultaneity.

Whereas Bloch devised this concept in his book *Heritage of Our Times* (*Erbschaft dieser Zeit* 1991) to explain the noncorrespondence between the economic base and the superstructure in historical materialism,[2] I intend to use it to examine the configuration of the ideological terrain in Korean politics, particularly focusing on a temporal dimension—that is, to illuminate the points of intersection and discrepancy between the world historical (standard) time and Korean local time and to highlight the suppression of the latter by the former, the repulsion by the latter, and, in particular, the subsequent mutation of the ideological terrain through mutual interaction. Thus the concept functions as a helpful tool to understand the formation of contemporary Korean political ideologies as distinct from that of modern Western ones.

Bloch developed the dialectic of nonsimultaneity to explain the appearance of Nazism in the Weimar Republic and the rise of reactionary right-wing nationalism in the progressive guise of National Socialism. He used the concept to explain Germany's discrepancy between the capitalist economic structure rapidly being formed and the archaic sociocultural formation "not yet disposed of," as well as the subsequent phenomena resulting from the mixing of the two. In the widest sense, the concept is similar to what we understand today as "cultural lag." According to Bloch, the economic and political transformation that was carried out in Germany in the absence of a bourgeois revolution was less radical than those in England and France in the sense that heterogeneous and outmoded reactionary social elements remained strong alongside a bourgeoisie much weaker than those of England and France. For him the problematic character of the past not yet disposed of manifested itself in the persistence of archaic (noncontemporaneous) mentalities among large sectors of the German population in the midst of rapid economic rationalization. In their reaction to this contemporary crisis, Germans resorted to myths, frustrated expectations, and irrational explanations inherited from a distant, noncapitalist past, which the Nazis later idealized and exploited adeptly to seize power. In order to explain the complexities underlying the enthusiastic support for Nazism on the part of the German masses, Bloch stressed the significance of the mythical, sacred, and irrational dimensions of human experience by attributing it to his concept of nonsimultaneity (Bloch 1991).

Speaking more broadly, *nonsimultaneity* refers to "a historical situation marked by an often confused constellation of coexisting economic structures and sociocultural formations from different epochs" (Durst 2002, 171). The dialectic of nonsimultaneity found in Germany, Japan, and other latecomer capitalist countries in Europe resonated more intensely in late-developing countries such as Korea, which gained independence only after the end of World War II. Thus Korean scholars from diverse academic backgrounds have often applied the nonsimultaneity concept. For example, Kang Jun-man, well-known Korean scholar of media studies, defines *nonsimultaneity* as a social context in which premodern, modern, and postmodern characteristics coexist in confusion. He then argues that the dialectic of nonsimultaneity is expressed more vehemently in Korean society due to extremely rapid social transformation over the last hundred years, analyzing the irrational structure of Korean society and the consequent amplification of diverse conflicts on the basis of the dialectic (Kang Jun-man 2013). Kim Jeong-hun, progressive sociologist, uses nonsimultaneity to criticize the behavior of a business conglomerate. In an article he contributed to a newspaper, he defines it as a phenomenon in which "social elements that supposedly must exist in different eras coexist in the same era" and suggests that the concept can be easily understood by observing that managerial control of the Samsung Electronics Co. is maintained by a premodern hereditary father-to-son transfer, even though the company boasts of the world's highest level of scientific rationality and economic efficiency (Kim Jeong-hun 2004).

In contrast, Kim Il-young, conservative political scientist, utilizes the nonsimultaneity concept to criticize candlelight demonstrations held at Seoul Plaza in 2008 to protest the Lee Myung-bak government's decision to import beef from the United States. First defining *nonsimultaneity* as a "phenomenon in which elements generate from different time zones, thus finding it difficult to coexist, and actually exist in confusion," Kim next suggests that the demonstrations began with "postmodern" characteristics displaying "postmaterialist, decentered, festival-like, spontaneous, nonviolent" aspects and then criticizes the gatherings, stating that they later revealed "modern and premodern" attributes hidden under the surface, such as "anti-American, antigovernmental, violent and whirlwind-like" tendencies (Kim Il-young 2008, 48–52). As these examples illustrate, the nonsimultaneity concept has been applied without much elaboration by Korean scholars to stress the bewildering coexistence of multidimensional time zones observed in Korean society. Both conservative and progressive scholars have used it to explain and criticize complex and contradictory sociopolitical phenomena or events.

Another scholar, Park Myeong-lim (1996b), further refines the application of the dialectic of nonsimultaneity in an essay examining contemporary Korean nationalism:

> This concept [the dialectic of noncontemporaneity] suggests the unevenness, partiality, and partial development of the consciousness and social change and indicates, for example, in Korea, the contemporaneous existence and uneven development of different agendas such as state-building and modernization, democratization and reunification, etc. Noncontemporaneous elements have existed contemporaneously in both South and North Korea, as seen in the existence of tradition and modernity in confusion due to their compressed social development in a short time period. This might be called the "contemporaneity of the noncontemporaneous." One of the dramatic displays of this in Korea is nationalism. The strongest ideological reference for a wide range of problems including state-building, modernization, and the reunification has been nationalism, but it has erupted in various appearances and different shapes. (60)

Once we accept Park's conceptualization, questions may arise as to how such various agendas originating from different time zones interact with one another and what dynamics or conflicts emerge from such interactions. It seems that most Korean scholars have not given these issues any serious theoretical reflection, being satisfied with merely identifying the phenomenon called *nonsimultaneity*.

Kim Dong-chun (1997a) seems to make a more advanced point in this regard. Applying the nonsimultaneity concept, he describes the social movement in non-Western latecomer countries such as Korea as the "third model of social movement" and finds its distinct characteristics in the variegated nature of movement agents and the ambiguity of movement objectives:

> Under this condition [in which nonsimultaneity prevailed] the social movement in the Third World does not exactly follow the Western path of "labor movement → building of the labor party → emergence of the new social movement."

This is due to the situation in which capitalist industrialization was launched on a full scale only in the late twentieth century and the developmental stages of history overlapped; that is, the nonsimultaneous were coexisting simultaneously. . . . Diverse resistance movements did not exist as sectoral ones, nor still as pure class struggles. Since Korea did not go through a bourgeois revolution as such, resistance movements overall retained the potential for power struggles or systemic transformation, and yet the agents were not necessarily confined to a single class such as workers, peasants, and so on. (71)

Following the insights of Park Myeong-lim and Kim Dong-chun, I define the structural characteristics of the contemporary Korean ideological terrain in terms of the dialectic of nonsimultaneity. Here the distinction between causal and teleological changes seems useful, as I previously addressed when discussing Korean democratization:

The Western-oriented modernization that Korean society has undergone over the last fifty years has exhibited both causal and teleological changes. As in most non-Western countries incorporated into the Western-centric world order, the necessity for change in Korea came from external pressure and dynamics, so that the change dictated was often opposed to or premature in regard to Korea's own internal dynamics. Thus . . . the transformations inevitably exhibited more teleological characteristics in the sense that they were propelled more by external dynamics than by any internal evolution. Korea had to conform to goals set or imposed by the outside world, with advanced Western nations as models. Therefore, whereas the changes Western nations experienced historically were caused predominantly by internal dynamics and logic, those in Korean society have exhibited a dualistic nature, both teleological and causal. This suggestion may apply to most non-Western nations that have pursued Western-oriented change in "catch-up" mode. (Kang Jung In 2004, 364–65)

As is well known, the process determines the outcome in causal change, whereas the goal (*telos*) determines (or directs) the process in teleological change. The causal and teleological changes have crisscrossed and brewed distinctive dual properties in the evolution of contemporary political ideologies in Korea.

The examination thus far suggested makes it clear that the political manifestation of nonsimultaneity in Korea did not derive from a discrepancy between a modernized capitalist structure and an archaic sociocultural structure in Bloch's terms but from an international clash of universal world historical time and local Korean historical time. The former imposed liberal democracy upon Korea; the latter lacked the capability to properly administer it. Accordingly, the nonsimultaneity observed in Korea does not presuppose the basic assumption of Marxist historical materialism—the superstructure conditioned or determined by an economic base. Rather, it focuses on the

interaction between world and local historical times and not on local historical time artificially separated from world historical time. The nonsimultaneity
observed in Korea considers the ideological clashes and conflicts originating
from the premature pressure of world historical time on peripheral countries, their stubborn resistance to it, and the outcome of such interactions.
Although Bloch's pioneering idea and its concept is deeply inspiring, the
use of the term *nonsimultaneity* in this chapter is distinguished from Bloch's
application. Herein I focus it on the world system, presupposing a distinction between the center and the periphery and their interaction; in terms of
perspective and subject matter, I examine only the interaction among ideologies and ideas rather than the interaction between the economic base and the
superstructure. Thus, in this chapter, the dialectic of nonsimultaneity focuses
on the dual political order of authoritarianism and liberal democracy and the
paradoxical coexistence of prematurity and belatedness regarding the state of
democracy in pretransitional Korean politics.

THE DUAL POLITICAL ORDER

The dual political order, an overarching characteristic of Korean politics
before democratization in 1987 that was dictated by the dialectic of nonsimultaneity, is particularly helpful in explaining the relationship between liberal
democracy and conservatism—that is, the ideological ambiguity of Korean
conservatism. Many Koreans would agree to refer to those regimes that were
headed and dominated by presidents Rhee Syngman, Park Chung-hee, and
Chun Doo-hwan as conservative. However, when we examine the political
aspects (rather than the capitalistic economic aspects) of Korean conservatism while remaining faithful to its definition, we are confronted with a question: *What was the status quo that conservatives were seeking to defend?* This
thorny question is raised because, except for the short-lived Second Republic,
Korean politics was ruled by a series of authoritarian regimes, although they
professed a liberal democracy that was also enshrined in constitutions, albeit
to varying degrees. Hence it seems rather self-evident that the essence of
Korean conservatism was authoritarianism. In an authoritarian political system, the leader exercises political power arbitrarily and frequently without
being subject to existing laws and institutions, and citizens cannot oust the
leader by free and fair elections. In fact, authoritarianism is diametrically
opposed to democracy. In this light, liberal democracy remains a professed
ideology rather than a stable practice in South Korea. Liberal democracy in
Korea is something yet to be realized rather than a status quo to be defended.

Seen from a different perspective, the dual political order was closely
intertwined with the paradoxical qualities of prematurity and belatedness,

displayed as a result of Korea's status as a peripheral latecomer. Speaking generally, prematurity is generated by the pulling of world historical time (teleological cause), whereas belatedness is brought about by the braking reaction of Korean historical time (efficient cause). These may be conceived in terms of the ideological dimension (prematurity) and the reality dimension (belatedness). In other words, teleological change leads to prematurity while providing us a reference point by which to recognize belatedness, and causal change gives rise to belatedness while providing us a reference point that triggers awareness of prematurity. When Choi Jang-jip (1996) examines the status of Korean democracy founded in 1948, he points to "premature democracy" and "variables for causing belatedness." "All these conditions," he writes, when expounding on the nature of the problem, "were far from being favorable to the development of democracy. Political turmoil was so severe as to approach civil war. The ideological spectrum was too narrow to allow broad political representation. Democratic institutions were introduced before any substantial progress of capitalist industrialization. Thus Korean democracy at that time was a premature democracy" (21). Here Choi Jang-jip presents his observation that, whereas democracy was prematurely imposed upon Korean society as a teleological change—that is, as a result of pressure from world historical time—its smooth operation was delayed due to the repulsion and braking of the Korean historical time resulting from the immature socioeconomic conditions. In this way prematurity and belatedness functioned as a mirror in which world and Korean historical times collided with, reflected, and recognized each other.

Contrary to the point made earlier that the essence of Korean conservatism was authoritarianism, Choi's observation also suggests that we cannot dismiss liberal democracy in pretransitional Korean politics as trivial and meaningless, for various reasons. First of all, as established earlier, the contemporary concept of authoritarianism tacitly presupposes the concept of democracy and is actually shaped by it. As a political system, democracy can be the opposite of authoritarianism: the leader exercises political power in accordance with the rule of law, and citizens can remove him or her through a free and fair election. However, we could also claim that contemporary authoritarianism is a kind of dual political order, with authoritarianism and democracy constituting two sides of the same coin. This duality is confirmed in reality as well as in theory.

Most authoritarian regimes in Third World countries, including South Korea, were constantly confronted with the issue of legitimation and subject to democratic pressure under the hegemonic influence of Western liberal democracy—that is, when world historical time was set to liberal democracy, excluding those proclaimed as a socialist or other kind of radical regime. In this way liberal democracy, which was implicitly used as a yardstick for measuring legitimacy and criticizing authoritarian regimes, was integrated into the Korean political reality. The fact that political reality and political discourses constituting authoritarianism were constructed, although disingenuously, using the rich vocabulary and concepts of liberal democracy demonstrates that, despite glaring violations of that type of governance, the authoritarian Korean regimes were still partly liberal democracies. The political discourses that explained and approved of governmental actions and aroused societal reactions were all conducted in the language of liberal democracy, including but not limited to "majority rule," "rule of law," "separation of powers," "guarantee of basic human rights," and "universal suffrage and fair election." In addition, the political rhetoric and criticisms from proponents of liberal democracy exposed, wittingly or unwittingly, the form and extent of the violations and distortions, further provoking democratic movements.[3] This irony that we encounter in pretransitional Korea resonates with most Third World countries where authoritarian regimes profess adherence to liberal democracy but are in actuality maintaining a dual political order, the result of nonsimultaneity.

On the contrary, antidemocratic and conservative ruling elites in nineteenth-century Western Europe—for example, the Tories in England; Napoleon I, the July Monarchy, and Napoleon III in France; Metternich in Austria; and Bismarck in Germany—did not have to legitimate their rule in the name of liberalism or democracy and thus dominated politics despite open hostility toward them. However, as in many other contemporary Third World countries, Korea's conservative regimes were faced with the uncomfortable dilemma of having to justify their authoritarian rule in democracy's name. Therefore the ruling conservative forces had to devise a rhetoric that incorporated these two mutually contradictory political systems, as witnessed with the Rhee, Park, and Chun regimes.

From this perspective, Korean conservatism before democratization may be defined as an ideology by which ruling right-wing forces justified and defended the authoritarian political order they believed was indispensable to protecting democracy against the impending communist threat and maintaining the political stability necessary for sustained economic development and strong national security. Thus authoritarian political leaders and their ideologues were highly sensitive to their lack of democratic legitimacy and were obliged to devise a political discourse that related national security and economic development to democracy. In other words, the advocacy of anticommunism had to be framed not as a defense of the actual authoritarianism but as a protection of a hypothetical democracy; likewise, the emphasis on economic development was not for the sake of maintaining authoritarianism but for the sake of building democracy on a sound base. The dual political order thus indicated that authoritarianism cannot secure legitimacy by and for itself and it would be granted only transitional or mediational, rather than durable or ultimate, legitimacy. Although these regimes adopted authoritarian rules to suppress communist movements or implement economic development, the ultimate locus of political legitimation for them was not authoritarianism per se but the defense and building of "democracy."[4] In this respect an inherent tension derived from the incongruence of means and ends: The authoritarian means were a flagrant violation of their own ends.

The concurrence of authoritarianism and liberal democracy helps us understand the somewhat paradoxical slogans used by the democratic movement in Korea, such as "defending the constitution," "opposing the [arbitrary] revision of the constitution," "protecting democracy," and "restoring democracy," most of which appear to be based on the premise that democracy is the status quo. Democratic activists used these slogans to highlight the purpose of maintaining or restoring the original constitution, whereas ruling elites attempted or initiated constitutional revisions to achieve their antidemocratic political goals. This suggests a duality whereby democracy and authoritarianism constituted the normative and actual realities, respectively. The activists launched democratic movements and initiatives, invoking the normative against the actual, and made frequent demands for constitutional revisions to restore democracy. Of course, there is no denying that these slogans contained conservative philosophy and rhetoric in the sense that radical democratic movements had to express themselves in moderate terms. Such a moderate tone was in part necessitated by the political reality, for prodemocracy leaders and activists sought to avoid oppression by the authoritarian regimes that frequently charged them with committing subversive communist activities. At the same time, such slogans were effective in enhancing the legitimacy of their beliefs because they were able to pretend that they did not demand something radical or revolutionary but only sought to defend and restore democracy.[5]

Through the preceding discussion it can be observed that the dual political order of authoritarianism and democracy as well as their complex interplay in general and the actual historical experience of authoritarian rule in particular, although facilitating democratic movements, led Korean democratization strongly in a conservative direction. Thus, in contrast to the radical experiments and diverse experiences of nineteenth-century Europe, there were hardly any democratic proposals based on daring visions or creative inspiration that envisaged participatory, socioeconomic, self-managing, or industrial democracies, except for crude emulations of Leninist socialist revolution. Thus, in addition to the harsh oppression of Korean democratic movements rendered by authoritarian regimes, the dual political order had deeply restrained their imagination.

In terms of the historical experience of authoritarianism, most Koreans, including opposition political and religious leaders, envisioned restoring or defending democracy; overall, democratic movements unfolded within the horizon of liberal democracy. In particular, as an experiential reaction to the targeting of preceding authoritarian regimes by democratic struggles, Koreans tended to identify democracy with opposition to prolonged one-person rule, indirect election of the president by the rubber-stamp electoral college, military rule via a military coup d'état, and so on. This is confirmed by the fact that "winning constitutional revision for direct presidential elections" was the centripetal slogan that mobilized and united the people in the democratic movement in the streets, culminating in the historic June Struggle for democracy in 1987. The slogan was little more than a call for restoring or defending liberal democracy.

As noted in chapter 1, this is the context for liberal democracy as both ruling and insurgent ideologies. The ultimately conservative nature of the latter aspect derived from this duality. Liberal democracy as ruling ideology functioned as an upper limit, restricting the ideational imagination and practical radicalness of liberal democracy as insurgent ideology. In turn, the latter aspect reinforced the legitimacy of the former. This brings to mind a familiar proverb: "There's no such a thing as a free lunch."

The concurrence was also responsible for the paradoxical evaluation given by the people to a series of democratic governments that came to power after democratization. Although people reacted lukewarmly or with indifference to sweeping democratic reforms and measures introduced by successive reformist democratic governments after a short period of acclamation, they became very sensitive to or easily disappointed with short-term political failures; democratic governments came under severe popular criticism, despite their valuable long-term contributions. People might have hailed various democratic reform measures with temporary support and enjoyed political confidence at the time; however, because democracy had long been present as a normative reality for most people, the reformed reality was soon taken for granted, as the actual reality approximated the normative. Or, to put it differently, given that most people had vicariously experienced the political reality of democracy in Western nations through education and the mass media, democratized Korean political reality was easily absorbed into the banal conservatism of everyday life. Thus people were overtaken by despair and cynicism after realizing that democracy, considered a panacea during authoritarian rule, failed to match their expectations and that Korean political reality would not soon catch up with the reality of advanced Western democracies. It may, therefore, be plausible to interpret the significant decline in turnouts at presidential and parliamentary elections since democratization in part as a reflection of such disappointment and cynicism.[6]

Furthermore, the concurrence has highlighted the political problem of "coping with past evils," a problem Korea shared with other newly democratized countries in the late twentieth century but was alien to Western democracies—namely, England and France. Western democratization was a transformation by a causal change in which democracy gradually gained legitimacy, not by a teleological change in which democracy had already secured legitimacy as the goal of transformation. The problem of coping with past evils, therefore, was not a public issue in Western nations when their democracy was finally consolidated. For example, the French Third Republic in the 1870s, which could be defined as a moderate democracy, did not face such a problem despite the massacre of workers during the June revolt soon after the February Revolution of 1848 and the slaughter of Paris citizens during the Paris Commune of 1871. In their contemporary perspective, struggles and conflicts between conservative and democratic or radical forces had been a struggle between each party for political mastery and legitimacy. Because no publicly recognized normative standard had been established, it might have been rather odd if the tasks associated with coping with past evils—such as truth finding, the punishment of wrongdoers, and the acquittal, rehabilitation, and compensation of victims—had been raised on grounds of political oppression once democracy was secured. These problems were raised vigorously, however, in newly democratized nations in the late twentieth century—notably, in South Africa, Argentina, and South Korea. Given that democracy had already established itself as the normative standard in the concurrence, political persecution and retaliation committed as part of the antidemocratic measures of authoritarian regimes became critical issues.[7]

OTHER CHARACTERISTICS

When liberalism, conservatism, nationalism, and radicalism, all of which are of Western origin, are introduced to a latecomer country such as South Korea in a compressed and simultaneous manner, what characteristics are displayed in their introduction and evolution as compared with Western Europe, where various ideologies emerged in an endogenous, gradual, and consecutive way? Bearing in mind that contemporary Korean politics belatedly adopted exogenous Western ideologies, let us examine Korea's ideological terrain.

Importation of Various Ideologies as Finished Products

The dialectic of nonsimultaneity brought about a phenomenon whereby political ideologies were imported as finished products from outside without the opportunity for autonomous and self-sustaining growth fueled by endogenous momentum. Roughly speaking, a historical survey of innovation of political ideologies shows an interesting contrast between the center and the periphery: innovation in the center tends to take place in an endogenous manner in response to the possibility of a breakdown of the paradigmatic political ideology, whereas innovation on the periphery is likely to take the form of importing and appropriating progressive external ideas and shying away from endogenous innovation of political ideology, to fight the threat to survival posed by foreign powers, and to satisfy various political needs to innovate the body politic or to introduce more effective political formulae for legitimation presumed as universal.[8] Therefore, societal change and innovation in political ideas tend to display strong attributes of teleological change in addition to those of causal change. In this process, political ideology pursued as an end on the periphery secures "borrowed legitimacy" due to the inflow from the "prestigious" center, more so than endogenous legitimacy won by its own struggle for acceptance.

If we apply this explanation to modern Korea's adoption of the four major ideologies of Western origin, this phenomenon is more pronounced in universal ideologies such as liberalism and socialism than in particularistic ideologies such as nationalism and conservatism, which tend to reflect the specific historical context of a given polity. As mentioned earlier, liberalism and socialism were imported as finished products, due to teleological change. As a consequence, liberalism, which appeared in South Korea after liberation in 1945, was not introduced in the form of an oligarchic ideology of the bourgeois republic but in the form of a liberal democracy that went through its own evolution, including its struggles with conservatism, socialism, and radical democracy, to reach its final stage of granting universal suffrage. Likewise, the mainstream form of socialism introduced into Korea during Japanese colonial rule was Marxism-Leninism, the version formulated after the Bolshevik Revolution in 1917, and not one of the other variants of Marxism. We may interpret this phenomenon as a *preemptive* or *progressive* effect brought about by the dialectic of nonsimultaneity.[9]

The same is true of conservatism and nationalism in liberated and divided South Korea. This country found itself obliged to hail democracy in its 1948 founding constitution due to the imposition of world-standard time. Conservatism in Korea, therefore, had to embrace liberal democracy, at least superficially; it was later added to contemporary Western conservatism, which had originally been opposed to liberalism and democracy in the nineteenth century. Nationalism in South Korea, too, embraced democracy as one of its cherished goals, although such was not the case with nationalism in various parts of Europe in the nineteenth century. In this way liberal democracy, which was the final product of long and violent struggles among proponents of various ideologies in the West, has shaped and mediated the development of conservatism and nationalism in contemporary South Korea since the mid-twentieth century.

The political ideas thus imported into a latecomer country on the periphery went through a historical trajectory different from those generated by countries in the center. We may illustrate this point with the evolution of liberalism in contemporary Korea. On the one hand, when liberalism appeared in England for the first time in history, it emerged as a rebellious or insurgent ideology, challenging the reign of "political absolutism," "religious conformity," and "ascriptive status" (Ball and Dagger 2004, 50–60); it finally rose (autonomously) to be the ruling ideology in the wake of strenuous political struggles and turmoil, including revolutions and civil and religious wars.[10] On the other hand, in latecomer countries, such as South Korea in 1945, liberalism was accommodated as the ruling ideology in the form of liberal democracy, the finished version of liberalism that enjoyed borrowed legitimacy, according to the preemptive direction of the global ideological terrain in general and to the overwhelming influence of the United States, which occupied South Korea at the end of World War II, in particular.

Thus the problem in Korea arose not before but after liberalism had ascended to the status of an official ruling ideology. Although it came to occupy this dominant status as a political idea and regime by being embodied and enshrined in the founding constitution, liberalism ended up functioning as more of a fictitious ideology to justify conservative authoritarian regimes until the time of democratization in 1987, primarily because politicians and the general populace were not equipped with the political competence to manage it properly—the immaturity of local historical time. Liberalism therefore had to descend to the position of a rebellious ideology, taking the form of a democratic movement before ascending to proper ruling-ideology status after successful democratization (Moon Ji-young 2009). This was a historical trajectory opposite to those of England and France.

In addition, the fact that liberal democracy was imported into South Korea as a finished product suggests that the probable tension between liberalism and democracy had not been recognized—at least not until democratization in 1987. In contrast, liberalism and democracy had been placed in a mutually reinforcing yet contradictory relationship in the process of democratizing England. Many proponents of liberalism in England, for example, were opposed to democratization, fearing that the extension of suffrage would bring about the tyranny of the majority, the danger of mediocrity, the stifling of the creative minority, and infringement of individual freedoms, including property rights. However, liberal democracy as the final version of liberalism was imported to South Korea without engendering any tension between liberalism and democracy due to the preemptive effect of borrowed legitimacy. Moreover, the mainstream of the opposition democratic movement demanded and carried out democratization without suspecting a contradiction between liberalism and democracy because authoritarian regimes violated both at the same time.[11]

Only after democratization—especially under the governments of reformist presidents Kim Dae-jung and Roh Moo-hyun—did Korean politics witness some acute tension between liberalism and democracy. Conservatives in the opposition, who rebranded themselves as liberals or the "New Right," pressured the two reformist governments by insisting on the rule of law, constitutionalism, the separation of powers, "small government and big market," and the protection of private property; they even tried to impeach the president through the Constitutional Court. At the same time, they developed a discursive offensive, stigmatizing the reformist governments as "populist" and "pro-North [Korea], left-wing." The conservatives cornered the government in order to oppose greater civic participation. They were eager to criticize the governments on liberal grounds, accusing them of mobilizing the populace and seeking the tyranny of the majority.[12]

Premature Ideological Clash and Precocious "Conservatization" of Liberal Democracy

Whereas major ideologies—such as liberalism, conservatism, and socialism—were imported in compressed and almost simultaneous ways in latecomer countries on the periphery, like Korea, these ideologies appeared gradually in Western European nations. For example, after liberalism and republicanism first appeared in England and France, conservatism as conscious traditionalism emerged in reaction; various kinds of socialism criticizing liberalism and capitalism arose as industrialization progressed. In this process, English liberalism had at least 150 years, until the mid-nineteenth century, to consolidate itself as a ruling ideology without being challenged by socialism. French liberalism (or republicanism) had considerable time—from 1789 until the revolution of February 1848—to establish itself as a hegemonic ideology while its supporters engaged in strenuous struggles with revolutionary dictatorships and conservative royalists.[13]

When socialism rose in Europe in the mid-nineteenth century, threatening both liberalism and conservatism (which originally had been opposed to each other), the two ideologies underwent mutation and bifurcation. Some among the conservatives and liberals began to gradually converge and form an alliance in fear of the rise of socialism. In other words, some liberals, feeling threatened by the emergence of socialism, became conservative, and some conservatives began to slowly and partially accept the reality shaped by liberalism, becoming more hospitable to liberalism in order to fight the more radical and threatening socialism. In addition, a sect of liberalism began to reconstruct itself partially through the appropriation of socialist elements, leading to the formation of welfare liberalism, a progressive version of the ideology introduced by Thomas Hill Green. Moderate socialism and social democracy also emerged, seeking a gradual transition to socialism along the parliamentary road and leading to the mutual convergence of liberalism and socialism.

In Germany, however, the building of the nation-state was delayed, and, unlike the lengthy development afforded France and England, the evolution of political ideologies as well as industrialization was compressed. Due to the need to forge a strategic compromise between liberalism and nationalism to achieve national unification and the premature rise of socialism, liberalism was not able to fully carry out its progressive potential (Langewiesche 2000, xiv–xvi). As a result, unified Germany fell prey to reactionary far-right nationalism, which appeared under the name of National Socialism (Nazism).

The case of South Korea differs from those of England and France but is close to the case of Germany. Yet Korea was forced to meet the challenge of modernization in a more belated and compressed manner than Germany was; hence clashes among diverse ideologies due to nonsimultaneity erupted more violently. Liberalism and socialism appeared almost simultaneously among independence activists during Japanese colonial rule in the 1920s, segregating them into bitterly hostile camps primarily over conflicts regarding a proper strategy for the independence struggle and the political blueprint for an independent Korea.[14] In addition to other factors, the premature confrontation with socialism made Korean liberalism more conservative and docile in the face of Japanese colonial rule. Similarly, the differences between the two ideologies as to how to build an independent nation led them to volatile confrontations even after liberation.

Given Korea's colonial heritage, however, the capitalist economic order and liberal democracy that President Rhee Syngman, the Korea Democratic Party, and other conservatives sought to introduce and institutionalize in the First Republic were not based on the existing order but were to be realized progressively through the radical reform of Korean society. The existing order—a (predominantly) premodern agricultural economy in which landlord-tenant farming was widespread—had to be reconstructed into a capitalist form of agriculture, whereas the autocratic political order fashioned by Japanese fascism was to be transformed into liberal democracy. The urgent task facing Korean conservatives was not to conserve but rather to build Korean society in an innovative way to implement capitalist industrialization and liberal democracy.

In this perspective, both liberalism and socialism had progressive potential in liberated Korea. But liberalism, once adopted as the ruling ideology, underwent "conservatization" at an early stage in reaction to the premature threat from socialism within and without (i.e., North Korea). Because the bourgeoisie was in an inchoate state, Korean liberalism was not accompanied and supported by a strong class and, therefore, did not maintain ideological vigor. Once liberalism confronted socialism with great mass appeal, it became reactionary in order to defend itself against socialism. The ruling conservative elite, moreover, were willing to give up liberal democracy as their top priority and instead justified authoritarian rule by stressing the necessity of anticommunism for national security against the impending North Korean communist threat and, later, the urgency of economic development for modernization.[15] For this reason, liberal democracy failed to reform Korean political reality in line with its own vision and remained mostly to justify an authoritarian regime pitting itself against communist North Korea.

Transcontextual Confrontation among Ideologies

As various ideologies simultaneously competed with one another for legitimacy by attacking one another on a speculative and transhistorical level rather than by criticizing one another within the concrete and historical settings, their clashes tended to become more vociferous and vehement. In the case of Western Europe, where divergent ideologies appeared gradually and consecutively, socialism emerged to challenge liberalism as the ruling ideology once liberalism had shaped society according to its own vision to a substantial degree and then bred its own contradictions. The confrontation between the two ideologies thus had more substantial and practical grounds. However, when socialism challenged liberalism in Korea before the latter successfully reformed and consolidated society, instead of criticizing liberalism's internal worth or logical coherence in light of the local setting, socialism manifested its radicalness and dogmatism by attacking liberalism in a more speculative and ideological dimension. An epitome of this was shown clearly when socialist-oriented intellectuals and activists followed Marxist criticism and defined Korean liberalism as bourgeois-class ideology and liberal democracy as bourgeois democracy and rejected them in toto. These intellectuals applied the Western context to Korea without careful or concrete analysis of Korean politics and society under military authoritarianism, in which the bourgeoisie in the Western sense was weak and dependent from the beginning, and core constitutional principles of liberal democracy, such as guaranteed human rights, the rule of law, and the separation of powers, had never been fully realized.[16] In these circumstances, both liberalism and socialism failed to control Korean society and merely remained in a speculative dimension. Their confrontation, therefore, lacked the vital element of reality, resulting in the eruption of a much stronger reaction or radicalism: a combination of substantial emptiness and dogmatic intensity. The violent ideological confrontation between the right and the left in the aftermath of liberation and the clamorous ideological controversies among leftist activists in the late 1980s and early 1990s are such cases.[17]

This phenomenon, familiar among Japanese intellectuals tormented by the rush to modernize, was keenly captured by Maruyama Masao, one of the most outstanding political thinkers of postwar Japan. Maruyama conceptualized the phenomenon as the "premature emergence of ideological critique" in the ideological terrain of latecomer Japan. He defined *ideological critique* as a "mode of criticism in which political ideas are criticized not from the perspective of their internal worth or logical coherence but from an external perspective." That is, they "are criticized by pointing to the sociopolitical roles—such as their function of concealing or prettifying reality—that political ideas were supposed to carry out or by unmasking the hidden motives or intentions lying behind them" (Maruyama 1998, 70).[18]

An ideological critique originally developed by Marx secured the historical context of contemporary European society for him, although it appeared partly as a "premature critique of the problems inherent in modern civil society and rationalism" (Maruyama 1998, 70). For Maruyama, however, the ideological critique by Japanese intellectuals ignored the historical context of contemporary Japanese society; it was launched from a point that took the European historical context as its standard—that is, from a Eurocentric perspective. He makes the point as follows:

> As the goal of evolution in Japan since the Meiji Restoration has been set as achieving the level of "advanced" Europe, so the Western complex and the progress complex are inseparably intertwined in evaluating political ideas. Consequently, their superiority and inferiority are examined not in terms of the actual significance they acquire in the Japanese ideological terrain but in terms of the historical sequence in which they were formed in Western history. . . . Under these circumstances, the discourse that the ideology of progressives is already outdated in Europe (or America) has been conventionally used [to criticize them]. A case in point is that Kato Hiroyuki attacked the illusion of naturally endowed human rights by opposing the theory of evolution [Darwinism] to the theory of natural rights. . . . [In these processes, Japanese intellectuals] sought to schematize historical evolution and the development of political ideas without examining all sorts of ideas in light of the Japanese reality, thereby deleting social context. (76–78)

Maruyama also points to the superficial radicalness and substantial emptiness illustrated by the bitter confrontation between left and right ideologies that erupted in the 1960s:

> Whatever ideologies are at issue now—liberalism, communism, and social democracy, for instance—were all imported from abroad and so were not formulated by the Japanese through their lived experience. Whereas democracy remains as a mode of life to Americans, the mode of everyday life in Japan

and these various ideologies exist side by side—indeed, without any substantial mediation. Although this basic fact has been pointed out repeatedly, Japanese intellectuals or pseudointellectuals actually forget it or deliberately turn away from it when examining the current political situation, so they end up tailoring Japanese political reality to the schematic confrontation of American democracy and Soviet communism. (Maruyama 1997, 181)

Similar to the situation in Japan described by Maruyama, ideological controversies and confrontations in Korea unfolded clamorously on the surface, displaying a tendency to proceed without the actual mediation of political reality. This intense ideological engagement has therefore failed to take root in the soil of everyday life in Korea (Kim Dong-chun 1997b).

Authenticity Controversy

In relation to the preceding point and as a consequence of the nonsimultaneity dialectic, the "authenticity" controversy surrounding diverse ideologies has occurred more frequently and intensely in latecomer Korea. In the West the process of forming political ideas was original and gradual: Ideas were not imported prematurely and preemptively from the outside, regardless of the sociohistorical context of the country. As a result, controversy surrounding the authenticity of various ideologies rarely arose. Examination of and reflection on the origin and development of any given political ideology were usually made with the benefit of hindsight and only after the ideology had matured; this left little room for controversy regarding authenticity in actual politics. The term *liberalism*, for example, was first used in the early nineteenth century when a faction of the Spanish legislature adopted the name *Liberales*. It then traveled to France and on to England, where the party known as the Whigs evolved into the Liberal Party by the 1840s (Ball and Dagger 2004, 43). For this reason, there has been no political or ideological controversy as to whether such thinkers as Locke, Montesquieu, Voltaire, Adam Smith, and James Madison were "genuine" liberals, except perhaps on rare occasions.[19]

The same is true of *conservatism*, a term that originated from the title of the short-lived French magazine *Le Conservateur* (1818–1820), published by F. Chateaubriand. The term traveled to England in 1835, and it became common currency in Germany in the 1830s (Klemperer 1972, 164). Almost thirty years before the coinage of the word, however, Edmund Burke, considered the founder of conservatism, articulated his conservative political thought in *Reflections on the Revolution in France* (1790) just after the outbreak of the French Revolution. Thus, formally speaking, Burke and his contemporary Tories could be regarded as "conservatives before conservatism."

Likewise, Joseph de Maistre, the French thinker who was violently opposed to the French Revolution, and American Federalists such as John Adams and Alexander Hamilton were also considered conservative, but the label was applied posthumously because they lived before 1820. It would, therefore, seem rather far-fetched to suppose that there was any sort of authenticity controversy over whether these figures were genuine conservatives. Even if such a controversy had been raised posthumously, it would have been in the form of academic research rather than political polemics. Marxism, however, constitutes an important exception, for it acquired a dogmatic and monopolistic quality like that of Christianity, not only in Marx's lifetime but also later on—that is, it has been converted, to use Maruyama's phrase, into a kind of "cult of theory," thereby condemned to suffer from the perennial controversies of orthodoxy and revisionism (or reneging).[20] It seems proper in Marxism to interpret the authenticity controversy as deriving from its unique characteristics.

Contemporary Korean politics, by contrast, has witnessed frequent and heated controversies regarding the authenticity of various ideologies. This appears to be due to certain general conditions prevalent in most latecomer countries as well as some unique Korean factors. Above all, we may surmise that many ideologies prevalent in the Korean political soil originated in the West and were imported as finished products, resulting in their universalization and frequent transhistorical idealization as eternal models by most Koreans. As a matter of course, however, the historical and political situation in Korea would not allow the exact reproduction and evolution of these ideologies, in terms of form and substance, as they had originally undergone in the West. Thus, above all else, it was the discrepancy between purportedly universal Western ideologies and ideologies actually realized in Korea that brought about the authenticity controversy.

To illustrate this authenticity controversy as it applies to discourses on liberalism in Korean society, I suggest beginning with the distinction between *anticommunist liberalism* and *liberal anticommunism* in Korean politics: The former is willing to sacrifice the essential components of freedom and the rights of individual citizens for the sake of anticommunism, whereas the latter would not admit such sacrifice, despite asserting anticommunism. Stressing the freedom of the nation or the state over that of the individual, the former has a close affinity with liberalism as ruling ideology and the latter with insurgent liberalism. Thus the insurgent liberals or radicals tend to criticize anticommunist liberals by engaging the authenticity controversy, frequently labeling them "pseudo," "sham," "fake," "spurious," "corrupt," "sycophant," and/or "subservient" liberals in contrast to "conscientious," "genuine," and "authentic" liberals. Such labels are meant to suggest that they are not proper liberals in the Western sense.[21]

At the same time, it is intriguing to find a reverse form of the authenticity controversy over liberalism in the "color offensive," a Korean version of the red-baiting discourse, which has been used frequently by conservative ruling forces or politicians to stigmatize their political enemies as "reds," "pro-North leftists," "impure leftists," "left-wingers," and "communist sympathizers," among other epithets, in an ideological terrain strongly dominated by anticommunism. From the perspective of anticommunist liberalism, those anticommunist rightists who engage in the color offensive simply dichotomize the ideological terrain of Korean politics into right-wing liberalism and leftist communism without admitting to any middle-of-the-roaders, and then they accuse their opponents of being communists incompatible with liberalism.[22] This strange logic may derive from the very same mentality that enables them to identify themselves as the only genuine liberals because "anticommunism equals liberalism." Thus their color offensive may be interpreted as containing an inverted form of the authenticity controversy, and their mentality may be the result of a kind of morbid anticommunism fetish, worsened by the South-North confrontation. They would consider liberalism tolerant of communism to be an oxymoron.

There are also caustic criticisms leveled by Korean liberals aiming to raise the authenticity controversy. Lee Geun-sik (2001), a well-known liberal Korean intellectual, for example, stresses that in Korean society, *liberalism (jayujuui)* has been "one of the most misunderstood words" among those imported from the West. He laments that reactionaries identify it with anticommunism, whereas progressives criticize it as greedy egoism. Lee maintains that such phenomena derive from a misunderstanding of liberalism, which was originally the "sound idea of modern citizens who overthrew oppressive and discriminatory absolute monarchies and traditional class structures and built modern civil societies characterized by democracy and the rule of law" in the West (13). Lee's argument, which stresses the prevalent misunderstanding of liberalism in Korean society and the subsequent need for correction, may be intertwined with his implicit complaint that a genuine liberal like him in Korean society is totally misunderstood. In this sense, his argument itself becomes implicated in the authenticity controversy.

Liberalism is not the sole concern of the authenticity controversy, which is also found in political, journalistic, and academic discourses on conservatism. In order to condemn conservatives in Korea, liberals and radicals who engage in democratic movements against authoritarian regimes often use such expressions as "reactionary conservative," "reactionary," and "slavish defender of the past" (*sugu*) in contrast to conservatives whose genuineness is recognized by an implicit standard—that is, by whether their brand of conservatism is in accord with that of the West, especially of a Burkean variety. Thus some conservatives attach such adjectives as *reformist, rational*, and *middle of the road* to the word *conservative* to avoid associated negative connotations.

However, controversy over genuine conservatism sometimes took place from the opposite perspective. In the fifteenth general election, held in April 1996, for example, the ruling Sinhangukdang (New Korea Party) and the conservative Jayuminjuyeonhap (Liberal Democratic Union) proclaimed themselves "the original conservatives," "the genuine conservatives," or "the orthodox conservatives" and competed to win votes of the conservative middle class, which cherished political stability and anticommunism. Simultaneously, they accused Saejeongchigungminyeonhap (National Union for New Politics), Kim Dae-jung's opposition party and professed reformist conservatives, of being "disguised conservatives," by which they meant that the party was a group of closet communists or communist sympathizers. Of course, this discursive strategy was intended as part of the so-called color offensive mentioned earlier. These phenomena illustrate the interestingly diverse forms of the authenticity controversy in conservatism.

Moreover, when the radical democratic movements bore the zeal of revolutionaries in the late 1980s and early 1990s, heated debates arose among radical activists over who represented genuine Marxism-Leninism. The debates were characterized more by the aforementioned dogmatic features of Marxism-Leninism than by the nonsimultaneity dialectic.

The authenticity controversy has also manifested itself rather vehemently in academic and political discourses about Korean nationalism. It typically has erupted over the question of whether the political activities and policies of specific politicians or political groups could be interpreted as nationalistic, focusing on such issues as the debate over the purge of pro-Japanese elements during the Japanese colonial period; the evaluation of Japanese colonial rule and whether it had a modernizing effect on Korea; Korea-Japan exchanges after independence, such as the normalization of bilateral relations; Japan's economic exploitation of South Korea; the national unification problem; and attitudes toward American imperialism. Of course, strong nationalism has prevailed as a universal phenomenon in newly independent states since the end of World War II. However, the humiliating loss of national sovereignty to the Japanese, whom Koreans had hitherto regarded as their inferiors, the painful division of the peninsula and its perpetuation, the June 25 (Korean) War, and the fervent national desire for reunification have driven Korean nationalism to become impassioned and overarching for both the South and the North.[23] This has resulted in the dominance of "sanctified" nationalism in Korea's ideological terrain. Such sanctified nationalism can never be blemished by political vicissitudes, whereas other ideologies, such as liberalism, conservatism, and socialism, are liable to political contamination.[24]

The authenticity controversy regarding nationalism developed at two levels: first between South and North Korea, then between contending political forces within South Korea. The regimes in South and North Korea have each professed themselves to be the only legitimate representative of the nation while accusing the other party of being a puppet of foreign (imperialist or communist) powers or a subordinate regime, a national traitor that initiated and now perpetuates national division, slavishly following the Soviet Union or the United States. In this way, each party refuses to recognize the other as a legitimate political entity.

Contemporary South Korean politics is not immune to the authenticity controversy, especially regarding the question of whether the rules of presidents Rhee Syngman and Park Chung-hee may be considered nationalist, either in terms of overall regimes or particular policies. Heated debates continue as to whether the preemptive establishment of the South Korean government initiated by President Rhee Syngman was antinationalistic because it resulted in the permanent division of the peninsula and whether President Park Chung-hee's modernization drive focusing on rapid economic development was antinationalistic because it excluded the well-being of the *minjung* (popular) strata, including peasants and workers, and rather made the Korean economy dependent on foreign powers such as Japan and the United States. Similarly, the North Korea policies initiated by the two presidents were labeled antinationalistic because they contributed only to perpetuating and strengthening division rather than seeking to facilitate the process of unification or alleviating the ills of division. One observer has accused presidents Rhee and Park of promoting "antinationalistic nationalism," an oxymoron, because they oppressed and persecuted other nationalistic leaders and activists relentlessly while spouting nationalist rhetoric and discourses (Park Myeong-lim 1996b, 66).[25] As such, nationalism in Korea has held the status of a political religion, to the degree that to denounce a certain political leader or group as a national traitor or antinationalist has effectively meant passing on them a political death sentence.

CONCLUDING REMARKS

This chapter examines the ideological terrain of contemporary Korean politics, in which diverse ideologies were adopted in a compressed and simultaneous manner from the West. This adoption of ideologies has been compared with the case of Western Europe, where various ideologies emerged in a gradual and consecutive manner. The overall ideological terrain and individual ideologies, however, have been examined only in a preliminary way and thus require more elaborate study. Our examination so far, however, has revealed many intriguing features, because various ideologies that evolved in the West over the more than two hundred years since the French Revolution in 1789 have come to acquire their basic shapes in South Korea only within the last seventy years, due to the compressed adoption characterized by the dialectic of nonsimultaneity.

It should be remembered, however, that the dialectic of nonsimultaneity and its derivative phenomena were widely observed among Korean intellectuals and activists during Japanese colonial rule as well. For example, Seo Sang-il, who underwent diverse political vicissitudes in the Rhee Syngman regime, once recollected his life experience in the 1930s. "There were frequent shifts in political opinions or positions whenever we all came across a new book," he writes, "since we were not familiar with new European knowledge. While sometimes discussing far-left political philosophy, we asserted the revival of feudal systems. While speaking of far-right political theory, we advanced the socialization of property" (Seo Sang-il 1957, 53).

The situation did not change much over the next thirty years. Koh Jeong-hun, who was imprisoned after the May 16 military coup in 1961 for his involvement in progressive activity, expressed a "bewildering hodgepodge of various ideologies" floating through his mind, written in his poem "Fragmented Thoughts in the Prison" in the 1960s:

I am a double-faced person, no, maybe a triple-faced

Head is a socialist, an idealist, a rationalist

Heart is a nationalist, a romanticist, an adventurer

Belly is a capitalist, a realist, a sensualist

This way, I am an existential man, a bundle of contradictions.

(1966, 34)

If we survey the current ideological terrain of Korean politics roughly in terms of the party system, we see that diverse political ideologies—displayed by a conservative liberal party, a reformist liberal party, a progressive social democratic party, and so on—decorate the political landscape of Korea. However, they have not undergone long maturation or saturated actual politics and everyday life as they have in Western Europe. So questions arise as to whether a politician or a political party espouses an ideology in a serious manner and seeks to put it into practice in daily politics. Does a Korean liberal politician combine individualism and economic and political liberalism consistently and seek to practice them in daily life as well as in the political arena? Does a Korean conservative make an effort to maintain and effectively adjust a conservative worldview to contemporary politics while also seeking to reappropriate Korean history, tradition, authority, and religion? Does a Korean nationalist properly seek to harmonize diverse goals of nationalism, such as prosperity, unification, and democracy? And, finally, does a Korean socialist or social democrat seek to mobilize the working class to challenge the dominating presence of neoliberalism by developing viable alternatives and policies while also coping with the thorny problem of North Korea, which is becoming an anachronistic, hereditary monarchy?

It does not seem easy to answer these questions in the affirmative. This is one factor in the perennial identity crisis of various ideologies and their professed adherents in Korean politics. The fundamental reason for such a situation lies in the contemporary predicament facing Korean politics: diverse ideologies were imported from abroad to meet the political needs of the elite and were exhausted as quickly as nondurable consumer goods rather than taking root in the Korean political soil and interacting with the general populace. It cannot be emphasized too strongly that the task of applying ideologies as productive goods, whereby diverse political groups seek to persuade people of their professed ideologies by developing and disseminating viable and differentiated policies, is long overdue despite Korea's democratic experiment over the last three decades.

NOTES

Chapter 2—though revised and adapted for this book—has been published previously, and I am grateful for permission to draw upon it. It is based on chapter 1, "The Ideological Terrain of Contemporary Korean Politics: From the Perspective of the Dialectic of Non-Simultaneity," pages 21–43, in Jung In Kang, ed., *Contemporary Korean Political Thought in Search of a Post-Eurocentric Approach* (Lanham: Lexington, 2014).

1. A more comprehensive picture of Korea's ideological terrain would be captured by comparing the Korean experience not simply with that of Western Europe but also with that of non-Western countries—notably, other East Asian, Latin American, or Eastern and Southern European countries. However, our mainstream convention of building knowledge remains quite Western-centric in the sense that knowledge about non-Western societies is obtained and accumulated primarily by examining their experience in light of Western experiences and concepts. This is, indeed, a regrettable academic practice to be overcome sooner or later.

2. The concept actually originated in art history (Schwartz 2001, 61–62).

3. This is easily confirmed in the criticisms leveled by opposition democratic forces when they condemned rigged elections, advocated the freedom of the press, and demanded the revision of the constitution to restore democracy. These criticisms, ironically, make sense because they presupposed liberal democracy as the normative reality.

4. For a detailed examination of Korean conservatism, see Kang Jung In 2009b.

5. However, radical activists led antigovernmental movements under the Chun Doo-hwan government in the 1980s; the movement thus became revolutionized to the

point that it was not satisfied to call itself merely a "restoring democracy movement." From then on its proponents defined it as a "democratization movement" in order to distinguish it from the moderate movement of the earlier period, thereby rejecting the conservative overtones of previous labels. At the same time, the new label bore the implicit orientation of criticizing liberal democracy as mere bourgeois democracy.

6. Voter turnout at presidential elections decreased from 89.2 percent in 1987, the year of the democratic transition, to 63.0 percent in 2007, when Lee Myung-bak was elected. The turnout at the presidential election of 2012, in which Park Geun-hye was elected as president, was unusually high, reaching 75.8 percent, and surprised many Koreans. The voter turnout at general elections decreased from 75.8 percent in 1988 to 46.1 percent in 2008, although the general election in 2012 witnessed an increase to 54.2 percent, which is nonetheless still quite low. However, the general election in 2016 under the current Park Geun-hye government witnessed an encouraging upsurge of 58.0 percent, which would in turn lead to a surprising victory for opposition parties.

7. The interpretation suggested here should not be understood as the assertion that newly democratized countries since the late twentieth century have successfully tackled the task of coping with past evils. In most countries in Southeast Asia and Latin America that were democratized like South Korea the task could be neither attempted nor carried out successfully due to the strong presence of authoritarian elements—including the military—remaining even after democratization. The point to be made here, however, is that a strong case for coping with past evils can be made for democratized non-Western countries in the late twentieth century, whereas such a case could not be made for Western democracies in the nineteenth century.

8. However, the difference between the center and the periphery in this regard should be considered a matter of degree, not of kind.

9. This does not mean that there were no social democrats in Korea. For example, Yeo Un-hyeong and Jo So-ang were notable social democrats and were active in seeking reconciliation between leftist and rightist politicians in the aftermath of liberation in 1945.

10. When liberalism in England was developed on a full scale and with a pioneering spirit, there was close interaction between England and other neighboring countries sharing the same historical space in Western Europe. Thus, although the latter were strongly influenced by England as its own liberalism evolved, the notion of nonsimultaneity used here would not apply.

11. Of course, this statement does not apply to the radical or people's democracy advocated in the 1980s by leftist activists who sought to go beyond liberal democracy to reach their ultimate goal.

12. Western democratic nations faced strong opposition from liberals when they tried to introduce social-welfare policies and Keynesian macroeconomic measures, for such policies would in turn strengthen governmental intervention in the market. See Hirschman 1991 for a fascinating account. Also, for the transformative evolution of conservatism and the clash of liberalism and democracy in South Korea after democratization, see Kang Jung In 2008a and Park Chan-pyo 2007b.

13. In 1848, when Marx and Engels issued the famous *Communist Manifesto*, the challenge of socialism to liberalism began to emerge on a full scale.

14. The origin of Korean liberalism can be located in the late nineteenth century, when Western-oriented reformist intellectuals in the Joseon dynasty sought to introduce Western enlightenment and liberalism, including constitutional monarchy.

15. For more detail, see Kang Jung In 2009b.

16. See, for example, Lim Young-il 1991, 76–77.

17. Ideological vehemence from radicals and leftists erupted more vocally after democratization in 1987 because their voices and opinions, long suppressed under authoritarian rule, now enjoyed opportunities for public expression. Here I think I must moderate my argument stressing the effect of the nonsimultaneity dialectic to a certain extent, given that the violent ideological confrontation between the right and the left reflects the Korean political reality of fierce ideological confrontation between South and North Korea with the worldwide Cold War in the background. However, it would be myopic to stress the influence of national division in Korea too strongly, for political scientist Maruyama Masao observed the same phenomenon in prewar Japan, which was not divided like Korea.

18. All Maruyama quotations in this chapter were originally written in Japanese; they have been translated from the Korean-language version of his works into English by the author.

19. For example, such academic questions as is Rousseau a liberal or a totalitarian?

20. In short, Maruyama defines "fetishism for political theory and ideas" as the "cult of theory." For more details, see Maruyama 1998, 118–21.

21. These words are drawn mostly from Kim Dong-chun 1996a and 2006a.

22. President Rhee Syngman did not hesitate to accuse even an avowed right-wing anticommunist politician of being a red when opposed by him in the 1950s.

23. All these factors are elaborated on further in chapter 3.

24. The sanctification of nationalism in Korean politics is addressed more fully in the next chapter.

25. Park also included North Korean leader Kim Il-sung as representing antinationalistic nationalism.

Chapter 3

The Sanctification of Nationalism

In order to understand the concept of the sanctification of nationalism as it applies to Korea, we first need to review the evolution of nationalism in Western Europe. There, notably in England and France, nationalism as a secondary ideology was forged, more or less, in a flexible cooperative relationship with other ideologies, without overwhelming them, in the process of building a modern nation-state. England and France succeeded in building modern nation-states on the basis of a rather smooth territorial integration and a protonation that had already achieved the stage of a dynastic state. Thus, in England, nationalism was able to combine with liberalism through the idea of popular sovereignty. In France it would coast smoothly on republicanism from the French Revolution to the late nineteenth century without showing its strong ideological fervor.[1] This is confirmed as well by the observation that *state of nature* or *civil society* did not address the formation of the nation as an important issue in the social-contract theory of Hobbes and Locke, which provided embryonic liberalism in England. This is also true of Rousseau's theory of the social contract, which decisively shaped French republicanism. In other words, Hobbes, Locke, and Rousseau, in their theoretical construct of the social contract, were all preoccupied with the desirable shape of a modern state that was able to protect the freedom and rights of its members, with the unconscious assumption that individuals in the state of nature had already formed a protonation, sharing the same language and culture in a given territory.[2]

Confronted with the prowess of and pressure from England and France, which had succeeded as pioneers in building a modern nation-state, and at the same time agonizing over the German backwardness characterized by the divided and scattered state of the German nation and the absence of a bourgeois revolution, Johann Gottlieb Fichte had to address the issue of the national problem as well as the bourgeois revolution. Thus, paying attention to the different moments of modern state-building, Fichte distinguished between the *contract state*, a legal community that free and rational individuals would enter by the mutual agreement of individual wills, and the *nation-state* (*Volksstaat*), which was based on the common will beyond individual choices, primarily formed by a common language. Whereas the former is based on the reciprocity of rational individuals, the latter is based on the commonality of the nation (*Volk*). Fichte then sought to comprehend these two ideas of the state in a unifying developmental process of human history.[3] In other words, roughly speaking, whereas the building of the modern state in England and France proceeded by centering on the class problem posed by the bourgeois revolution on the basis of the protonation and territory already consolidated, that in Germany was confronted with the simultaneous solution of dual problems (i.e., the liquidation of feudal class relations and the unification and integration of scattered protonations into a modern nation-state).[4]

In contrast to the experience in Western Europe, however, modern Korean history witnessed the appearance of nationalism as a result of the dialectic of nonsimultaneity. Faced with the intrusion of Western powers into Northeast Asia in the late nineteenth century, Korean society under the Joseon dynasty aspired to modernization, while feeling inferior and backward vis-à-vis modern Western civilization. Thus, on the basis of the protonation and the territory stably formed in a traditional dynastic state, Koreans invoked nationalism by setting up the nation, rather than the bourgeois class or the traditional ruling class, as the subject of modernization (Schmid 2002). However, such a dynamic was first witnessed in Eastern Europe. Partha Chatterjee (1986) describes the appearance of Eastern European nationalism as follows:

> "Eastern" nationalism . . . had appeared among "peoples recently drawn into a civilization hitherto alien to them, and whose ancestral cultures are not adapted to success and excellence by these cosmopolitan and increasingly dominant standards." They too have measured the backwardness of their nations in terms of certain global standards set by the advanced nations of Western Europe. . . . There is also a fundamental awareness that those standards have come from an alien culture and that the inherited culture of the nation did not provide the necessary adaptive leverage to enable it to reach those standards of progress. The "Eastern" type of nationalism, consequently, has been accompanied by an effort to "re-equip" the nation culturally, to transform it. But it could not do so simply by imitating the alien culture, for then the nation would lose its distinctive identity. The search, therefore, was for a regeneration of the national culture, adapted to the requirements of progress but retaining at the same time its distinctiveness. (2)[5]

In addition to the dialectic of nonsimultaneity, particular historical experiences that gave birth to Korean nationalism imprinted the sanctification of nationalism on the Korean ideological topography. In the late nineteenth century, Korea was confronted with the task of building a modern state by undertaking modernization to meet the challenge of incoming Western powers; however, the country lost its national sovereignty as a result of Japanese imperial annexation, which put an end to Korea's efforts at modernization. Thus the national question (i.e., national survival) overwhelmed the social question (i.e., the problem of social class) until the introduction of socialist ideology in the early 1920s under Japanese colonial rule.[6] In the process of undergoing such national crises and frustrations, Korean nationalism coagulated into a racial form stressing the biological bloodline. It was further reinforced by the addition of the ideology of *danil minjok* (a single and pure nation), an ideology insisting on national-racial homogeneity that is unique to the Korean nation.[7] Finally, unlike other non-Western states that shared colonial experiences with Korea, the country unexpectedly met with national division after liberation and, subsequently, the fratricidal June 25 War. It was thus unable to achieve the building of a national state in the full sense.

Due to the complexities incurred by such trauma, nationalism in Korea has now grown into an ideology with greater and heavier political symbolism than any other, acquiring an air of inviolable and infallible sanctity in the minds of most Koreans. Of course, sanctification is not a phenomenon confined to Korean nationalism. While surveying the trajectory of nationalism in the last part of twentieth century, Eric Hobsbawm (1990) ended his book *Nations and Nationalism since 1780* with an unusual prediction of its gradual decline. Yet he has still noted this aspect of nationalism (i.e., sanctification), saying, "Above all, where ideologies are in conflict, the appeal to the imagined community of the nation appears to have defeated all challenges" (163). In addition to the task of belated modernization that contributed to the strengthening of nationalist fervor, it should be noted that South Korea had to carry out capitalist modernization as if it were a life-and-death struggle, to secure national legitimacy in desperate competition against North Korean communist brethren, and to achieve national unification by defeating them. This intranational aspect has added another intense dimension to the already-serious international struggle for national dignity and recognition. Thus nationalism has become all the more fervent and sanctified.[8]

Nationalism, therefore, has exerted a unique and powerful influence on the country's ideological landscape. Its sanctification is demonstrated by the titles of books criticizing politicians who have dared to violate it—titles like *Bigeugui Hyeondaejidoja: Geudeureun Minjokjuuijainga Banminjokjuui-jainga* (Tragic Contemporary Leaders: Are They Nationalist or Antinationalist?), *Baebandanghan Hangungminjokjuui* (Korean Nationalism Betrayed), and *Minjokjuuineun Joeaginga* (Is Nationalism a Sin?), a defensive yet ironic title. The phenomenon can also be confirmed, paradoxically, in a phrase that defines former president Park Chung-hee's nationalist discourses as "statism in a divided state on the pretext of nationalism," which is premised on the infallibility and sanctity of nationalism (Kang Man-gil 1987, 27).[9] Lim Ji-hyeon (1999), by contrast, has reacted strongly against this sanctification by publishing a book provocatively titled *Minjokjuuineun Banyeogida: Sinhwawa Heomuui Minjokjuui Damnoneul Neomeoseo* (Nationalism Is Treason: Beyond the Myth and Emptiness of Nationalist Discourses). In the book, Lim states that "in modern and contemporary Korean history—a history of failed attempts to build a modern nation-state—the nation is a standard for moral and historical judgment" that has enjoyed dominant status as "a moral categorical imperative and social standard imposed on Koreans by history" and has become "an ideology and religion embodied in the life of each individual" (6). Lim defines this phenomenon as "a corneous and mythological understanding of the nation" and notes poignantly the ill effects this has brought about. The provocative title of his book could be taken as an expression of his conviction that there is a need to "bust or debunk the nationalist myth" (5–6).

This chapter discusses the effects of the sanctification of nationalism on the contemporary Korean ideological terrain, primarily focusing on the period before democratization. To examine these effects, I divide them into two distinct but interrelated concepts: (1) the overdetermination of other ideologies by nationalism and (2) the overpowering presence of one task over the other tasks of nationalism. First, through the concept of overdetermination, I investigate the way nationalism, as a source of (ultimate) legitimacy, has overdetermined conservatism, liberalism (and liberal democracy), and radicalism, the other three of the four ideologies that have shaped contemporary Korean politics.[10] Then, through the concept of overpowering presence, I explore how one task among various tasks of nationalism—for example, overcoming division (or reunification), economic development (or modernization), anti-communism (or national security), and democracy—acquires supreme importance and marginalizes the other tasks. This phenomenon takes place in the discursive struggles over nationalism by various political protagonists when a certain group presents, stresses, and imposes one task over others as the top priority and seeks to win a viable hegemony among the general populace, even if they do not acquire the consensus of the majority. Here overdetermination focuses on the reciprocal relationship among conservatism, liberalism, radicalism, and nationalism and approximates the structural and objective phenomena that have an influence beyond the subjective wills of political actors. In contrast, overpowering presence is concerned with the competitive relationship among diverse advocates of nationalism within the autonomous sphere allowed by the ideological terrain, stressing the subjective position of ideological protagonists and the subsequent hegemony (consensus reached by intellectual and moral leadership in a Gramscian sense) they seek to acquire and impose on others. On the basis of this distinction, the chapter examines overdetermination first and then overpowering presence.[11]

THE OVERDETERMINATION OF OTHER IDEOLOGIES BY NATIONALISM

As discussed in the previous section, nationalism through its sanctification has established itself in contemporary Korean politics as both the common denominator of all ideologies and the fundamental language for evaluating the authenticity of all political entities (Kim Dong-chun 1996a, 301; Lim Ji-hyeon 1999, 52–53; Ha Sang-bok and Kim Su-ja 2009, 208).[12] It has, in other words, reigned as the "supreme ideology" or "ideology of all ideologies," overwhelming and justifying all others; this is what has caused it to overdetermine other ideologies as the ultimate source of legitimacy.

Nationalism does not have a self-sufficient ideational structure in itself; rather, it bears strong hallmarks of being an "ideology on a blank sheet of paper"—in other words, a secondary ideology that is frequently combined with other ideologies, thereby reinforcing them and making them more effective and vigorous (Lim Ji-hyeon 1999, 24).[13] Accordingly, it has a tendency to expand its goals and agenda, varying with changes and development in the modern and contemporary world, thus overlapping with other ideologies and transforming into a more comprehensive ideology itself.

Until the end of the nineteenth century, however, the main aim of modern nationalism was generally limited to building an independent and strong nation-state according to the principle of national self-determination; or, to use Ernest Gellner's (1983) expression, "a political principle which holds that the political and national unit should be congruent" (1). Nationalism did not, therefore, necessarily have to incorporate liberal or democratic ideology. Nationalism in early-comer nations such as England and France contained elements of liberalism or republicanism as espoused by its main agents, the bourgeoisie. Yet the nationalism of politicians who contributed to building a rich nation with strong military power in other parts of the world did not adhere to liberalism or republicanism but conservatism, statism, or even fascism. Such ideological inclinations, however, do not cause their exclusion from the scope of nationalism. As good examples we may cite Bismarck, who contributed to German unification and the establishment of the German Empire, or the Japanese oligarchic elite, who successfully led the Meiji Restoration.

The states that gained independence with the end of World War II, however, were obliged to set up diverse and often conflicting tasks as the goal of nationalism and undertake them almost concurrently: the acquisition of status as a modern, independent nation-state, economic self-sufficiency and prosperity through economic development and industrialization, the realization of a democracy that embodies popular sovereignty and equality among citizens, the unification and integration of the nation, the establishment of national identity through the preservation and regeneration of national culture, and the revival of past glory by advancing to become a powerful nation. It was the successful accomplishment of these tasks that would contribute to the independence, unification, and development of nations. This combination of goals, deemed necessary ingredients of nationalism in newly independent states, made it inevitable that Korean nationalism, too, transformed into a multifaceted ideology. This is the defining characteristic that distinguishes the nationalism of latecomer countries in the late twentieth century from that of nineteenth-century Western Europe. In this sense Park Myeong-lim has noted nationalism as the ideology that condenses nonsimultaneity most intensely in Korea, as cited in chapter 2.

Under these circumstances, politicians of various stripes in Korea competed and conflicted over the proper way to accomplish these tasks. Liberals, conservatives, and radicals clashed politically due to their differences prioritizing the tasks at hand, ways of interpreting them, and their various strategies and agents of change. As part of this process, they called on both their own respective ideologies and sanctified nationalism for justification; as a result, nationalism became the common denominator of the various ideologies, ultimately overdetermining conservatism, liberalism, and radicalism alike. In other words, conflict that originated with differences between ideologies transformed into a struggle among right-wing nationalists (conservatives), radical (populist or socialist) nationalists, and liberal nationalists. As a result, politicians from diverse ideological backgrounds ended up clashing just as much over who could claim authentic or orthodox status as a true nationalist as over whose ideology is more worthy of leading the country. We now examine this phenomenon with regard to each ideology.

Conservatism and Nationalism

With regard to the overdetermination of conservatism by nationalism, all the political discourses advanced by South Korean conservatives to defend authoritarian regimes have been linked to nationalism: anticommunism and unification (including "unification by marching forward to the North," "unification by defeating the communist North," and "unification by exterminating the communist North"), national security, modernization (economic development), and liberal democracy.[14] Conservative regimes throughout South Korean history have claimed to be the only legitimate government representing the Korean nation as a whole, declaring the North Korean regime a "puppet clique" that blindly followed the Soviet Union and started the internecine June 25 War. For them, accordingly, the presence and aggressive potential of the antinational North Korean puppet was a direct threat to the independence, unification, and development of the nation. Thus "anticommunism" and "national security" in opposition to the North Korean communists and the Soviet Union, which controlled North Korea behind the scenes, was in itself nationalistic in the sense that it aimed to protect the survival and independence of the nation and preserve the orthodoxy of South Korea in the lineage of national history. In this way anticommunism was elevated to *guksi* (state doctrine), the supreme principle of protecting the nation. Such nationalism in which anticommunism is elevated to the status of state doctrine may well be called "anticommunistic nationalism."[15]

In his speech to mark the opening of South Korea's first National Assembly on May 31, 1948, for example, Rhee Syngman proclaimed the Republic of Korea as the legitimate successor in the national orthodoxy because it succeeded the historic March First Movement of 1919 and the Provisional Government of Korea (Gongbocheo 1953, 1).[16] In a statement on June 20, 1950, calling for people's support for the government, Rhee branded North Korea an antidemocratic, antinational regime that existed as "a slave that has fallen under the influence of communism, become a state subordinate to another country, and given up all national independence and popular freedom" (Gongbocheo 1953, 35). If South Korea were subverted by the North and became a communist state, he claimed in another speech, "we, too, would become a subordinate state and live the life of a slave."[17] In this he justified anticommunism with the cause of nationalism.

Park Chung-hee, too, branded North Korea the "antination," as opposed to the Korean nation. To Park, North Korean communists subserviently followed foreign powers such as the Soviet Union, were hell-bent on warmongering to massacre the brethren of the same nation, trampling on the nation's conscience, and denied "our" national history and unique cultural tradition.[18] The corollary implication of this was that the South Korean anticommunism opposing them was an indispensable force when it came to national survival and independence and was unquestionably nationalistic because it defended the nation's conscience and the orthodoxy of the national history. This can be interpreted as a process of transforming the anticommunism directed against the North Korean regime into nationalism and, furthermore, as the overpowering presence of anticommunism over other tasks of nationalism, which I address later.[19] According to this logic, it is rather natural that the anticommunism, national-security measures, and unification discourses adopted by South Korean conservative regimes be regarded as nationalistic.

Just as anticommunism was transformed into nationalism, North Korean communists—the "reds"—were converted into "antinationalists." Given that the racist notion of nation was superimposed on the reds, the reds did become *another race of a different kind*, not *the same nation with a different ideology*. Thus numerous massacres that the South Korean government and their soldiers committed upon innocent civilians in the June 25 War and on other occasions, simply branding them as reds, took on the characteristics of genocide. The Korean expression "Wiping out the seeds of reds" speaks tellingly of this mentality of ethnic cleansing. In other words, the political ideology (i.e., anticommunism) was the decisive criterion by which to distinguish the nation from the antination or "nonnation," overwhelming conventional objective attributes of nation like ethnicity, culture, religion, language, history, and so on. In this way anticommunism overdetermined the nation.[20] Furthermore, anticommunism thus converted into racism justified unconsciously committing genocide against the same nation, a kind of ethnic cleansing.[21]

When it comes to the link between nationalism and modernization (or economic development), the economic development and ultimate economic self-reliance that was a fundamental aim of the Park Chung-hee regime onward was a nationalist goal due to both the national prosperity it aimed to create and the assumption that democracy and unification (also goals of nationalism) would only be possible once such economic development had been achieved. As early as 1962, in his book *Uri Minjogui Nagal Gil* (The Path for Our Nation to Take), Park Chung-hee made it clear that modernization was a core priority of nationalism, writing, "The historical task of modernization lies before our nation." Then he cited "liberating the nation from poverty and achieving economic self-reliance" as the top priority for Korean modernization (128–29).

South Korean conservatives, moreover, have considered the liberal democracy they sought to defend in the face of the North Korean communist threat as a system that guarantees the liberty of a nation as a whole and individual members' freedom; by this logic, it is unquestionably a nationalist goal. Park Chung-hee also claimed the need for the "'Koreanization' of democracy," adding a nationalist element to democracy (1962, 130–31).[22] The transformed "national democracy" and "Korean-style democracy" thus called for by Park Chung-hee as part of the Koreanization of democracy were adaptations, therefore, of Western-style democracy to suit Korean tradition and history for the sake of continued economic development and national security against the North Korean communists and to strengthen national autonomy and subjectivity in accordance with Korea's specific historical situation. They can be regarded as ideological devices designed to fill the vacuum left by a lack of democratic legitimacy by appealing to nationalism.

Radicalism and Nationalism

Radicalism (of socialist orientation) in South Korea has also been subject to overdetermination by nationalism. In terms of its historical origins in Europe, Marxist socialism began by claiming universalism and internationalism, starting from the premise that the development of capitalism would neutralize ascriptive individual identities such as the nation and religion. This internationalism, however, met with the challenges posed by nationalism within the German socialist movement even during Marx's own lifetime.[23] Following the outbreak of World War I, moreover, socialist parties and trade unions in each European country reversed their original opposition to war and began supporting the positions of their respective governments and offering active cooperation. This led, ultimately, to the collapse of the Second International, a dramatic case in which nationalism overwhelmed socialist internationalism. The subsequent formation of Comintern after the Russian Revolution saw the emergence of difficult theoretical and practical questions that had to combine socialist revolution with national liberation from colonialism. History has shown, however, that, since the Russian Revolution, successful socialist revolutions outside Europe—China, North Korea, Cuba, and Vietnam—have been combined, irrespective of the official rhetoric deployed by the revolutionaries themselves, with nationalist goals such as liberation from the yoke of imperialism or colonization and the establishment of autonomous nation-states and that such revolutions have only succeeded when able to make effective appeals to nationalism. This point, at least, allows the interpretation that, outside Europe, socialism has been overdetermined to a great extent by nationalism.

This phenomenon can also be witnessed in contemporary Korean political history. In the case of Korea, most radical political activists were forced from the start to consider class issues within the context of the establishment of a nation-state, due to the country's experience as a colony of Japan and to its division following liberation.[24] Accordingly, the "August Theses" of 1945, which had been issued by the Communist Party of Korea under the leadership of Park Heon-young immediately after liberation, announced a bourgeois democratic revolution aimed at "complete national independence," thereby appealing primarily to nationalism. At the same time, however, it displayed idealist and dogmatic characteristics by declaring an excessive prioritization of class struggle by excluding the national bourgeoisie from the forces of revolution (Kim Nam-sik 1985). Here, too, however, the term *class enemy* was infused with the "nation versus antination" structure and can be taken to mean "national enemies" who blindly followed Japanese or US imperialism. The Communist Party of Korea's powers of popular mobilization, thus, derived more from nationalist rhetoric attacking pro-Japanese Koreans and the US

Army Military Government in Korea, which protected them, than from revolutionary class slogans. Moreover, once the system of national division had been further entrenched as a result of the June 25 War, radicalism found itself oppressed by the dominance of extreme anticommunism and muzzled thoroughly from speaking in explicit class languages for a long time.

As good examples, we may take a brief look at Cho Bong-am and his Progressive Party, the greatest manifestation of radical political power during Rhee Syngman's presidency, and at the radical movement that erupted temporarily at the time of the Second Republic (1960–1961). These two examples also confirm that the popular influence exerted by these movements was due more to their unification-oriented nationalism in the form of calls for peaceful unification, negotiation between South and North, and neutral reunification (as opposed to Rhee Syngman's calls for "unification by marching forward to the North" and the Second Republic's unification policies such as anticommunist reunification and the doctrine of "construction first, then unification") than to the social-democratic measures—such as political democratization, nationalization of key industries, and planned economy—that they suggested.[25] However, Park Chung-hee's presidency saw no noteworthy eruptions of radicalism with mass appeal, due to tighter suppression of radicalism of any kind.

Radicalism experienced a revival as part of the democratization movement of the 1980s, which was ignited explosively as a result of the ruthless suppression by the new military government of the Gwangju Democratization Movement in May 1980. In this process, radical activists shared their overall commitment to a socialist revolution but were divided into two broad camps—more clearly after 1989—in terms of emphasis and strategy: (1) that of national liberation, which emphasized the eradication of domination by foreign powers (i.e., nationalism), and (2) people's democracy, which focused more on the abolition of Korea's monopoly capitalism subordinate to American imperialism (i.e., class liberation) (Lee Jae-hwa 1990). The main driving force behind the radical movement, however, was anti-imperialism, which considered the United States and its proxy government in South Korea to be the main culprits behind national division, dictatorship, and subordinate capitalism.[26] Of course, underlying this anti-imperialism was nationalism. In the case of the radicalism that developed in South Korea following national division and the establishment of two states, calls for revolution and alternative systems were shaped by the stress on simultaneous and overlapping class and national problems.[27] It is apparent, however, that nationalism came to overdetermine socialism in this process. The specific details are as follows.

The nationalism of democratic activists under the Yusin regime in the 1970s took populism (*minjungjuui*) and democracy as its main constituents. This nationalism was characterized not only by the goals of "escaping dependency, opposing foreign powers, and achieving national subjectivity but also by a brand of *minjung* [populist] nationalism aimed at resolving domestic class conflict." In this case, however, opposing foreign powers signified "criticism of and resistance to the externally dependent politico-economic structure" rather than inherent political aspects of actively opposing or entering into direct conflict with foreign powers (Kim Dong-chun 1996b, 166–67). Accordingly, this nationalism lacked a clear awareness of the interrelatedness between the structure and perpetuation of national division and foreign powers. The democratization movement under the regime of Chun Doo-hwan in the 1980s, however, began to acquire a radical streak that sought to achieve revolutionary change. The experience of a second authoritarian military regime after eighteen years' iron rule by Park Chung-hee caused the democratization movement "to take a step beyond the goal of superficial reform to achieve regime change, the establishment of a civilian government or the abolition of dictatorship, or the realization of liberal democracy. The movement developed into one that demanded a resolution to the structures of contradiction within Korean society themselves." This development took place due to "a social-scientific [Marxian] awareness of imperialism and capitalism" and was specifically triggered by the massacre of democratic protesters in Gwangju by the new military government (Kim Dong-taek 1992, 491).

As a whole, however, the democracy movement of the 1980s saw a boost in anti–foreign power (particularly antiAmerican) consciousness in both ideological and practical terms. As a consequence, it appears, the nationalist ideology and faction (the national liberation faction) ended up overwhelming the socialist ideology and faction (the people's democracy faction). This is easily confirmed by the addition of the adjective *national* to refer to the democratization movements of various stripes among activist circles, thereby calling them the "national democratic movement," "national democratic revolution," or "national democratic struggle," terms commonly used at the time. Whereas movements resisting the dictatorship in the 1970s had been collectively termed a "restoration of democracy" and the "protection of democracy," those of the 1980s were officially labeled collectively as the "national democratic movement," despite regarding themselves as "revolutionary movements" (i.e., seeking class liberation as well).

Such labeling seems to suggest the addition of two new meanings. First, as demonstrated by many of the pamphlets and tracts circulated during this period,[28] members of the resistance understood the origins and development of their movement for revolution from a long-term historical perspective of "anticolonialism, antifeudalism and antidictatorship national movements" that went back at least as far as the Donghak peasants' revolt in the late nineteenth century and had continued since then through the "anti-Japanese struggle for national liberation, the April Student Revolution and the May Popular Struggle [Gwangju Democratization Movement]" ("Declaration for the Founding of National Youth Association for Democratic Movement: For Democracy, Minjung [People], and National Unification," September 30, 1983, found in Shindonga Pyeonjipsil 1990, 36). Unlike in the past, furthermore, they understood national division by foreign powers to be directly linked to the perpetuation of dictatorial regimes and exploitation of the Korean *minjung* (people) and regarded the goals of achieving democracy, securing the right to subsistence for the *minjung*, and peaceful unification of the Korean nation as mutually inseparable in an organic relationship, in accordance with the "three-mins ideology" that identified national unification (*minjoktongil*), democracy (*minjujuui*), and people's liberation (*minjung-haebang*) as its three main goals (ibid.). Dictatorial regimes were regarded, accordingly, as "antidemocratic, antinational" forces that reproduced the system of national division and exploited and suppressed the *minjung* by siding with foreign powers (or as the tool of foreign powers) (ibid.). As a result, resistance movements that aimed to overthrow antidemocratic and antinational dictatorial regimes were conceived of not just as democratic movements within a single state but as comprehensive national movements that aimed to "establish an autonomous, democratic, and unified nation-state" through national liberation, which would overcome the foreign interference and suppression that had been maintained for the last one hundred years (United Association for Democracy, Unification, and Minjung Movement, "Declaration for the Movement for Democracy, Unification, and Minjung," May 10, 1985, found in Shindonga Pyeonjipsil 1990, 38).

The second thing this labeling suggests is that, because desire for national subjectivity and anti-American sentiment ran high within the radical student movement in the mid-1980s, doctrines of direct struggle against foreign powers, especially the United States, emerged across the board as a strategy. This phenomenon was spurred on by belated revelations that the United States had somehow approved of or acquiesced to the new military government's brutal suppression of the Gwangju Democratization Movement. Until the 1970s, Koreans' feelings toward the United States had been generally amicable. The country was seen as a liberator that had saved Korea from oppression by imperial Japan, a benefactor that had saved South Korea during the June 25 War and supported its recovery effort afterward, and a "defender of democracy" that had played a positive role in helping to bring about the fall of the Rhee Syngman regime during the student-led April Revolution and had applied constant pressure to curb human-rights abuses by the Park Chung-hee regime (Minjuhwaui Gil 1989, 50). Accordingly, in democratic movements before the 1980s, the United States had been seen more as a "friendly entity" than an "object of resistance" (Cho Hui-yeon 1989, 20). Facts later revealed, however, that the United States had approved the deployment of military reinforcements to put down the Gwangju Democratization Movement, thereby revealing that images previously held of the United States were false. Furthermore, as Koreans became aware that the United States subsequently offered active support and approval for the Chun Doo-hwan regime, many— angered by their government's merciless actions in Gwangju—felt betrayed and began to harbor anti-American sentiments.[29] As a result, some members of the radical student movement began claiming that in order to achieve democracy it was necessary to struggle not only against the military regime of Chun Doo-hwan but also against the United States, which controlled or protected the regime. Accordingly, the democratic movement acquired an even stronger character as a struggle for national liberation. This explains why radical activists in the 1980s referred to their movement as the "national democratic movement." We now examine this second aspect more closely.

The gradually increasing anti-American sentiments of the 1980s were manifested through intermittent but significant episodes involving student activists, such as the printing in 1980 of a pamphlet at Seoul National University titled "Is America Really Our Friend?," an arson attack in 1982 on the US Cultural Center in Busan, the burning of the Stars and Stripes in the same year by students at Kangwon National University, and in 1985 a sit-in occupation of the US Cultural Center in Seoul. The phenomenon of anti-American sentiment also spread widely among Korean farmers due to pressure from the United States to open Korean import markets to US goods, including agricultural produce. A national liberation movement armed with such anti-American sentiment had not been launched, however, on a full scale in the early 1980s. On the contrary, members of the radical movement in the early 1980s were actively engaged in Marxist research; around 1985 an intense controversy arose regarding the class base for revolution—the so-called CNP controversy. This controversy saw competition among doctrines of civic democratic revolution (C), nationalist democratic revolution (N), and people's (*minjung*) democratic revolution (P). The controversy ended up establishing a doctrine of nationalist democratic revolution. It defined Korea's social formation as "neocolonialist state monopoly capitalism" and highlighted that the "main contradiction in Korean society was that between military fascist powers, based on imperialism and monopoly capital, and the Korean *minjung*." Thus it advocated the development of a struggle "against foreign powers to achieve national subjectivity and autonomy and against the military dictatorship to achieve democracy," by means of an alliance between the leading capacity of basic "*minjung* classes such as workers, peasants and the poor, and the middle classes" (Cho Gwang 1989, 182–84).

Within this controversy, the ruling bloc—which consisted of "monopoly capital," "fascist state power," and "the foreign powers protecting this system of collusion between fascism and monopoly capitalism"—was taken to be the object of revolutionary change. But "a systematic awareness of the reciprocal relationship among these three was lacking" (Cho Hui-yeon 1989, 19–20). Thus, applying Marxist methodology, the radical activists sought to synthesize "the defining power of imperialism and the particularity of Korean capitalism" (Cho Hui-yeon 1992, 233, 239). Here, emphasizing imperialist influence contained a nationalist element because it was related to pursuing national liberation from the United States and the proxy Chun regime, whereas noting the contradiction of Korean capitalism meant seeking radical class revolution. However, how to reconcile the national contradiction and the class contradiction in a dialectical way remained a thorny question among radical activists.

In the general election held in February 1985, however, a stunning victory was won by the Sinhanminjudang (New Korea Democratic Party), a hard-line opposition party that had been formed hurriedly just before the election, who then emerged as the largest and the most powerful opposition party. Enjoying full popular support, the Sinhanminjudang launched into a struggle for constitutional revision. Student activists within the radical movement now began engaging in debates about whether to participate in this struggle and what strategies to use. At the time, "the general trends within the student movement converged into a 'doctrine of struggle to abolish the fascist constitution,'" as represented by the stance of South Korea's largest federation of student unions. But the sudden appearance of a pamphlet that leveled a frontal attack on their "struggle to achieve a *minjung* democratic constitution" and called for a direct, anti-imperialist struggle stirred huge turmoil (Cho Hui-yeon 1989, 26). The pamphlet criticized the constitutional revision for being a conspiracy by foreign powers to stabilize a colonized fascist regime and asserted that antifascist struggles should be converted to an anti-American struggle for national subjectivity and autonomy (i.e., direct struggle against "American imperialism, the substantial agent of fascist rule over the Korean *minjung*"; "A Prologue for Liberation" by Kang Cheol, 1985, quoted in Shindonga Pyeonjipsil 1990, 128).[30]

This stance of anti-imperial direct struggle was continued by a group of student activists called the Committee for the Struggle against America to Achieve Independence and the Struggle against Fascism to Achieve Democracy (the so-called Jamintu); the committee formulated an official National Liberation–People's Democratic Revolution doctrine that prioritized anti-imperialist national liberation, which had previously held secondary status due to the priority given the antifascist and prodemocracy struggle as the realistic front. The committee's stance characterized Korean society as colonized and semifeudal and branded the state as "neocolonial fascist" and a "puppet regime" controlled "by US imperialists, subordinate capitalists, and landowners to rule the Korean *minjung*" (Yun Seok-in 1989, 345). Another student group with another stance, the Anti-Imperialist, Anti-Fascist Committee for National Democratic Struggle (the so-called Minmintu), took the social formation of Korea to be at "the stage of monopoly capitalism subordinate to neocolonialism" and identified its main contradiction as that "between military fascism–US imperialism and the Korean *minjung*." This committee espoused a "doctrine of national democratic revolution against imperialism and fascism" (344).

Though a more detailed discussion lies outside the scope of this chapter, it must be noted that these two committees differed considerably, not only in terms of their analysis of the social formation in Korea but also in terms of the target, stage, and strategy of revolution (Yun Seok-in 1989). In terms of the immediate target for their revolutionary attack, however, the Minmintu "emphasized class contradictions" and "identified the political-military authorities . . . which enjoyed relative autonomy from foreign powers as its principal enemy," whereas the Jamintu instead "identified foreign powers, the overall agents behind Korea's subordination—especially the United States—as its principal enemy," thus prioritizing the struggle against foreign powers (348–49). Even so, both committees developed their doctrines of social formation, agents of revolution, and strategy on the basis of the aforementioned doctrine of national democratic revolution established within the radical movement early in 1985. They shared the ultimate goal, therefore, of opposing foreign powers to achieve national liberation and of opposing the dictatorship to achieve class liberation. Given this, the radical movement's socialist revolutionary ideology can be regarded as having been overdetermined by nationalism, albeit with significant differences among factions.

Beyond the horizons of such abstract, sophisticated ideological disputes, however, the stance that effectively became dominant in the practical movement after the mid-1980s was the one that took South Korea to be a colony occupied by the United States and advocated the creation of a unified sovereign state by establishing an independent national regime through a national liberation movement against imperialism (Kim Dong-chun 1996b, 168). Writing on this subject, Kim Dong-chun claims, "Analyses of the reality and activism strategies based on class theory in Korean social activist circles were confronted with considerable problems in organization and mass mobilization, provoking an even stronger backlash," and "now the anti-imperialist nationalist movement was no longer treated as one moving in parallel to the democracy movement but was regarded as a higher-ranking, comprehensive movement that had absorbed the democracy movement." Kim also points out that around the time of the collapse of the socialist bloc, under the influence of North Korea's Juche ideology, "the movement transformed and acquired a national supremacist character" (170–72). Korea's radical movement, then, despite identifying class contradictions as the basic contradictions of Korean society, ended up acquiring still greater public influence by appealing to nationalism. It can therefore be said that radicalism in its practical dynamic, too, became overdetermined by nationalism in the reality of Korea's national division.[31]

We have witnessed how conservatism and radicalism, fierce rivals in the period before Korea's democratization, made appeals to nationalism from different directions, thereby jumping on the bandwagon of sanctified nationalism to reinforce their respective legitimacy on the one hand and becoming overdetermined by sanctified nationalism in that process on the other. This must be considered an intriguing feature of Korea's ideological landscape that sets it apart from the West. Whereas conservatism in Western countries—for example, in England—depended on conservative philosophy that aimed to protect the interests of the aristocratic and propertied classes while developing a universal logic of skepticism regarding equality, the importance of social elites, the necessity of authority and religion, and the undesirability and futility of radical reform,[32] authoritarian conservatives in South Korea asserted the need to build a self-reliant economy through development and modernization, to develop state power, to oppose communism, and to maintain national security while appealing to nationalism in order to justify these policies. Similarly, Western socialists, despite admittedly harboring nationalist tendencies to a certain extent, have sought socialist revolution by the working classes as a matter of priority, whereas Korean radicals, rather than aiming for a proper socialist revolution, have appealed to the nationalistic desire to establish a unified nation-state after bringing to power an autonomous nationalist government of a populist or socialist variety by overthrowing dictatorial Korean governments that are subordinate to foreign powers.

Liberalism and Nationalism

If the process by which liberalism, too, has been overdetermined by nationalism is to be understood, it is necessary to emphasize the particular characteristics of Korean nationalism once again. As mentioned in the previous section, mainstream Korean nationalism was formed organically through a primordial and perennial understanding of the concept of nation on the basis of a "single and pure nation" (*danil minjok*) ideology. It grew stronger along with the tragic loss of national sovereignty to Japan and in the grip of fascist rule by imperial Japan. For this reason, ethnic nationalism was combined with strong statism by the regimes of both South and North Korea. Consequently, this inseparable, monolithic organic state nationalism came to overdetermine Korea's ideological landscape.[33] In these circumstances, it was liberalism that suffered the most damage. Liberalism, which holds individual freedom as its most important value, is based on individualism in terms of both political and economic freedoms. It was Korean nationalism, however, that deprived rational individualism, an essential element of liberalism, of the space to grow and reach maturity. It maintained and reinforced the collectivism that had already materialized as part of the Confucian tradition of the Joseon period (1392–1910) in opposition to the pressure from modernization (e.g., economic development, industrialization, urbanization, rationalization) to dissolve traditional collectivism.[34] This is why South Korean liberalism after national liberation and division was overdetermined by nationalism. Measured by the yardstick of Western liberalism, South Korean liberalism was effectively forced to undergo severe refraction and distortion.

Bearing in mind the aforementioned distinction between liberalism as a ruling ideology and as an insurgent ideology—the dual character of Korean liberalism—let us first examine "anticommunist liberalism," which falls into the category of ruling ideology.[35] As mentioned earlier in chapter 2, classical Western liberalism acquired a progressive character in the historical process wherein the bourgeoisie set liberation from religious conformity, political absolutism (absolute monarchies, in the case of Europe), and ascriptive status as its political agenda and engaged in consequent struggles, thereby growing into a dominant ideology. South Korean anticommunistic liberalism, in contrast, made the protection of liberty from the communist threat of internal subversion and external aggression its foremost goal, due to the establishment of a communist regime in North Korea and formation of the Cold War order. In effect, seen from the perspective of propertied classes, the potential bearers of South Korean liberalism, communism was the foremost threat to liberty (including the right to private property); to the majority of the general public, too, single-party communist dictatorship—a contemporary form of political absolutism—was the biggest threat to both individualism and political freedom, despite its ostensible socioeconomic progressiveness.

It was from this perspective that Rhee Syngman declared that the "communists, the essence of barbaric evil of a sort never seen before in the history of humanity," aimed only for "world domination," which would mean "the end of all freedom and liberation," "ideological control of everyone," and the "eradication" of "all the value that has been built up over thousands of years of civilization." In this way Rhee emphasized that communism constituted an absolute denial of all values, including liberty, and that anticommunism was therefore a struggle to defend all values, including liberty (Rhee Syngman 1954 and 1955). Accordingly, Korean liberalism, as the ruling ideology of which Rhee spoke, made anticommunism its primary goal. It was politically legitimate in its own way, as far as ruling conservatives were concerned.[36]

A serious problem with the "anticommunist liberalism" advocated by South Korean governments, however, was that it prematurely acquired a reactionary character while turning away from creating conditions in which ordinary citizens could properly enjoy freedom (to an extent where anticommunism actually meant anything substantial). Anticommunist liberalism soon became subject to abuse and corruption. Under the pretext of defending liberty from communism, South Korea's ruling forces cruelly suppressed the civil liberties of ordinary citizens in general and political liberties in particular, including those necessary for citizens to engage in political opposition (such as freedom of the press, publishing, association, thought, and conscience), in order to maintain their own power. As a result, liberalism as a ruling ideology ended up such an empty shell that it was not even sufficient to justify anticommunism.

In a situation, moreover, where the security of the state, the "guardian of the nation," was under direct threat from antinational North Korean communists and attempts were being made to mobilize the entire populace in efforts to develop economic self-reliance, there was no room for individualist liberalism. Park Chung-hee branded the nation and the state "big self" and the individual "small self," claiming that the two shared the same inseparable fate ("New Year's Press Conference," January 9, 1970, 3:686). He also defined the freedom of the nation and the state as "greater freedom" and that of individual citizens as "lesser freedom," asserting that sacrificing or exercising restraint with regard to the lesser freedom for the sake of the greater freedom was inevitable ("Admonition to Armed Forces Day," October 1, 1974, 5:312).[37] In terms of the economy, too, just as many other late-developing nations had to do, successive Korean governments before democratization pursued state-led economic development, rather than creating market-led laissez-faire economic policies, in order to achieve catch-up-style modernization. This also left no room for economic liberalism. Because Korea's bourgeois and middle classes benefited from state-led economic development, however, they did not feel the need to assert economic liberalism overall until the Korean economy matured along with democracy, despite any partial dissatisfaction they might have felt with state control and regulation of the economy.[38] From this perspective, it can be said that anticommunism, national security, and the need for economic development stunted the healthy growth of liberalism in pretransitional South Korea. These agendas have been justified in the name of national survival (and prosperity) and national security, as shown in the preceding examination of the relationship between conservatism and nationalism. It can therefore be said that liberalism in South Korea has been overdetermined by nationalism and statism.

Insurgent liberalism in South Korea, too, is no exception in this respect. This ideology, in the process of consistently struggling to achieve democratization and overcome national division, became overdetermined by nationalism. By way of explanation here I offer a reinterpretation of the three characteristics of insurgent Korean liberalism, as put forward by Moon Ji-young (2009). "First," he writes, "Korean liberalism emphasizes the 'nation' or '*minjung*' as a whole rather than the 'individual' as the bearer of rights and the agent of resistance. . . . Second, it emphasizes equality, distributive justice, and welfare rather than an autonomous market or the absolute nature of private property. . . . Third, it is weak as a class-based ideology and has been oriented toward liberal *democracy* from the start" (159–61; emphasis mine). It must be noted that the first of these characteristics—"nationalism" or "populism" (*minjungjuui*, people-centered ideology)—has overdetermined and weakened liberalism both as a ruling and as an oppositional ideology. This is easily illustrated in the thoughts of opposition intellectual Chang Chun-ha and of liberal opposition politicians Kim Dae-jung and Kim Young-sam, who opposed Korea's dictatorial regimes and developed an intense democratic movement.

Chang Chun-ha was an anticommunist, liberal democrat and editor of the magazine *Sasanggye* (World of Ideas). He made his name in the struggle for democracy under Park Chung-hee but died under suspicious circumstances in 1975. In September 1972, two months after the announcement of the historic July 4 Joint Communiqué between South and North Korea, Chang published a famous topical essay titled "Minjokjuuijaui Gil" (The Way of the Nationalist) in which he emphasized that political freedom was a means of securing national freedom while recognizing the importance of a struggle for political freedom as such in the democracy movement: "We have fought until now to secure political freedom. This, in itself, is a fundamental thing, but it is all the more important as a means of securing greater national freedom [unification]" (Chang Chun-ha 1985, 58).

For Chang all freedoms were reduced to "freedom for the unification movement," which sought to break through the national division, the greatest cause of people's poverty and lack of freedom, and thus freedom for the unification movement provided the genuine beginning of national freedom (Chang Chun-ha 1985, 49). This emphasis on national freedom demonstrates how Chang's liberalism was overdetermined by nationalism. Thus his kind of nationalism harbored the potential for demanding the sacrifice of individual freedom for the sake of national freedom, as we examine later.

In 1983 liberal opposition politicians Kim Dae-jung and Kim Young-sam felt the need to join forces in opposition to the Chun Doo-hwan regime. As the first manifestation of this effort, they published "The Kim Dae-jung and Kim Young-sam August 15 Joint Announcement," subtitled "The Struggle for Democracy Is the Struggle for National Independence and Liberation." When the democracy struggle they pursued was conceived of in this way, the "free space" in the liberal democracy they sought inevitably would be compromised. Their statement therefore used a logic similar to Park Chung-hee's distinction between lesser and greater freedoms—that is, between the small self and the big self—inevitably revealing an antiliberal or illiberal orientation in their thinking. The announcement read, "Just as the struggle of independence activists for liberation and independence was one of abandoning their own egos and devoting themselves to the bigger 'I'—the nation and the country—our struggle for democratization must be one of abandoning our personal egos and throwing ourselves forward for the sake of democracy in the fatherland. We must be able to throw our own egos aside and surrender everything we have, our desire, even our lives" (Shindonga Pyeonjipsil 1990, 31).[39]

Seen in this light, to Park Chung-hee, who made the distinction between greater and lesser freedoms, it was nationalism in the form of securing a self-reliant economy in order to accomplish national liberty that overdetermined liberalism. To Chang Chun-ha, on the other hand, it was unification with the aim of securing national liberty and the freedom to engage in the unification movement—namely, unification nationalism—that overdetermined (political) liberalism. Kim Dae-jung and Kim Young-sam, meanwhile, who devoted themselves as opposition politicians to the democratic struggle against the dictatorship of the time, regarded the struggle against the regime as a "struggle for national independence and liberation." By conferring nationalist legitimacy on the democracy struggle, they contributed to the sanctification of nationalism while showing, in turn, how the liberal democratic movement was overdetermined by nationalism.

Moon Ji-young (2009) does not link the second and third characteristics of insurgent liberalism that she identifies directly to nationalism. Rather, she offers appropriate explanations for them by citing other factors such as the influence of Confucianism, the tides of world history, socialist influence, and the adoption of liberal democracy by South Korea, as a latecomer nation, in "ready-made" form (160–61). There is nothing wrong, however, with interpreting these second and third characteristics as influenced by the multifaceted nationalist tasks faced by latecomer countries, as discussed previously. As we have seen, nationalism in the politics of South Korea, a latecomer country, weakened economic liberalism and individualism by overdetermining liberalism. In addition, because ideologies of Western origin were imported as a finished product due to the dialectic of nonsimultaneity, Korea can consequently be seen to have adopted a form of liberalism that emphasized equality and redistributive justice in accordance with the ideology of modified capitalism (or social liberalism), which grew more powerful in the mid-twentieth century, while skipping the stage of classical liberalism of a free, competitive market economy. The South Korean liberalism embraced in the country's founding constitution of 1948 was not nineteenth-century oligarchical bourgeois liberalism but liberal democracy accompanied by recognition of universal suffrage; this, too, can be explained by the same logic. It can be said, then, that liberal democracy with its weakened original bourgeois character was accepted as a desirable political system for the entire nation. The three characteristics of insurgent liberalism suggested by Moon Ji-young, then, may be understood to be the result of the dialectic of nonsimultaneity and, at the same time, the result of certain forced compromises in terms of individual, economic, and political freedom due to overdetermination by nationalism.

Summary

My intention in this section has been to demonstrate that the sanctification of nationalism brought about the phenomenon whereby conservatism, radicalism, and liberalism were overdetermined by nationalism. Kim Dong-chun (1996a), too, describes the overdetermination of liberalism and socialism in Korean politics from the end of the Japanese colonial period until 1990. "Ultimately," Kim writes, "in Korea, any modern social ideology that inherited Western enlightenment traditions was only able to come to life by combining with nationalism rather than existing as an independent, self-contained ideology. This in itself indicates that such ideologies were unable to overwhelm the authority and morality of nationalism" (301).[40] Linking this description from Kim with the conventional characteristics of nationalism as a secondary ideology incapable of standing alone (i.e., an ideology on a blank sheet of paper), as suggested earlier, we reach a very interesting paradox: liberalism and even socialism in contemporary Korean politics have been unable to function as ideologies complete in themselves due to the sanctification of nationalism.

OVERPOWERING PRESENCE OF ONE TASK OVER OTHERS IN NATIONALISM

In order to discuss the overpowering presence of one national task over others in Korea's ideological topography, it is necessary to recognize that nationalism has evolved into a multifaceted comprehensive ideology in the contemporary world. It is also mandatory to investigate the phenomenon that, either potentially or actually, problems of national division and unification became the decisive factor in multidimensional tasks of nationalism, so they exerted an enormous influence in the ideological terrain. This is because the unexpected national division after liberation decisively frustrated the realization of the basic task of nationalism—namely, the congruence of the political and national unit.

As mentioned earlier, most newly independent states in the mid-twentieth century had to simultaneously undertake many tasks to achieve modernity—for example, state building, industrialization, democratization, national integration, and national unification—and set them as nationalist goals and agenda in a catch-up mode of modernization. A clear difference is found, however, between Korea and other non-Western countries in the task of nationalism. In most of them, the basic task of nationalism as a distinct political ideology was usually settled with the achievement of formal independence, insofar as they were not confronted with separatist movements by ethnic minorities. South and North Korea, however, failed to achieve this basic task. After liberation, both South and North Korea met with unexpected national division and its subsequent entrenchment. This caused nationalism (which sought to break through this deadlock) to acquire an inviolable sanctity nearing that of religious faith.

In this way the task related to unification accumulated enormous potential to overpower other tasks of nationalism in terms of priority in the evolution of Korean nationalism.[41] However, it turned out to be a project whose successful undertaking lay beyond the will and capacity of an individual regime due to the continuation of the Cold War system and the hostile confrontation between South and North Korean regimes. Moreover, the two Koreas had to undertake other secondary nationalist tasks such as modernization (industrialization), the development of democracy (or socialism), and the establishment of national identity and subjectivity even in a state of national division (while acting as if each state represented the whole nation without being impaired in any way by the division). The history of national division would show, however, that carrying out two kinds of tasks in South Korea can be mutually conflictual as well as mutually reinforcing.[42] Here note the conflictual aspect in which the unfulfilled unification might bring about conditions that would make the undertaking of secondary tasks difficult, whereas the successful undertaking of these secondary tasks would create a condition that would make fulfillment of unification difficult or even unnecessary.[43]

Overpowering of nationalism by the task related to national unification began to be observed more explicitly with the emergence of an extreme version of a reductionist argument asserting that whether certain policies or positions were genuinely nationalist enough to gain national legitimacy should be decided solely by their ability to contribute to solving problems of division and unification while putting aside other national tasks. This monistic position was developed more visibly by some progressive historians and oppositional political dissidents in the early 1970s. But, at the same time, it should be noted that the life-and-death struggle between South and North Korea beginning with the national division had not allowed unification-oriented nationalism to develop smoothly. The dictatorial regimes of Rhee Syngman,

Park Chung-hee, and Chun Doo-hwan, which took the lead in initiating and entrenching the national division, had oppressed the eruption of unification-oriented nationalism in the name of anticommunism, economic development, "construction first, then unification," and so on.[44] So it is reasonable to point out that the overpowering of nationalism by the unification task had been suppressed during the long authoritarian rule. However, unification-oriented nationalism expanded its influence on a full scale in the 1980s, beginning with the Chun regime. It refused to grant the conservative elite in South Korean politics—including most politicians in opposition parties as well—the status of nationalists.[45]

However, given that I do grant nationalism to the political ideology of the conservative elite (although I think they were passive and lukewarm rather than active and progressive toward unification), I prefer to interpret and define their ideological position as division-maintaining *nationalism*, as I did do in earlier chapters, for the following three reasons.[46] First, because the international political situation and interaction with North Korea are as important as or more important than South Korea's stance, we cannot attribute the responsibility for the initiation and subsequent entrenchment of the division solely to South Korea's conservative elite. Second, their nationalist discourses also included a program for unification either by military or peaceful means, such as "unification by marching forward to the North," "unification by defeating the communist North," "construction first, then unification," and unification by holding a general election for North Korea only or for the whole of Korea under UN monitoring. Thus we have to accept the fact that just as it was natural that North Korea's program for unification was anticapitalist and socialist, so was it natural that South Korea's was anticommunist. So it is one thing to criticize South Korean conservatives' program as passive and lukewarm, but it is another to declare that their nationalist discourse was antinational for that reason. The third reason I interpret and define their ideological position as division-maintaining *nationalism* is that their discourses on nationalism should not be denied nationalist status merely because they gave other nationalist tasks such as anticommunism, national security, and economic development priority over unification. Here again it is one thing to criticize their nationalism for their priority-setting of nationalist tasks, and it is another to deny their nationalist discourses a nationalist character completely. In other words, conservatism as well as liberalism and radicalism have displayed both positive and negative aspects in Korean politics. Furthermore, nationalism is not free from any immanent ills or fallacies, as some Korean nationalists or students of nationalism would like to suppose.[47]

On the basis of this discussion I now examine in more detail how the overpowering presence has manifested itself in contemporary Korean politics. Looking back over the history of contemporary Korean politics, division-maintaining nationalism like anticommunism and modernization dominated the nationalist discourse during the long authoritarian rule, and unification-oriented nationalism has expanded its influence and posed a serious challenge to hegemonic division-maintaining nationalism since the beginning of the great transformation era.

Suppression of Unification-Oriented Nationalism by Division-Maintaining Nationalism before 1980

Before examining the upsurge in unification-oriented nationalism, it is necessary to examine the long domination by division-maintaining nationalism. The ruling elite did develop and propagate various discourses on unification, as I mention previously. However, South Korean governments branded the Soviet Union the "red imperialist" and North Korea its puppet regime; they consistently claimed that the government in South Korea was the only legitimate government standing against the "red desires" (i.e., the desire to subvert the government in South Korea by staging a communist revolution). In this way they solidified the divided state and aimed to achieve unification by absorbing the North into the South. At the same time, they systematically avoided formulating progressive and active policies regarding unification and relentlessly suppressed free discussion of the unification matter outside the government. By sternly stigmatizing those who advanced alternative proposals as "communist sympathizers," they sought to monopolize unification discourses and policies.[48] Thus they might be judged as division-maintaining in the sense that they perpetuated and entrenched the national division.

As a solution to cope with the division and achieve unification, the Rhee Syngman regime proposed both military and peaceful means, asserting without a doubt that the Republic of Korea should represent the only legitimate government on the Korean Peninsula. As for military means, it consistently advocated "unification by marching forward to the North." As for peaceful means, it only asserted, in fact, the peaceful absorption of North Korea into South Korea by holding an election in North Korea. For example, the Rhee regime proposed a plan "to expand South Korean sovereignty to the North by holding an election [only] in North Korea with UN monitors after the complete withdrawal of the communist army from North Korea" (the Resolution of the National Assembly in 1953) or "the measure to hold a free election [in the North] with UN monitors and to let the North Korean brethren decide their own destiny for themselves" (quoted in Hong Seok-ryul 2001, 30, 50).[49] As the truce became a fait accompli and the peaceful coexistence of the United States and the Soviet Union was settled in the late 1950s, the ruling Jayudang (Liberal Party) as well as the opposition Minjudang (Democratic

Party) came to realize that military means of unification was neither desirable nor feasible in reality, so it was virtually given up (40, 50).

If we take into consideration that neither the military nor the peaceful means of unification proposed by the Rhee regime was at all feasible, not only from the present perspective but also from the perspective of that time, Rhee's unification policy might well be criticized for being only division-maintaining in the sense that it does not give any serious thought to the unification matter, paying it lip service only. From the perspective of the Rhee regime, however, the advocacy for unification by marching forward to the North and/or holding a general election only in the North aimed to solve the problem deriving from the "forceful occupation of North Korea by the 'red imperialism'" by means of the "liberation of North Korea." So it was unquestionably based on the "strong nationalist logic" succeeding the "spirit of the March First Movement" and following the "principle of national self-determination" (Hong Seok-ryul 2001, 32). Thus it was something that could not be compromised by the unjust reality, regardless of whether it was feasible. Of course, behind this nationalist logic lay the strong creed that had been asserted since the establishment of the government in South Korea with the official name—the Republic of Korea. It held that the Republic of Korea was the only legitimate government on the Korean Peninsula that also represented the orthodoxy of the national history. According to this creed, then, North Korea could not be recognized as an active partner of the unification but only its object. It was not a legitimate political entity but an area of rebel occupation to be recovered either peacefully or militarily.

Seen from official political discourses, however, it should be noted that nationalism had been identified widely with "anti-Americanism" and "sympathy for communism" in the aftermath of liberation in 1945 (Kang Man-gil 1987, 17–18). Nationalism was also frowned upon as the "catchword that was used by communists to infiltrate backward countries," so that "*nationalism* was a taboo word" in the Rhee regime (Song Geon-ho 1986, 17; cf. Seo Jung-seok 1983, 270). Furthermore, "the nationalist discourse that emphasized that South and North Korea are the same nation had to disappear for a while," as "extreme hostilities were developed between South and North," particularly after the June 25 War. Thus politicians, bureaucrats, the military, and the police of the Rhee regime, most of whom had cooperated faithfully with the Japanese colonialists and later with the US military government, were at the forefront of "suppressing nationalism, putting up the cause of extreme anticommunism and anti–North Koreanism" (Park Chan-seung 2010, 232). Of course, they appealed to nationalist logic and sentiments to justify their anticommunism and anti-Japanese posture. At the same time, however, they did not welcome the discourses on nation and nationalism that the oppositional activists put forth to advocate independence and unification but took them as rebellious. Thus, instead of the polluted word *nation* associated with the left, "more neutral terms for the nation, like *kukka* (nation-state) and *kungmin* (national citizenry), whose meaning could be restricted to imply loyalty to the southern state alone," were widely circulated (Schmid 2002, 264; *kungmin* is transliterated herein as *gungmin*).[50]

Nationalism revived as the discourses on democracy and unification were invigorated among intellectuals and students in the Second Republic, which was inaugurated after the student-led April Revolution in 1960. However, this temporary revival of nationalism was stifled by the military government that took power through the coup d'état in May 1961. The military regime suppressed forward-looking unification proposals like South-North negotiation and "unification by neutrality" as communist-sympathetic and antistate (antigovernmental). As such it was almost impossible to expect unification-oriented nationalism to recover its momentum in the public realm during the Park Chung-hee regime, just as in the Rhee regime. Throughout his reign Park condemned the North Korean communists for being antinational, while putting forth anticommunism as the state doctrine. Of course, the basic plan for unification in the Park regime succeeded that of the Second Republic, which had given up military means of unification and had put forth a policy to achieve peaceful unification by holding a general election in both South and North with UN monitors.

Accordingly, Park basically maintained the unification plan (i.e., "construction first, then unification") he had inherited from the Second Republic. In a more concrete form, he presented "economic development" as the "immediate task," "modernization of the fatherland" as the "interim goal," and "unification of the divided territory" as the "supreme task" (September 245, 1969, 3:571). In this way, although he presented unification as the supreme goal among nationalist tasks in terms of importance, he still gave utmost priority to economic development. Thus he asserted that the "five-year economic development plan is in itself the unification movement" (October 1, 1968, 3:326). Elsewhere he stated, "Unification must be sought in the process of strengthening state power through building an autonomous economy and cultivating democratic capacity" (August 15, 1967, 3:25). Overall, Park's nationalism could be interpreted as overpowering nationalism by economic development and modernization.

Most intellectuals in the mid-1960s seem to have agreed with the nationalist tasks and the priorities set by Park. For example, Cha Gi-byeok, eminent Korean theorist of nationalism at that time, shared Park's formula in a 1965 article. Cha stated that the essence of "modernization" was "industrialization"—that is, "building the economy"—stressing that it was "building the economy" by utilizing "nationalism as its driving force," which would prepare the "ground for democracy" and provide the "right measure for the unification of the notional territory in the future"(Cha Gi-byeok 1965, 106). Ahn Byeong-uk (1968), well-known philosopher at the time, also noted that "modernization" was the "nationalist effort" that would fill "political independence" with the "content of economic independence" (139).[51] Thus most intellectuals at that time seem to have agreed with or conformed voluntarily to the division-maintaining nationalism of the Park regime.

Thus a study that analyzed the nationalist discourses in the 1960s drew this conclusion: "The content of nationalism constructed in the historical context of Korea's 1960s admitted nationalist elements congruent with the goal of economic development, but nationalist discourses opposing the interference and subordination by strong foreign powers or asserting national unification were diluted or ruled out by the official nationalism of the regime" (Hong Seok-ryul 2002, 181). In this context, both ruling and opposing forces share "capitalism," "developmentalism," and "anticommunism," and thus unification-oriented nationalism had to be muzzled.[52] This situation persisted into the 1970s. Thus most scholars who contributed their essays to the 1976 book edited by Jin Deok-gyu, *Hangugui Minjokjuui* (Nationalism in Korea), approved of the anticommunist (division-maintaining) nationalism put forth by the Park government. They branded North Korea antination(al) while vesting the orthodoxy of the national history in South Korea, and they advocated the unification of the territory after achieving industrialization and democratization—that is, "construction first, then unification" (Cheon Gwan-u 1976; Hwang Seong-mo 1976; Jin Deok-gyu 1976b; Lee Geuk-chan 1976; Lee Hong-gu 1976; Yang Ho-min 1976).[53]

On the basis of such wide agreement and support, Park Chung-hee set strengthening state power like economic development and self-reliant national defense as top priority among nationalist goals and flatly branded North Korea and domestic political elements opposed to such goals as antination(al) or communist sympathizers. In this way Park's nationalism displayed a strong preoccupation with the "economy-first policy" ("development supremacy") or "anticommunism supremacy" (national security first), confronting "unification supremacy" or "division reductionism" (to refer to an argument to explain all the evils rampant in South Korea in terms of national division). Such a position was held and raised by dissident leaders like Chang Chun-ha and Ham Seok-heon during Park's reign and would be strongly invigorated in the 1980s by radical activists. In other words, among nationalist goals, Park gave top priority to anticommunism and economic development, and he marginalized democracy and problems related to the division and unification, giving them low priority. In this sense, just as unification overpowered nationalism in unification-oriented nationalism, anticommunism and economic development overpowered Park's nationalism, albeit from the opposite direction. The former exerted its force to break through the division, whereas the latter mobilized its strength to maintain the national division, the status quo. For the former, the division was the historical phenomenon *never to be accepted but to be overcome desperately*, whereas for the latter it was historical reality *to be accepted, first of all, as a fait accompli and thus to be acted on for an indefinite period whatsoever.*

Unification-Oriented Nationalism and Its Overpowering of Nationalism since the 1980s

Whereas division-maintaining nationalism was based on the rigid dichotomy of "nation versus antination," unification-oriented nationalism sought to transform, break, and reverse the dichotomous concept that justified the perpetuation of the division. Unification nationalism, which had been occasionally raised from below in the period of long authoritarian rule, stored up its energy and expanded its influence strongly enough to confront division-maintaining nationalism in the era of great transformation in the 1980s. Going through its radicalizing phase in parallel with the democratic movement rapidly making a revolutionizing left turn, it had also shifted from a defensive to an offensive posture, making a deep impact on nationalist discourses. Let's examine this in more detail.

When we survey the seventy years of history since the division from the perspective of unification-oriented nationalism, we see it had to undergo bitter ordeals and frustrations from the beginning. Unification nationalism had reached a climax in April 1948, when Kim Gu, Kim Kyu-sik, and other South Korean political leaders went over to North Korea to hold a historic South-North negotiation with North Korean leaders—among them Kim Il-sung and Kim Tu-bong. The talk was held to discuss the matter of building a unified government in the whole of Korea to prevent the establishment of separate governments in South and North Korea, just before the historic first general election, scheduled for May 10, was to be held only in South Korea.[54] But it turned out to be a sheer failure. So, after the establishment of separate governments in South and North Korea, unification-oriented nationalism fell into a rapid decline—all the more so as the iron castle of anticommunism was built with the June 25 War. It temporarily recovered its influence in 1956, however, when Cho Bong-am and his Progressive Party advocated peaceful unification. Later, radical political forces also raised diverse unification discourses such as South-North talks and unification by neutrality with vigor in the free atmosphere of the Second Republic. They tapped the shift in the dichotomous conception of the nation by accepting the North Korean government as partner in dialogue while maintaining a baseline of anticommunism. But, during their respective regimes, Rhee Syngman and Park Chung-hee cracked down on them.

However, as the historic South–North Korea Joint Communiqué of July 4, 1972, pushed the progressive space for unification wide open, unification-oriented nationalism began to show strong indication of revival. Although the joint communiqué was later found to be abused by the South and North authorities for their political purposes, it cannot be denied that it did open the sluice for unification nationalism blocked by the stubborn bank of the division. It is Chang Chun-ha who spoke most ardently for unification nationalism at the time. In his article "Minjokjuuijaui Gil" (The Way of the Nationalist) published in September 1972 immediately after the joint South-North communiqué, Chang described his own brand of nationalism, which prioritized unification above all else, as follows:

> Is all unification good? Yes. There is no categorical imperative above unifica-tion. Unification means a divided nation becoming one, and if this means prog-ress in the history of the nation, all valuable things will be naturally fulfilled as part of this. None of these, such as democracy, equality, liberty, prosperity, and welfare as well as communism, can acquire their genuine substance insofar as they are opposed to unification. When all truths, all morals, and all goodness are opposed to unification, they are nothing more than false pretexts and cannot be truths. Our unification is at least this; if it is not, it will not ultimately become a reality. (Chang Chun-ha 1985, 54)

Although this vision of unification invoked by Chang showed passionate and utopian zeal, it also displayed the quintessence of unification-supremacist nationalism, which claimed that all kinds of tasks in Korean politics should be undertaken and judged in terms of achieving unification.

But the nationalist fervor for unification burning hot for a while soon abruptly abated after its manipulative use by the authorities in South and North Korea and the subsequent oppression of the unification movement. Unification-oriented nationalism was, however, to expand its influence in the academic and ideological realms first. It is Kang Man-gil, historian, who has made a pioneering and lasting contribution to articulating unifi-cation nationalism academically. Setting the (academic) contribution to achieving a unified nation-state as the sacrosanct goal of nation-centered historiography, Kang has designed and developed the basic ideas of unifica-tion-oriented nationalism most articulately since the mid-1970s. In an article titled "Minjoksahangnonui Banseong: Gwangbok 30nyeon Guksahagui Banseonggwa Banghyang" (Reflection upon Nation-Centered Historiogra-phy: Reflection upon and Guidelines for Korean Historiography Thirty Years after Liberation), originally published in 1975 and later included in a book, Kang openly declared unification-oriented nationalism top priority, claim-ing that the "guiding idea of our national history since liberation" should be "national unification." Accordingly, he maintained that "the independent sovereignty and modernization that emerged as the supreme task of the national history since the late nineteenth century cannot be accomplished ultimately without the establishment of a unified nation-state" (Kang Man-gil 1978, 35). In another article Kang further argued that, just as the period of the forced occupation by the Japanese was commonly called "the colonial era" to be overcome or "the era of the independence movement" to overcome it, so the "postliberation age" should be defined as the "age of the division" or the "age of the unification movement" from the perspective of unification-oriented nationalism (14–15).

However, it was regrettable, Kang maintained, to observe the following phenomenon. "Most of the Korean nationals," he wrote, "underwent the rapid cooling-off of the nationalist mission for unification that had boiled up at the time of division, with the experience of the internecine war, and then they became indifferent to the system of the national division or took it for granted as the unavoidable reality and jumped on the bandwagon of national division. As a result, they ended up contributing to prolonging this tragic history" (Kang Man-gil 1978, 15). In this way Kang criticized directly the anti-communist or division-maintaining nationalism pervasive in South Korea. He summarized his argument, stressing that the essential purpose of naming "the age of the division" or "the age of the unification movement" was "to guard against complacent settling for the system of the national division by accepting it as a fait accompli, to urge in earnest that it should be overcome, and to explore the proper direction for overcoming it" (ibid.).

In 1979, at the end of the Yusin regime, Hangilsa, one of the major publishing companies in Korea, published *Haebang Jeonhusaui Insik* (later renamed *Haebang Jeonhusaui Insik 1*, or, Understanding History before and after the Liberation; Song Geon-ho 1979). It would turn out to be a hugely successful, historic publication that provided a systematic and objective analysis of the cause and process of the national division for the first time since liberation by focusing on the period before and after liberation, and thus it stimulated concern for unification-oriented nationalism, widely circulating the idea among the informed public. The book consisted of such themes as "the US military government and the national division, the real state of pro-Japanese collaborators and antinational elements, and the economic structure in the aftermath of liberation." However, the military authority in charge of the martial law declared just after Park's sudden assassination in October 1979 prohibited sale of the book by censoring it. Hangilsa resumed publication of the series *Haebang Jeonhusaui Insik* (Understanding History before and after the Liberation) in 1985, when nationalism advocating national liberation and *minjung* (people's) liberation erupted as a result of the radical-democratization movement. The series, consisting of five volumes (1985–1989), attracted unusual attention among readers who were interested in contemporary Korean history. As a result, the academic concern about the history of "before and after" liberation increased rapidly and widely, such that research on the cause and process of the division and its historical implication expanded and deepened. Accordingly, the fervor for unification-oriented nationalism experienced a great upsurge. Therefore the 1979 publication of *Haebang Jeonhusaui Insik* and the publication of subsequent volumes in the series may be duly interpreted as historic events.

In this historical context Kang Man-gil's unification-oriented nationalism was expressed more clearly in "Haebangjeonhusa Insigui Banghyang" (The Proper Direction for Understanding History before and after the Liberation), his preface to the 1985 book he edited, *Haebang Jeonhusaui Insik 2* (Understanding History before and after the Liberation 2). First, Kang indicates as the cause of the national division extranational variables such as "US–Soviet army's joint occupation of the Korean Peninsula by division" and the subsequent development of international situations such as the outbreak of the Cold War. At the same time, however, he equally stresses "divisive maneuvers by politicians within the nation jumping on the bandwagon of US–Soviet occupation in order to seize power even in a divided state" (Kang Man-gil 1985b, 9, 12). In addition, whereas the ringleaders of the maneuvers tried to "justify" or "cover up" such "divisive maneuvers . . . within the nation" seeking to build divided states, he maintains they emphasized the "inevitability of the division," advocating "the determination of the division by foreign influence," or sought to exempt themselves from their own share of responsibility for the national division by transferring it to their political opponents—Northern communists, in the case of South Korea. Kang then criticizes division-maintaining nationalism by the ruling elements in the South not only for oppressing, in the name of anticommunism or communist sympathizers, "political movements aiming to establish a unified nation-state," but also for denying their historicity by destroying their historical records and sending them into complete oblivion (12–13). He suggests that this phenomenon was brought about by statism in a divided state, which presented the South Korean state as if it were the whole Korean nation, and thus advocates that the "perspective of such statism be elevated to the stage of unification nationalism" (14).

Kang's perspective of unification nationalism stipulates that "whenever we recognize all the political, economic, social, and cultural phenomena as historical facts, we have to set as the standard of their evaluation whether they have made positive or negative contributions to the problem of achieving the unified nation-state" and we have to agonize over what kind of directional change is needed to make them contribute to unification once they are found to be negative (Kang Man-gil 1985b, 14–15). As a result, the national division calls for the "awareness of times that all the political action, economic and social development, and cultural activity in general in the age of division cannot acquire their historicity until they are in line with the road toward national unification" (15). When we follow Kang's unification-oriented nationalism, we can understand why the anticommunist nationalism or division-maintaining nationalism advocated by Rhee Syngman and Park Chung-hee is defined as "statism in a divided state on the pretext of nationalism."

From the perspective of this unification-oriented nationalism, it is rather natural to observe that the division-maintaining nationalism from above and the unification-oriented nationalism from below collided with each other not only over the issue of national division and unification but also over that of modernization via economic development engineered by the Park regime. For instance, the advocates of unification-oriented nationalism, though acknowledging the need for economic development as such, put forth a critique that economic development under the Park regime was "not in line with the progress of nationalism by contradicting national unification as well as sacrificing the operation of democracy" (Kang Man-gil 1987, 29). From a similar viewpoint, Song Geon-ho (1986) offered criticism that "the problem of unification would be further complicated" if economic development were achieved by dependency on overseas powers and on condition of the perpetuation of the national division because the beneficiaries of economic development would harbor an antinational orientation, colluding with foreign powers and sitting complacently on the national division (213).[55]

Thus unification nationalists such as Chang Chun-ha, Song Geon-ho, and Kang Man-gil did acknowledge economic development and democracy as the important objectives of nationalism and subsequently reviewed and criticized the accomplishments of Rhee Syngman, Park Chung-hee, and Chun Doo-hwan accordingly. But, more important, these unification nationalists evaluated the validity of these goals and the methods to achieve them in light of the ultimate goal of overcoming national division and achieving national unification. Thus, although they would not deny the importance of democracy, nevertheless democracy would seem to only hold a place secondary to national reunification. They might have been willing to accept the suspension of democracy to a certain extent if it had been deemed necessary for national unification.[56]

Such a position held by unification nationalists shows a paradoxical similarity to that of most intellectuals in the mid-1960s. They were willing to give top priority to economic development and concentrate on it, marginalizing the importance of democracy and the problem of national unification. In other words, they approved "the logic of modernization advanced by the Park regime to a substantial degree," took "economic growth as the supreme and urgent task of the state," and were prepared to accept and rationalize "the restriction of freedom to sustain the divided state, state intervention, and the suspension of freedom for economic development"—that is, restraints on liberal democracy and laissez-faire capitalism (Kim Dong-chun 1994, 230, 236). In the same way, but with a different set of priorities, unification nationalists would have been ready to temporarily accept the restriction on important elements of democracy in the process of solving the problem of national division. In other words, we may harbor strong doubts as to whether they could have raised strong opposition to the restriction of democracy when it was inevitable that national unification (nationalism) and democracy would collide.[57] It seems to me that they did not so much justify national unification in terms of democracy as democracy in terms of national unification.

Moreover, unification nationalists held the view that the dictatorial system in South Korea beginning with the Rhee Syngman regime and continuing through the Chun Doo-hwan regime had been perpetuated ultimately by the structure of the national division and the support and acquiescence of foreign powers. Thus their position led to the conclusion that the division structure should be overthrown even to achieve democracy. Furthermore, their position on Korean politics tended to tilt toward so-called division reductionism, which interprets all the contradictions and evils of South Korean society as deriving from the structure of the national division.[58] This point was well confirmed by Song Geon-ho (1986) when he designated the national division as the "foremost enemy to democracy," enumerating the evils it brought about (221).[59] Of course, such a stance harbors the strong potential for "unification supremacy." This was revealed in Chang Chun-ha's previously quoted statement—"Is all unification good? Yes. There is no categorical imperative above unification." For Chang (1985), national unification was imagined as a utopia that meant the fulfillment of all values such as "democratization of political institutions," "the securement of national homogeneity" including the guarantee of welfare for *minjung*, "the development of the national common ideals," and so on (47–49). Thus, Chang was able to demand that individual members of the nation devote everything to the fulfillment of such a utopian vision—that is, the accomplishment of all things good. "Only those," writes Chang, "who are willing to shake off political ideas, living conditions, even private life, and their attachment to these things—once they are found to be impediments to national unification—are entitled to speak of national unification and join the unification movement" (40). Ham Seok-heon (1984) also preached in the aftermath of the South–North Korea Joint Communiqué, writing, "Just as a person is not a person if one's personality is not unified, so a nation is not a nation if it does not attain a unified country" (34).

Thus the argument of the unification nationalists boils down to the following: "The nation has existed precisely because the national unification movement has persisted" in the era of national division, just as the nation existed during Japanese colonial rule precisely because there was the national independence movement (Chang Chun-ha 1985, 44). The argument put forward by Chang and Ham might contain significant historical insight and an awak-ening voice. It is also a compelling rhetorical expression aiming to remind most Koreans, who were in the habit of forgetting the importance of national unification, of its urgency. Nevertheless, it is hard to deny that such advocacy had the tendency to brand not only ruling elements adhering to division-maintaining nationalism but also most Koreans who, consciously or uncon-sciously, took national division for granted, those stuck to the reality who were unable to shake off everything for the sake of unification or who lived a schizophrenic national life. Indeed, it contained the danger of "unification supremacism" to stigmatize such Koreans as "nonnation" or "antination." In this sense it is proper to interpret tasks related to division and unification as dominant over other tasks of nationalism (e.g., modernization and economic development, democracy, anticommunism) in unification-oriented national-ism. Just as authoritarian ruling forces headed by Rhee Syngman and Park Chung-hee imposed a dichotomous scheme of nation versus antination (or nonnation) according to whether a person was for or against their political objectives of anticommunism and/or economic development, so did advo-cates of unification-supremacist nationalism articulate their own dichotomous scheme of nation according to whether a person was for or against the unifica-tion advocacy they presented. In other words, they essentially reproduced the nation-versus-antination scheme from a different direction.

Dissident intellectuals like Chang Chun-ha, Song Geon-ho, and Kang Man-gil articulated and led unification nationalism in a pioneering but anguished spirit, even at the risk of their lives, when Park's iron rule of Yusin reigned supreme in the 1970s. Although nationalism stressing anticommu-nism still held sway in the official political arena of the 1980s, beginning with Chun Doo-hwan's seizure of power,[60] unification-oriented nationalism began to revive itself in the arena of radical political movement, stored up its power, and expanded its sphere of influence, despite severe oppression by the govern-ment. When the "antinational" feature of Chun Doo-hwan's military clique was exposed so blatantly by their ruthless and bloody suppression of the Gwangju Democratization Movement in May 1980, radical democratic move-ments thereafter attributed to American imperialism the responsibility for the origin and perpetuation of national division as well as chronic dictatorships in Korean politics, thereby displaying strong anti-American sentiment for the first time in Korean history. They also returned the arrow of "antination" to Chun's military regime, which had perpetrated an unprecedented iron-fist rule and had perpetuated the national division by jumping on the bandwagon of US imperialism. When the Chun regime was branded subservient to US imperialism, it became rather natural to characterize the opposition move-ment as pursuing national liberation as well as democratization. In particular, the radical faction stressing national liberation revealed a strong tendency toward "unification supremacism" or "nation supremacism" (Kim Dong-chun 1996b). This overpowering presence of the tasks related to the division and unification in Korean nationalism became conspicuous in the 1980s as a result of the vehement struggles against the Chun regime, thus going on to revolutionize and radicalize the ideological terrain of Korean politics.

Thus unification nationalism had overwhelmed the Park Chung-hee–style modernization nationalism in radicalized discourses since 1980. This phenomenon was quite salient among progressive Korean historians. Unification discourses and the unification movement have been invigorated more actively in the public arena with more freedom since democratization in 1987. This was made possible by the weakening of the severe oppression of unification nationalism and democratic governments' more progressive and flexible attitudes toward unification, although there were substantial variations in their attitudes. Unification nationalism reached its climax with visits to Pyongyang by Reverend Moon Ik-hwan and university student Lim Su-kyung, one after another, without government approval in 1989, immediately after democratization. Their visits, which were made at the risk of governmental prosecution and persecution, took the political elite as well as the general public by surprise, thereby succeeding in graphically demonstrating the cause of unification nationalism to the world as well as to Korea.

In this way unification nationalism sanctified nationalism as much as or perhaps far more than Park Chung-hee's modernization nationalism had done.[61] Due to the overpowering weight of the unification task in nationalism, official nationalism advocated and circulated by the Rhee, Park, and Chun regimes was considered as contributing to the antinational (un)reality of consolidating and reproducing the national-division system by the advocates of unification nationalism. In short, Rhee's and Park's nationalist discourses were denied the status of nationalism, even retroactively. In this way, linking the ideas and policies of Rhee and Park to nationalism became as good as an oxymoron. They were considered at best a quasi-nationalism or pseudonationalism. Kang Man-gil, as if foreseeing such a situation, said as early as 1978 that "the task of the highest stage through which Korean national historiography can contribute to the liquidation of the age of division is to clearly and thoroughly overcome antinational and antihistoricist features of nationalist theories that have been mobilized to sustain the system of divided states and to set up nationalist theories that pursue the establishment of a unified nation-state. This point must be confirmed all the more indisputably" (1978, 21).[62]

Critical Review of Unification-Oriented Nationalism

Division-maintaining nationalism and unification-oriented nationalism have been examined thus far in order to show the overpowering presence of one task over others in Korean national discourses. Because the oppressive and ill effects brought about by the former have been criticized sufficiently by the latter,[63] some serious problems contained in the latter deserve critical attention now in order to restore ideological balance in the study of Korean nationalism.

To do this we need to note Kim Bo-hyeon's outstanding work (2006), which characterizes nationalist discourses produced by progressive Korean intellectuals as the "mythification of nationalism" and makes a critical scrutiny of them. Confronting the arguments advanced by unification-oriented nationalists, Kim relates the establishment of the Park regime to the emergence of a new nationalism. He draws our attention to "the condition of mass impoverishment, the foremost grievance during the April Revolution" in 1960, as a matter of highest priority among nationalist tasks (19). Then Kim argues that the period of Park Chung-hee's rule should be understood "as the age of not antinationalism but nationalism" because "the economic development embarked upon by the Park regime was the promoter of Korean capitalism as part of a nationalist project." Kim maintains that, as a matter of fact, the regime "not only aimed to seek but also promoted the development and self-reliance of the national economy" (15, 17). At the same time, he stresses that the contradictions brought about by Park's economic growth should be accepted as "contradictions of nationalism" and "contradictions of development" (15). Furthermore, Kim advances the argument that Park's policy of "unification by defeating the communist North" on the basis of the slogan "construction first, then unification" should not be interpreted as an indicator of antinationalism. The policy stressed, above all, the "promotion of state power via economic development as a preparatory stage for unification," although we cannot deny that it clearly "functioned as an oppressive discourse" by blocking the free discussion of unification issues. Besides, Kim argues, "unification by defeating the communist North" constitutes a "prototype of 'unification by absorption' [of North by South Korea] considered highly feasible since the 1990s, aside from its normative desirability and validity" (20).

Thus Kim Bo-hyeon criticizes progressive scholars' nationalist discourses, stating that they have privileged the image or the vision of the desirable nationalism they favor and then committed "ideological dogmatism [by] asserting normatively that 'only this is nationalism'" and fallacies to brand "situations, figures, and forces" contrary to their own image of nationalism as antinationalist. As a result, Kim further maintains, they unduly narrow the scope of nationalism and evaluate overall modern Korean history, including Park's reign, as the "oppression, failure, and frustration of nationalism" (2006, 28–31).

We may summarize the debate over nationalism between the conservative ruling elite and the progressive oppositional intellectuals and activists in the following way: Dictatorial regimes in South Korea forcefully asserted that the division-maintaining nationalism they presented and imposed, whether anticommunist or modernization nationalism, was the only correct nationalism, and they branded as antinational other kinds of nationalism different from their own (e.g., North Korea or communist sympathizer) and suppressed them. Likewise, the progressive camp also claimed that their vision and interpretation of unification-oriented nationalism was the only genuine nationalism and stigmatized other varieties as antinational. At the same time, progressive intellectuals breathed a more sanctified and infallible utopian vision into the nationalist discourses they built. The infallibility and sanctification were realized by banishing nationalist discourses they were opposed to from (genuine) nationalism and branding them as antinational. In this sense, conservatives and progressives in their discursive struggles over nationalism reflected or reproduced each other's argument in an inverted form.

As mentioned earlier, Kim Bo-hyeon stipulates the nationalism that progressive nationalists have drawn in this way to be the "mythification" of nationalism. However, it cannot be emphasized too much that nationalism is a multidimensional ideology forced to carry out multiple tasks such as national independence, national security, anticommunism, modernization and economic development, economic self-reliance, national unification, and so on. History has also shown that the newly independent states in the mid-twentieth century were compelled to carry them out simultaneously and that these tasks often conflicted during implementation. Seen from this perspective, the various tasks of nationalism could be seen, at best, as evaluative criteria by which diverse policies, ideas, and figures of would-be nationalism (or what passes for nationalism) are judged in terms of their respective strengths and weaknesses but are not necessary or defining conditions of nationalism. In conceptualizing the ideology, we have to broaden our horizons flexibly to accept that there is good and bad nationalism—instead of clinging to a dichotomous contrast between nation(alism) and antination(alism). According to this suggestion, then, we should discuss nationalism not in terms of a monistic dichotomy but in terms of diversity and plurality.

Just as socialist fundamentalists advocate the infallibility of socialism, regardless of the actual state of "historical socialism," and libertarians insist on the flawlessness of liberalism without giving any attention to the flaws of actualized liberalism, unification-oriented nationalists in South Korea who have made a decisive contribution to the sanctification of nationalism seem to reject all ideas and realities contrary to their idea of nationalism as antinational and thereby succeed in preserving the integrity and infallibility of their own nationalism. However, it is still a baffling paradox to observe the dualistic attitude in which they keep silent or are not forthcoming about the antinational as well as antidemocratic nature of the North Korean regimes in which the Kim dynasty reigns supreme, while clamorously criticizing the antinational features of dictatorial leaders in South Korea.

CONCLUDING REMARKS

Thus far the sanctification of nationalism has been examined as one of the notable features of the ideological topography of Korean politics, focusing mainly on the period before democratization. In order to understand its impact on the topography, the impact has been divided into the overdetermination of other ideologies by nationalism and the overpowering presence of one task over other tasks within nationalism. In this book's final chapter we trace the trajectory that nonsimultaneity and sanctification have drawn since democratization in 1987. Now, however, this chapter concludes by exploring the relationship between overdetermination and overpowering presence. *Overdetermination* refers to the phenomenon whereby the legitimacy of conservatism, radicalism, and liberalism are overdetermined by nationalism in the end, although the three ideologies appeal to nationalism in order to complement their deficits in legitimacy or to reinforce their legitimacy with a certain degree of success. Here the overdetermination thesis assumes that the three ideologies are distinct and autonomous from nationalism. In contrast, *overpowering presence* intends to conceptualize the phenomenon that takes place when diverse tasks constituting multidimensional nationalism—such as anticommunism, economic development (modernization), national unification, and democracy—are engaged in intense competitive struggles to gain top priority within nationalism.

In the midst of these struggles, conservatives assign top priority to anticommunism and economic development; liberal democrats, to democracy; and the radical advocates of unification, to the task related to division and unification. They also marginalize or disregard other nationalists who prioritize differently and even stigmatize them as being antinational. Thus overpowering presence can be interpreted as the contentious striving of diverse nationalist tasks to gain top priority within nationalism. Seen from another perspective, however, this may be interpreted as conservatives, liberals, and radicals engaging in discursive struggles, this time not outside nationalism but inside it. In other words, if *overdetermination* presupposes the distinctiveness and autonomy of the three ideologies from nationalism and their competition without nationalism, *overpowering presence* describes the dynamic by which the three ideologies struggle for hegemony within nationalism by bringing their primary tasks—such as anticommunism, economic development, democracy, and unification—into nationalism.[64] In this respect, overpowering presence does not treat the three ideologies as distinct but, rather, incorporates them into nationalism. In conclusion, although these two phenomena have taken place in the midst of ideological struggles among diverse political actors, each seeking hegemony by jumping on the bandwagon of the sanctification of nationalism, they also have contributed to strengthening it.

NOTES

1. See Lee Hwa-yong 2010 for the English experience. See Hong Tai-young 2010 for the French; however, right-wing nationalism did emerge at the end of the nineteenth century in France and threaten republicanism, as shown in the affairs of George Boulanger and Alfred Dreyfus (174–84).

2. Due to this assumption, which overlooks the formation of the nation, social-contract theories have been frequently criticized for being ahistorical.

3. See Fichte's *Foundations of Natural Right* (2000) for his concept of the contract state, his *Addresses to the German Nation* (1922) for his idea of the nation-state, and "The Characteristics of the Present Age" (1999) for his later thoughtful examination of the relationship between the two ideas of the state.

4. In this sense, it was no accident that the sanctification of the state by Hegel and the glorification of the nation (and the state) by Nazism emerged in Germany. This has great implications for the appearance of the sanctification of the nation and nationalism in contemporary Korean politics.

5. Chatterjee, however, critically examines John Plamenatz's famous distinction between Western and Eastern types of nationalism. For Chatterjee, the Western type has emerged "primarily in Western Europe" while the Eastern type is found "in Eastern Europe, in Asia and Africa, and also in Latin America" (Chatterjee 1986, 1).

6. Of course, the Donghak (Eastern Learning) peasants' revolt at the end of the nineteenth century raised the issue of class problems with the cause of antifeudal reform as well as the antiforeign issue in defense against Western powers and Japan.

7. According to Park Chan-seung's survey (2010), the doctrine of "a single and pure nation" Koreans have long taken for granted "emerged actually for the first time after liberation." It was used to oppose the decision of the trusteeship by the three powers, to warn of the South-North division in the aftermath of liberation, and to stress the imperative of reunification after the formalization of the national division (22, 103–16). However, as evidenced by common expressions such as "The twenty-million nation are the descendants of the same Dangun" (legendary founder of the first Korean state), the vague idea that the Korean nation maintained "single-blood lineage" had existed for a long time (104–5).

8. The sanctification of nationalism now applies all the more strongly to North Korea, which has developed the Juche ideology and the "Unitary System" (*yuil cheje*). North Korean stress on nationalism has become much more pronounced with the appearance of the slogan "Our Nation Number One" after the collapse of socialist regimes.

9. Cho Hui-yeon (2003b), a well-known progressive sociologist, also joins the sanctification of nationalism and the authenticity controversy by defining Park

Chung-hee's discourses on nationalism as "pseudonationalism" that appeals to "pseudonational sentiments" (73–74).

10. I borrow the concept of overdetermination from Louis Althusser's (1979) work. He is opposed to the schematic interpretation of Marx's theory of historical materialism as the determination of superstructure ("the State and all the legal, political and ideological forms") by economic structure (the forces and relations of production). Instead he proposed the concept of overdetermination to explain the complexity of historical change. Noting uneven social development, he stressed the "relative autonomy of the superstructures and their specific effectivity," while asserting "the economy is determinant, but in the last instance" (111–12).

However, the concept is widely used in a loose sense beyond the Marxist circle. For example, when Ella Shohat and Robert Stam discuss the concept of the West in their examination of Eurocentrism, they note the contemporary parlance in which Israel is considered a Western country, whereas Turkey, Egypt, Libya, and Morocco, which lie to the west of Israel (a substantial portion of Turkey also lies to the east of Israel) are all "Eastern" and Latin America is often excluded from the West. Moreover, we often observe that Japan is included as part of the West in political discourses and the media. So Shohat and Stam state that "politics overdetermines cultural geography" (1994, 13). In this sense, it can be said that today *the West* refers mostly to the regions or countries in which advanced capitalism and liberal democracy prevail. Thus, in this chapter, *overdetermination* is also used to refer to the ideological phenomenon in which various ideologies such as liberalism, conservatism, nationalism, and radicalism have competed for their legitimation in the ideological terrain of contemporary Korean politics. All these ideologies have maintained their relative autonomy in the source of their legitimation, but nationalism has overdetermined the legitimation of other ideologies in terms of providing the ultimate source due to Korea's structural and historical conditions.

11. *Overpowering presence* may well appear to be the same as *overdetermination* to those who share the same political ideology, but it may also appear to be merely the outcome of an exaggerated notion to those who do not. This suggests that the consequence of overpowering presence is fluid, indeterminate, or controversial, contrary to that of overdetermination.

12. In contrast to the position here, Lim Ji-hyeon (1999, 5–6) and Kim Bo-hyeon (2006, 28) use phrases such as "mythical understanding of the nation" and "mythification of nationalism," usually pointing to the progressive discourses on nationalism. But as is examined in chapter 6, the sanctification of nationalism is observed in Park Chung-hee's discourse on nationalism as well.

13. There is some controversy among Korean scholars over the question of whether nationalism is a distinct and self-sufficient ideology for its own sake or merely an instrumental one to help other ideologies realize their own ideas and values. See Park Chan-seung 2010, 237–39, for an examination of this debate.

14. As briefly discussed in chapter 1, the *ilminjui* (doctrine of a unitary nation) imposed on the populace as the ruling conservative ideology during Rhee's rule contained an explicitly nationalist character. Thus it is not addressed here. See Kim Hye-su 1995, Seo Jung-seok 2005, and Yeon Jeong-eun 2003 for a detailed examination of it.

15. As I address later, this phenomenon has brought about the overdetermination of the concept of nation by anticommunism, which overwhelms the ethnicity in nation, and the overpowering presence of anticommunism, which marginalizes other tasks of nationalism.

16. This speech was cited earlier in chapter 2.

17. Rhee Syngman 1948.

18. For a detailed examination, see chapter 6, where Park Chung-hee's discourse on nationalism is scrutinized.

19. This is often called "anticommunist nationalism" (Kim Jeong-hun and Cho Hui-hyeon 2003; Seo Jung-seok 1996).

20. In contrast, for Kim Gu, who viewed the nation as a permanent entity, ethnic elements such as "blood lineage" overdetermined the concept of nation, overwhelming the ideological element, as is addressed in the concluding chapter 7.

21. Such anticommunist genocide committed during the June 25 War has been critically analyzed in detail by Kim Dong-chun (2006b).

22. This point is further elaborated on in chapter 4.

23. Contrary to the internationalist Marx who asserted that the working class has no homeland, Ferdinand Lassalle, leader of the United German Labor Party and, at the same time, Marx's main rival for the theoretical and intellectual leadership of the German socialist movement, was an ardent advocate of nationalism. He held that workers of every nation should seek their own paths to socialism (Dagger and Ball 2004, 142).

24. Of course, there emerged some Korean internationalist communists who in the early 1920s during Japanese colonial rule gave priority to universal class liberation over nationalism. They took the Korean public by surprise, issuing a statement in a newspaper that "they would cooperate with Japanese workers, setting Korean nationalists as their enemy" (quoted in Lee Kyeong-nam 1981, 187).

25. In addition, it seems that their advocacy for peaceful unification that accepted North Korea as a partner for dialogue and unification was more shocking to right-wing adherents of anticommunism as the state doctrine than their election manifesto for social democracy. The Democratic Party government of the Second Republic advocated as their unification plan "construction first, then unification," putting forth "economy first," while still maintaining anticommunism as the state doctrine, like the First Republic.

26. However, the direct target of anti–US struggle was not usually the American government but the Chun Doo-hwan regime. This suggests that the nationalist anti–US struggle had erupted in the form of a radical democratization movement against the dictatorial government. I elaborate on this point later.

27. Of course this was also true of the Japanese colonial period.

28. Many pamphlets and tracts were circulated during that period. But here special focus is placed on the founding manifestos of the National Youth Association for Democratic Movement and the United Association for Democracy, Unification, and Minjung Movement, which were founded in 1983 and 1985, respectively. These two associations as centripetal bodies of the then-radical democratization movement led and organized various rallies and demonstrations such as the great June Struggle

in 1987 and the constitutional-revision movement for direct election of the presidency, as well as numerous *minjung*, democratization, and unification movements that erupted after the Chun government had to shift to an appeasement policy in 1983 to prepare for the impending general election in 1985.

29. In addition, insulting remarks regarding Korean democratic forces as well as the general Korean population were made in 1980 by John A. Wickham, commander of the United States Forces Korea, and in 1982 by Richard Louis Walker, then–US ambassador to South Korea, which fueled anti-American sentiment among the Korean populace (Minjuhwaui Gil 1989, 51).

30. Kang Cheol's "Prologue," published in late 1985, and written in lucid and appealing style, is considered one of the representative pamphlets asserting direct struggle against imperialism (see Kang Cheol 1985).

31. This point is confirmed by an opinion survey of college students conducted in 1989, two years after democratization. In the survey, 59 percent of the students responded that anti–US sentiment was "the majority opinion and valid," and 89 percent of the students evaluated "the US role in Korean unification" to be negative (quoted in Kim Dong-chun 1996b, 167). Even more than twenty-five years after democratization, this legacy continues to be confirmed by various public opinion polls establishing that among South Koreans, an important indicator of being "progressive" is sympathy toward North Korea while being critical of the United States.

32. However, if we remember that most British and French intellectuals and politicians justified their colonialism and imperialism in terms of a "civilizing mission," the "white man's burden," and/or "the glory of the British Empire" and if we take Western imperialism and colonialism as a variety of overblown nationalism, it may seem simply naive to deny that their conservatism contained a nationalist streak. This point may well apply to their liberalism as well. At the same time, it should be noted that some French conservatives in the late nineteenth century and German conservatives throughout the nineteenth century harbored strong nationalist sentiments.

33. State nationalism is addressed further in chapter 6.

34. In this regard the influence of traditional culture should be considered seriously. Collectivism remains much stronger than individualism in East Asian nations with a Confucian tradition, in comparison with Western countries. This phenomenon still persists in so-called newly industrialized entities like Taiwan, Hong Kong, and South Korea, as well as Japan (Cho Geung-ho 2006, 34–35).

35. Here the examination of "anticommunist liberalism" as a ruling ideology overlaps with that of conservatism to a great extent, given that pretransition Korean politics is characterized by the dual political order of authoritarianism and liberal democracy, as discussed in chapter 2.

36. My interpretation here is not intended to disregard the point raised by progressive scholars. They usually assert that most conservative Korean political leaders—such as Kim Seong-su and Song Jin-wu, who advocated liberal democracy—had pro-Japanese careers and thus wanted to cancel or mitigate them by advocating anticommunism. But we need to be reminded that leaders of the overseas independence movement—like Rhee Syngman, Kim Gu, Lee Beom-seok, Shin Ik-hi, and Chang Chun-ha, who were all free from such pro-Japanese blemish—were strongly opposed

to communism. In this respect the two groups forged a strong anticommunist alliance, despite their significant differences in pro-Japanese careers.

37. Such antiliberal elements in Park Chung-hee's political thought are analyzed more closely in chapters 5 and 6 when his conservatism and nationalism are addressed.

38. In connection with this, it is worth recalling that 60 percent of Korean intellectuals in the 1960s responded positively to the suggestion that "freedom may be restricted for the sake of economic development" (quoted in Kim Dong-chun 1994, 236).

39. Furthermore, the two politicians stressed strong solidarity in democratic struggles, appealing to nationalism: "Just as the whole nation had to be united to be one in the struggle for national independence, so must we be united to be a harmonious whole in the struggle for democracy" (Shindonga Pyeonjipsil 1990, 31). They concluded their announcement by declaring that "the two of us . . . solemnly pledge that we will devote all we have to the altar of nation and democracy" (35).

This passage reminds us of Park's resolute remark, declaring the October Yusin (Revitalizing Reform) in 1972: "As for myself, I have already devoted everything to the altar of the unification of the fatherland and national regeneration for a long time" ("Special Declaration on October 17," 1972, 4:301). After all, varying with the times, Park devoted himself to "the altar of the unification of the fatherland and national regeneration" and the two Kims to "the altar of nation and democracy." All in all, the two opposing forces—one represented by the two Kims as well as Chang Jun-ha and the other by Park Chung-hee—both engaged in a life-and-death struggle to a great extent in the political arena, ultimately appealing to "nation" and "nationalism" to establish the legitimacy of their political action.

40. In the quotation, Kim Dong-chun uses "modern social ideology" to refer only to liberalism and socialism, excluding conservatism. Kim, who stresses the progressive understanding of nationalism, does not examine the conservatism of the South Korean elite in the essay quoted here in terms of nationalism because he denies Korean conservatives nationalist status. Here he interprets the political thought of Rhee Syngman and Park Chung-hee overall as statism, expounding elsewhere that "the supreme logic of [their] rule was the maintenance of the state order, and so nationalism (= unification = national subjectivity) contrary to the maintenance of the state order was rejected [by them]" (2000, 301; cf. 1996a, 304).

41. Park Chan-seung (2010) expresses this point in a telling way: "No words have exerted more powerful influence than *minjok* [nation] in the Korean history of the twentieth century. The realities of colony and national division have made 'the independence of the nation,' and 'the unification of the nation,' respectively, the supreme task of twentieth-century Korea" (21; cf. 24).

42. Of course, simultaneously carrying out even secondary tasks like rapid economic development and implementing democracy may lead the tasks to collide with each other.

43. Given the example of South Korea, we may cite two kinds of arguments to explain the first point: (1) the argument raised immediately after the division that the imbalance between the industrial structures of South and North Korea (agricultural

South versus industrial North), which had formed during Japanese colonial rule, would make successful industrialization in the South difficult and (2) the diagnosis made by some democratic activists in the late 1970s that "the division posed a fatal obstacle to democratization in the South." The second point may be illustrated by the development of two possible circumstances: (1) the situation in which one partner of unification would become passive or negative toward unification if the overall power imbalance between the two Koreas widens, so that a partner with an inferior status might fear unification by unilateral absorption, or (2) the circumstance in which a partner that might feel confident of its economic success does not want unification any longer because it would demand a high cost and confusion. In contrast, the doctrine of "construction first, then unification" was based on the assumption that the successful implementation of the secondary tasks of nationalism would facilitate the attainment of unification.

44. Seo Jung-seok (1995a) argues that, as successor to Rhee's policy of "unification by marching forward to the North," Park Chung-hee's policy of "construction first, then unification" played the role of blocking and prohibiting public discussion of unification as well, pointing to the fact that there was no public discussion of unification, let alone any unification movement, after the May 16 coup d'état (335).

45. Thus Kang Man-gil (1987) distinguishes between "statism in a divided state" and "unification nationalism." He argues that discourses on nationalism advanced by Rhee Syngman and Park Chung-hee were merely "insistence on anticommunism as if it were nationalism" and nothing but the "statism of a divided state" that stressed the "subjectivity of the nation in a disguised manner" while bringing about "serious subordination economically and culturally" (27).

From a similar perspective, Kim Dong-chun (2000), too, asserts that "the history of South and North Korea has actually restrained 'nationalism' under the principle of 'statism' while using [apparently] nationalist discourses" (300; cf. 301, 340). Following this logic, Kim never mentions the nationalism of Rhee and Park when he surveys the history of Korean nationalism after liberation (Kim Dong-chun 1996b).

46. Kim Il-young (2006b) divides nationalism into four types in an essay dealing with Korean nationalism during Park Chung-hee's reign: "defensive-modernization nationalism," "unification-oriented nationalism, "nationalism oriented to a nation-centered economy," and "anti–US nationalism." Then he classifies Park Chung-hee's nationalism as defensive-modernization nationalism. In the essay he points out that it is "wrong to insist that a particular nationalism among the four" can "monopolize the concept of nationalism." Then he wants to show that Park's doctrines—such as "growth first, then distribution" and "construction first, then unification"—can be duly regarded as a proper kind of nationalism (224).

I agree with Kim's position and thus conceptualize the nationalism of the conservative authoritarian elite including Rhee and Park as division-maintaining nationalism in contrast to unification-oriented nationalism. Such a conception as mine may well be considered a kind of oxymoron by those who claim that only unification-oriented nationalism is genuine nationalism. In this regard it is clear that such naming as "division-maintaining nationalism" is in a disadvantageous position vis-à-vis unification-oriented nationalism in terms of the conceptual frame. If we accept this, we may change the name of ruling authoritarian conservative nationalism from division-maintaining nationalism to "anticommunist nationalism" or "modernization (or industrialization) nationalism." Just as "anti–US" and "anti-Japanese" nationalism is a proper expression, I think "anticommunist" nationalism is too. Jin Deok-gyu and Lee Seon-min characterize Park's nationalism as "modernization nationalism" (Jin Deok-gyu 1992, 153–54; Lee Seon-min 2008).

47. However, progressive scholars of nationalism who insist on unification-oriented nationalism tend to refuse to acknowledge the immanent ills or fallacies. For instance, in his book addressing nationalism in South and North Korea, Park Ho-seong (1997) writes that "nationalism is a window, and its evil effects likely to be produced are something like frost covering the window" (23–24). Just as a window and frost are separate and distinct entities, so are nationalism and its evils. In this way he distinguishes nationalism from its contingent ills and sticks to the infallibility of nationalism.

48. Because communist sympathizers accepted communism and benefited antinational North Korea, they were naturally branded "antination."

49. Opposition parties during the Rhee regime had been consistently docile toward its unification policies (Hong Seok-ryul 2001).

50. *Gungmin* (國民 in Chinese characters) in Korean literally means "state subjects" or "people belonging to the state." It has been used in Korea as a substitute for English words such as *general citizens, citizenry,* and *people.* But the use of *inmin* (another Korean word for "people") has been avoided because it has been widely used by communist North Korea. During the authoritarian rule before democratization, the term *gungmin* had a strong authoritarian, vertical, and exclusive connotation similar to *subjects*—especially so when it was used by presidents Rhee Syngman and Park Chung-hee—but it was also widely used among the opposition politicians and intellectuals as well as among the general populace to mean "the whole people of the state." It has changed since democratization, however, to explicitly bear a more egalitarian, horizontal, and open connotation.

51. Of course, Ahn elevated modernization to a spiritual and moral revolution going beyond mere economic growth (Ahn Byeong-uk 1968, 139–40).

52. As a notable example we may cite the episode of Hwang Yong-ju, then-president of the Munhwa Broadcasting Corporation. In November 1964 he published an article proposing arms reduction, the joint entry of South and North Korea into the UN, and other similar measures to ease hostilities between the two Koreas. But he was indicted for his writing by opposition as well as ruling-party members of the National Assembly because he allegedly praised and encouraged the unification doctrine of the Northern puppet (*bukgoe*) (Kang Jun-man 2004a, 323–28).

53. One notable exception was Lee Geuk-chan's essay (1976). Although he approved anticommunism, Lee criticized Park's Yusin system indirectly by arguing that only a true democrat who believed firmly that freedom meant "independence, autonomy, and criticism" could be a true nationalist (26). As a matter of fact, Lee's position can be interpreted as a good example of the overpowering presence of democracy in nationalism.

54. In this respect, Kim Gu should be duly acknowledged as the precursor to unification-oriented nationalism. His famous remark made when crossing the thirty-eighth parallel for the South-North Talk in 1948 is worth quoting: "I shall not cooperate with

building a separate government to pursue ignoble comforts of my person. Fighting my way to build a unified father country, I will rather perish and die lying with the thirty-eighth parallel as my pillow" (page 181 of "Appealing with Tears to the Thirty Million Brethren," found in Kim Gu 1973).

55. Furthermore, they made a frontal attack on rapid economic development itself. Song Geon-ho (1986), for example, characterized the economic situation in the 1970s and 1980s, which focused on economic growth while ignoring the issue of unification, as a swelling of foreign debts, the hypertrophy of chaebols (family-controlled business conglomerates) and widening rich-poor gap, a deepening overseas dependency, an increase in the relative poverty of the working class and labor disputes, and the extreme poverty and accelerated exodus of the population in rural areas (28–29).

56. A good example is found in Chang Chun-ha, who revealed a wavering political attitude in the aftermath of the South–North Korea Joint Communiqué of July 4, 1972. When the Joint Communiqué was announced, taking the general Korean populace by surprise, Chang showed enthusiastic support for it and preoccupied himself with the unification problem for a while, pushing aside the domestic political situation, wherein Park Chung-hee strengthened his dictatorial power and prepared for the Yusin Constitution after declaring a state of national emergency in December 1971. When the South-North talks turned out to be only temporary and deceptive, Chang returned to his original position of vehement opposition to Park's Yusin regime. Chang had also shown temporary support for Park's military coup d'état in 1961. Of course, the coup was an outright antidemocratic violation of the constitution. Pointing to the extreme political confusion at the time, however, Chang approved of the coup as the last resort to "strike a way out of national crisis," calling for the "sincere support of the Korean people," while urging the military to "accomplish the revolutionary task as soon as possible and hand over the power to those conscientious politicians with an air of freshness within the shortest period of time" (Chang Chun-ha 1961, 34–35).

57. In this context it is important to note that the nationalism they espoused was not so much civic or liberal nationalism as populist (*minjung*), one of the collectivist kinds. In this way the democratic creed of most intellectuals as well as the general populace (except for some intellectuals and dissident activists) was not that strong in the 1970s, let alone in the 1960s.

58. Bearing this kind of criticism in mind, Paik Nak-cheong (1994) advanced a more sophisticated and discriminating argument in early 1990. He predicted that democratization would be restricted in the division system even if it took place and that a more full-fledged democracy would not be achieved until unification. "We must distinguish," he writes, "between the minimum democracy we have to win in the process of the movement to overcome the division and the democracy of a higher dimension we will be able to achieve by overcoming the division, and we must think of both at the same time" (115). Considering that the current state of Korean democracy is stagnant, without continuing to make much progress, his prediction has turned out to be prescient and insightful.

59. Although we may well offer criticism that the current state of democracy is not quite satisfactory, we cannot deny that South Korea has still made substantial and

solid progress in democracy since 1987, contrary to Song Geon-ho's argument or prediction.

60. For example, in October 1986 during the Chun regime, in a speech to the National Assembly Yu Seong-hwan, National Assemblyman of the opposition party, criticized the regime for setting "anticommunism" as the doctrine of the state, instead proposing "unification" as its substitute. His statement was then indicted for being "communist-sympathetic," and he was tried in court for it. Although the court did not convict him of being a communist sympathizer, he was convicted on another charge (Kim Sam-ung 1994, 209–11).

61. Chapter 6 addresses how Park's modernization nationalism contributed to the sanctification of nationalism.

62. Here it is clear that "nationalist theories that have been mobilized to sustain the system of divided states" refers to nationalist discourses produced and circulated by authoritarian ruling forces such as Rhee Syngman, Park Chung-hee, and the like.

63. Representative of such criticism are the works of Kang Man-gil, Song Geon-ho, and Seo Jung-seok thus far cited and discussed. We may add Seo Jung-seok's detailed examination of the antinationalist character of the Rhee Syngman and Park Chung-hee regimes (1995b, 2005, and 2009). Jeon Jae-ho's survey of the controversy over the Park regime's nationalist character and the literature he cites in his work are also helpful (1997, 4–12).

64. It should be noted that the word *radicalism* used here has different denotations, varying with the context. *Radicalism* used with respect to overdetermination mostly refers to an ideology and movement pursuing class liberation and national liberation (national unification), whereas *radicalism* with respect to overpowering presence usually refers to those pursuing unification-oriented nationalism. Although the latter also stresses the guarantee of people's right to subsistence, note that its proponents do not directly assert the vision of socialist class liberation.

Part II

THE POLITICAL THOUGHT OF PARK CHUNG-HEE

Chapter 4

Discourses on Democracy

Part 2 examines Park Chung-hee's political thought by analyzing his discourse on democracy, antiliberal conservatism for modernization, and nationalism, while at the same time reviewing how and to what extent his discourses embodied the concepts of nonsimultaneity and sanctification. Accordingly, chapter 4 analyzes discourses on democracy produced throughout Park Chung-hee's presidency, from his seizing of power through the military coup d'état in 1961 to his assassination in 1979.[1]

First, this chapter must begin with the understanding that determining whether and to what extent the politician Park Chung-hee would be defined as a democrat is not its primary concern. Instead I argue that, even when Park Chung-hee infringed on democracy or publicly expressed opposition to it in order to defend his authoritarian rule, his expression necessarily remained within the frame of a democracy discourse due to the compelling structure of the dual political order that characterized Korean politics. With this premise, analyze discourses regarding democracy by focusing on Park's writings and speeches and examine how and how effectively Park Chung-hee's authoritarian rule made up for its absence of or deficiency in democratic legitimacy through these discourses.[2]

To do this, two characteristic concepts of Korean politics applicable to the basic frame of analysis (i.e., dual political order and authoritarianism dressed up as democracy) are first discussed. Next, the continuity and change in the content of Park's discourse on democracy are examined by focusing on three concepts: administrative democracy (military government), national democracy (the Third Republic), and Korean-style democracy (the Yusin regime).[3] Park offered these to justify his authoritarian rule and to express his shifting concerns regarding the "Koreanization of democracy," which varied with the phases of his reign. In other words, to fulfill his political goals and meet the Korean political reality, Park devised and used the three concepts to modify *political democracy*, which then institutionalized the competition and conflict among the political elite through election, political parties, and the parliamentary system. Thus the concepts are analyzed in contrast to Park's view of Western (or political) democracy. Finally, this chapter closes by comparing and contrasting the three concepts.

DUAL POLITICAL ORDER AND AUTHORITARIANISM DRESSED UP AS DEMOCRACY

In order to analyze Park's discourse on democracy, I pay specific attention to a distinctive feature of Korean conservatism—which had to legitimize the authoritarian government in the name of democracy—as well as to how the democracy discourse expressed by Park reveals this characteristic. In chapter 2, bearing the dual political order in mind, I define Korean conservatism before democratization as "an ideology by which ruling right-wing forces justified and defended the authoritarian political order they believed was indispensable to protecting democracy against the impending communist threat and maintaining the political stability necessary for sustained economic development and strong national security." Similarly, the dual political order—authoritarianism and democracy—can also be seen as a distinct feature faced by authoritarian conservative governments that ostensibly professed democracy in other non-Western countries. Due to the phenomenon of duality, authoritarian regimes could not acquire legitimacy in and of themselves. In other words, they were only able to gain transitional, mediational, or implied legitimacy by linking themselves with democracy, the ultimate source of legitimacy. Thus Park Chung-hee used all means available to cope with the gap between democracy and authoritarianism—that is, the absence of democratic legitimacy during his reign. As a result he had to continuously produce discourses on democracy.

In other words, in the name of anticommunism (national security) and economic development (modernization), or by attributing Korea's particular historical background or cultural traditions, Park emphasized the necessity of establishing a de facto authoritarian government but could not explicitly justify use of the term *authoritarianism*. Thus, as has already been pointed out in chapter 2, developing diverse justifications and rhetorics, Park had to produce discourses that linked various causes and reasons to democracy in order to secure democratic legitimacy. For example, if he stressed national security and anticommunism, he had to argue that they were necessary in order to protect democracy, instead of contending that national security and anticommunism made authoritarianism indispensable. Or he had to maintain that economic development was a necessary condition for the achievement of a democratic order rather than admitting candidly that it required authoritarianism. In addition, Park did not argue explicitly that it was necessary to introduce and maintain an authoritarian regime to suit Korean cultural tradition; rather, he held that a dressed-up democracy was suited to Korean history and tradition. As a result, using the idea of the Koreanization of democracy, Park's authoritarian regime attached modifiers to *democracy*—such as *administrative, national,* or *Korean-style*—in order to borrow democratic legitimacy. During this process, although the important theoretical elements or concepts of democracy may have been maintained in form (appearance), the content was reinterpreted or redefined in order to meet the need for authoritarianism. In this way, the Park regime was granted legitimacy through the appearance of this democratic form, and the substantial goal of authoritarianism was achieved through such transformed content or terms.

Thus during the Park administration the dual political order ultimately appeared in the form of Korean-style democracy (i.e., authoritarianism dressed up as democracy), a type of masquerade. Although this authoritarianism disguised as democracy was legitimized to a certain extent, at the same time, due to the fact that the endless inner clashing and tension between democracy and authoritarianism could be patched up only temporarily and never fully resolved, it remained in an unstable and fluid state.[4] Accordingly, the Korean democratization movement paid special attention to this inner clash and tension, and exposing this hypocrisy was one of its foremost strategies. In reality, such continual inner conflict provided an advantageous line of attack for the democratization movement. If Park Chung-hee had openly and unabashedly denied the legitimacy of democracy as had Lee Kwan Yew of Singapore, while explicitly arguing, defending, and propagating that the concentration of power in his authoritarian system was desirable and necessary for the purpose of economic development, national security, anticommunism, and/or reunification, then leaders of the democratization movement could not have leveled the criticism that the Park regime was in fact antidemocratic and authoritarian, contrary to its purported goals. Accordingly, whereas Park's authoritarian regime enjoyed partial legitimacy through its own pretension of democracy, at the same time it became fatally bound to democracy. In other words, to Park Chung-hee, democracy was a double-edged sword, and this has been demonstrated historically.

The dual order is expressed in Park's discourse on democracy as well. Even though Park realized the pressure of the normative reality called *liberal democracy*, at the same time he countered that the reality of Korean society did not allow for the full realization of such liberal democracy and implicitly suggested the inevitability of the authoritarian system. He consistently argued this position from the time of his military government through the establishment of the Third Republic and up to the Yusin system. For example, in *Gukgawa Hyeongmyeonggwa Na* (The state, the revolution, and I) published in 1963, Park stated his dualistic feelings about democracy. "In Korea," he wrote, ". . . there are restricting limits to the [fundamental] revolution in this regard, and this will involve factors in every direction that will put the brakes on the momentum of this revolution. We cannot escape the need to oppose communism and establish liberal democracy. As long as we adhere to an espousal of democracy, the freedom of public opinion cannot be blocked" (28). In this quote, after Park refers to the "restricting limits" to the fulfillment of the modernization revolution that he is pursuing and the "brakes" that will slow its momentum, he brings up anticommunism and liberal democracy. He continues, "The freedom of public opinion cannot be blocked." Thus we may notice vague but somewhat negative phrases, like "cannot escape," phrases with cumbersome and negative nuances regarding revolution fulfillment, like "restricting limits" and "brakes," and phrases expressing reluctance, like "cannot be blocked." These subtle dualistic phrases imply Park's overall inwardly negative or reserved attitude regarding liberal democracy, together with the inevitable acceptance that democracy cannot be rejected altogether.[5]

In *Gukgawa Hyeongmyeonggwa Na* (The state, the revolution, and I; 1963), Park used democracy as a standard for critiquing other politicians, although he himself felt it burdensome as well. Park criticized the politics of the Liberal Party in the First Republic and the Democratic Party government in the Second Republic, calling them a "distorted 'disguised democracy'" (281). But in *Uri Minjogui Nagal Gil* (The path for our nation to take), published in 1962, before *Gukgawa Hyeongmyeonggwa Na*, Park argued that Western democracy could not be fully realized in Korea due to economic poverty, the threat of North Korea, and other historical and cultural particularities, and he hinted, in essence, that an authoritarian system was inevitable and that a "distorted 'disguised democracy'" was necessary. He claimed an absence of "objective conditions that would allow for democracy to come to fruition" in Korea and noted Korea's fundamental differences from the West, such as "historical background" and "cultural traditions," severe poverty and large-scale unemployment, "widespread illiteracy in rural areas," and an inadequate level of industrialization (Park Chung-hee 1962, 221–22).

Due to such restrictive conditions, Park proposed that, until the objective conditions necessary to realize Western democracy could be met, the country instead should practice a democracy that fit the Korean context. Thus in *Uri Minjogui Nagal Gil*, after criticizing the preceding governments' failed attempts at democracy, Park argued, "Even if we import the form of democracy, we cannot import its roots." In addition, Park proposed "grafting the 'Koreanization of democracy' onto the subjectivity of the history of Korean thought" on the basis of "the emergence and cultivation of new leading groups" (Park Chung-hee 1962, 130–31). Actually, Park's belief that it would be difficult to directly apply Western democracy to Korean society continued throughout his rule. Even in his New Year's press conference on January 19, 1979, during the last year of his rule, Park argued, "Western democracy is certainly great and desirable, but nations that are receiving it must consider their own historical background and social environment. In other words, it cannot be successful without considering the climate and implementing a cultivation method suitable to it" (16:46–47).[6]

However, considering Korea's status as a peripheral latecomer nation in a Western-centric world, it would be historically difficult to separate the influence of foreign powers from a discussion of Korean democracy. Such an attempt would be a grave mistake, because it assumes a Korean polity that is self-sufficient in the production and circulation of political ideas.[7] In addition, although Korea has felt the pressure of the universality of the democracy originating in world historical time, more concretely it has been tightly placed under the direct and continuous influence of the United States since liberation. In other words, although it is true that democracy was a universal political idea that had already had great influence on independence-movement activists even during the Japanese colonial period, after liberation, "liberal" democracy began to exert itself in full force, with US backing (Park Chan-pyo 2007a).

In this context, Choi Jang-jip (1996) defines the democracy founded in South Korea as a "premature democracy" and emphasizes the influence of the United States as the "institution builder of a divided nation." Through an interesting concept called the "American boundary line," Choi finds that the role carried out by the United States in the institutionalization of democracy in South Korea "has an upper and lower limit." Choi explains, "The American boundary line was able to be conceptualized due to the American demand that South Korea as a divided country be both anticommunist and democratic. That is, it was faced with implementing these two tasks simultaneously—both so difficult that they could be seen as contradictory when considering the reality at the time. In other words, this refers to the political space between the lower limit of the minimal stability of a divided nation and the upper limit of the minimal maintenance of democracy" (22).

The contradictory tasks of creating a state that is anticommunist and developing a democratic system were imposed by the "American boundary line" and falls perfectly in line with the declaration by Park, mentioned earlier in this chapter, that "we cannot escape the need to oppose communism and establish liberal democracy." In other words, the US–imposed requirements of becoming both anticommunist and democratic were internalized by Korean political leaders. Thus, during the era of the authoritarian governments of Rhee Syngman, Park Chung-hee, and Chun Doo-hwan, anticommunism, which had been the lower limit, was promoted to state doctrine. Of course, as long as the anticommunist authoritarian governments did not encounter nationwide resistance, and thus create serious political unrest, the United States generally overlooked the undemocratic character of the regimes.

Park Chung-hee, of course, was already well aware of the "American boundary line" even during the rule of his military government. In *Gukgawa Hyeongmyeonggwa Na*, Park estimated the support and role of the United States as positive overall in his discussion of the relationship between Korea and the United States. At the same time, he argued that Western democracy could not be imposed on Korea, saying that "first of all, the US must understand that Western democracy is not suitable to our reality" (1963, 226–27). From this perspective, Park also consistently criticized Korean politicians who were proponents of implementing Western democracy exactly as is in Korea, calling them "flunkeys" and "fake democrats."

Keenly aware of the dual political order, Park had expressed his concerns about liberal democracy since the earliest days of his military government. In *Uri Minjogui Nagal Gil*, regarding whether Korea would be able to implement liberal democracy, given its political situation at the time and particularly keeping in mind the need for economic development, Park's stance was hesitant and fluctuating. Actually, among political leaders of the time—Rhee Syngman, Yun Posun, Chang Myon, and so on—Park was a rarity, the first to express his serious concern regarding the (in)compatibility of the need for economic development and liberal democracy. In this regard, it can be said that Park was ahead of his time given his unusual insight. In other words, Park was a trailblazer for being concerned with the relationship between industrialization and democratization, generally an important point faced by the American modernization theorists in general as well as by future Korean-studies scholars in particular when they would later discuss the merits and demerits of the Park regime. Thus the conventional understanding of Park—which is based on his Japanese colonial education and military experience as well as the political situation at the time, his belief in the urgency of creating a powerful state and economic development, and his sporadic declarations that democracy impeded national integration and wasted state power—is not accurate. The fact that Park Chung-hee was not a democrat does not necessarily mean that "Park was not concerned with democracy from the outset" (Kim Kap-sik 2007, 13).

Accordingly, Park focused on the poverty of various Asian countries, including Korea, and, regarding the relationship between economic development and democracy, stated, "In order to achieve effectiveness in the attempts and efforts to improve the living conditions of the people, it is nearly impossible for the government to become a people's government as described in the West, because it seems natural that nondemocratic emergency measures must be used more often than not" (Park Chung-hee 1962, 226). He went on,

"Democracy that rests on the true support of the people cannot mature in a country that has not achieved the economic condition or foundation that is the prerequisite of political democracy" (228).

By jointly analyzing these two statements, two interrelated conclusions can be drawn: First, in developing countries (such as Korea during the Chang Myon government), although it is possible for democratic governments to temporarily come to power, sustainable democracy cannot be expected in countries where economic development has not yet taken place. Second, in developing countries that need to overcome economic poverty, the strategy of economic development requires nondemocratic emergency measures. Thus it can be understood that Park's original intent is to argue that "in Korea's current political situation, a nondemocratic or authoritarian government is mandatory in order to resolutely carry out economic development."[8]

However, unlike the situations France's Louis-Napoléon III or Germany's Bismarck faced in nineteenth-century Europe, Park could not directly and publicly speak negatively about democracy in Korea, where democracy still secured normative legitimacy due to the dual political order. The result is that Park spoke vaguely and ambiguously on both sides of the relationship: "The success or failure, as well as the future, of true democracy in Asia, not only for Korea, will only depend upon, ultimately, . . . how successfully economic development can be achieved there under the ideology and system of liberal democracy (even if only in appearance) imported from the West" (Park Chung-hee 1962, 229). Such subtle and vague references suggest to an extent the probability that, although it might be difficult, economic development is possible even while maintaining liberal democracy. Nonetheless, as he predicted early on and as he later historically and personally proved through his oppressive authoritarian control, in Asia, "the road to liberal democracy cannot help but be a thorny path" (227).[9]

THE KOREANIZATION OF DEMOCRACY

During his eighteen-year rule, Park Chung-hee held a steadfastly consistent stance on democracy, which can be seen in the fact that the statements he made regarding democracy after the Yusin regime are almost the same as the references to democracy he made in both *Uri Minjogui Nagal Gil* (1962) and *Gukgawa Hyeongmyeonggwa Na* (1963). This fact continues to be confirmed in his application of his proposed Koreanization of democracy and the sequentially contrived concepts of administrative, national, and Korean-style democracy. A startling similarity and consistency can be found among them.[10] These three concepts of democracy are examined alongside Park's criticism of (an imitation of) Western democracy.

Administrative Democracy

After seizing power, Park advocated temporarily a somewhat-vague notion of administrative democracy in order to make up for a lack of legitimacy in the military government. In his May 16 "Pledge of the Revolution"—although the pledge regarding democracy was buried under other promises, such as upholding "anticommunism," the "eradication of corruption and old evils," and "overcoming poverty" and only appeared as the last provision through the insertion of the line "the greatest efforts will be made . . . in order to achieve the firm foundation of a new democratic republic"—he made clear his commitment to democracy (Kim Sam-ung 1997, 258).[11] At the time, because Park had illegally overthrown the constitutional Chang Myon government by military coup d'état, he needed to seek legitimation by any means. During his speech on Constitution Day in July 1961, immediately after the coup d'état, while sternly denouncing first the nondemocratic situation that had unfolded from the establishment of a divided government until early 1961 and then the politicians who were responsible for that situation, Park justified the coup d'état as an emergency measure, likening it to a doctor's resolute choice to perform surgery on a critical patient:

> Politicians' selfish struggle for power has brought on the unhappiest corruption of parliamentarism . . . all of the provisions in the constitution, which must be objectively observed, were violated frequently for the conveniences of those in power at the time . . . the result of this was that the morale of the people hit rock bottom, illegality and corruption were rampant, and the poverty of the people spread, bringing about a forsaken reality that could not be treated without applying some kind of drastic operations. In other words, since the founding of the country, the state doctrine of our society has been anticommunism, but . . . this became like a lamp without oil . . . in danger of flickering out at any time. Here we see the inevitability of the May 16th military revolution and its historical significance. Just as a patient with a serious illness needs decisive surgery, so must emergency measures be taken when there is an issue of security and survival for a state and its nation. ("Constitution Day Speech," July 17, 1961, 1:13)

In addition, just as "a doctor sends a recovered patient back home" (Park Chung-hee 1962, 216), Park, of course, had to emphasize the temporary nature of the military government. Hence, he declared that, inasmuch as "the goal of revolution is to protect at all costs the basic democratic order of the existing constitution," the partial suspension of constitutional provisions by the law of state-reconstruction emergency decrees was merely a temporary phenomenon lasting until the tasks of the revolution had been fully carried out ("Constitution Day Speech," July 17, 1961, 1:13).

In *Uri Minjogui Nagal Gil*, Park devoted a considerable amount of space to criticizing the corruption and distortion of the party politics rampant in the era of the Liberal Party (the First Republic) and the Democratic Party (the Second Republic), pinning the responsibility on corrupt politicians. Park advocated an alternative to such corrupt and distorted party politics: "democracy of the revolution period" (i.e., military government phase), "not Western democracy but democracy that matches our sociopolitical reality"—or, in other words, "administrative democracy" (Park Chung-hee 1962, 231). The goal of administrative democracy was, above all else, to improve the "political competence" of the people and the "self-governing ability 'from below'" to achieve this (232).[12] Park emphasized that the main agents of an administrative democracy are ordinary citizens and that the goal is human reform in order to realize social reform. He wrote, "If the immediate goal is to realize social justice by eradicating past corruption and strengthening the people's self-governing ability, this will not be done by the immediate achievement of democracy politically but, rather, must be realized administratively while in the transitional phase. As a method for this, we must implement a democracy not descending from the 'top down' but growing 'from the bottom up,' democracy awakened from below, democracy by which the people correct their past mistakes on their own, starting anew" (231).

In this context, regarding the relationship between liberal democracy and administrative democracy, Park argued that the former is the ultimate goal, whereas the latter is transitional democracy during the phase of revolution. "From the perspective of the ideological demand to cultivate democratic values and discipline in order to reestablish democracy," he wrote, "although we are in a phase of the revolution where we cannot enjoy complete political liberal democracy, at the very least the basic democratic principles are to be adhered to at the administrative level, and the opinions and rights of the people must be respected on the basis of these democratic principles" (Park Chung-hee 1962, 232).

He offered a more concrete description of the proposed administrative democracy, writing, "Administrative democracy does not block but welcomes the reasonable criticism and suggestions of the people regarding the government. It should be understood as democracy in which the government's performance will be judged by public opinion and (in the case that there is) government wrongdoing, it will be corrected based on the reasonable opinions of the people. . . . Each exercise of the government's authority, even during the revolutionary period, must fall under democratic process and principle" (Park Chung-hee 1962, 232). In this regard, during the time that political democracy was suspended in the military-government phase, "although criticism of the governmental legitimacy or leaders was restricted, that of policy was allowed and public opinion respected" in administrative democracy (Cho Gab-je 1999, 158). This indicated that, "at the very least, at the administrative level," democracy would be maintained (Park Chung-hee 1962, 232).

Similarly, Park explained the reason political democracy must be deferred in the military-government phase. "In reality," he wrote, "the organizational corruption and dishonesty of party politics has infiltrated all the cells of our society, due to the abnormal pressure of party politics. Thus, even if we held an election tomorrow in the name of resuscitating political democracy, that would not mean that the bad elements of the past will simply disappear overnight" (Park Chung-hee 1962, 231). As the phrase "abnormal pressure of party politics" suggests, from Park's perspective the corruption and distortion of party politics was not simply caused by a specific corrupt politician or party but, rather, was due to the overall inadequacy of the economic or cultural conditions needed to properly practice political democracy.

Accordingly, comparing the crippling of Korean parliamentary politics with the experience of England, Park understood the reality of the Korean situation to be inevitable due to the premature institutionalization of the party system brought about by the dialectic of nonsimultaneity.

> Even if we look to England, the home of parliamentary politics, representative politics developed alongside the Industrial Revolution and, in a sense, can be seen as a product of the Industrial Revolution. . . . On the other hand, in representative politics of an undeveloped democracy, the country has not undergone stable industrialization and is only imitating the appearance of Western democracy from an institutional facade. Thus the corruption of political parties and its adverse effects have already emerged to the fore even before the establishment of the modern party system needed in a modern nation-state in the strictest sense. (Park Chung-hee 1962, 222)

However, although attention should be paid to Park's concern with the negative effects of Korean party politics at the time and, furthermore, his agony over the impossibility of advancing party politics, it is also important to note that Park continued to acknowledge the inevitability of liberal democracy and party politics as its foundation in principle and resolved to implement the latter. "The party system is the foundation of modern liberal democracy," he wrote. "If modern liberal democracy cannot do without the parliamentary system, party politics is vital. . . . If modern liberal democracy is the only system by which we can live and prosper, then we must set out to create a healthy party system by all means. We must possess political parties of the people [*gungmin*], those of the nation, which engage in mutual criticism and fighting over policies and ideologies while respecting certain limitations and restraints" (Park Chung-hee 1962, 22; refer also to Park Chung-hee 1963, 75).

However, Park had no intention of restoring political democracy at the time, as can be seen in subsequent political conflicts and his repeated changes of heart regarding the transfer of power to a civilian government. It seems clear that Park planned to maintain a military government for a comparatively long period of time. He proposed such a plan through administrative democracy, but in actuality it was not implemented and remained an empty assertion because the transfer of power to a civilian government was hurried and carried out faster than the initial plan due to great pressures exerted by public opinion and the US government. Concretely speaking, even in the speeches given by Park during the time of the military government, specific proposals or plans regarding administrative democracy, such as the cultivation of ordinary citizens' self-governing ability or democratic competence, are rarely found.[13]

With the impending handover, Park came to found and participate in the Democratic Republican Party in 1963. Reflecting the experience of the Liberal and the Democratic Party governments, he himself was skeptical and negative about party politics. But his founding of a new party can be explained as an attempt to promote the innovation of party politics. Thus, before the Third Republic was fully established, in his Constitution Day speech in 1963, he praised the overall revised Third Republic constitution as a model democratic constitution and stressed that the foremost task of the incoming new civilian government was "the establishment of a modern party system that could secure the stability of the political situation and the efficiency of the government" (July 17, 1963, 1:463–64). Thus it can be seen that, ahead of the planned presidential election on October 15, 1963, Park embraced hope and expectations regarding party politics to a certain extent, anticipating the upcoming inauguration of the Third Republic over which he personally would preside.

National Democracy

In his campaign for the 1963 presidential election, Park countered his opponent Yun Posun by arguing for "national democracy."[14] In a campaign speech he asserted that "independence and self-reliance are the essential goals of the Third Republic" and that "those without national consciousness are sure to always misinterpret liberal democracy and are unable to properly digest it." He also emphasized that "proper democracy can only be achieved after gaining a national consciousness of independence and self-reliance." In addition, advocating national democracy, he defined the election as a showdown of "false liberal democratic thought devoid of national ideology and liberal democratic thought full of strong national ideology" (September 23, 1963, 1:519–20).

Yun Posun criticized Park Chung-hee for holding heterogeneous thought or heterogeneous democratic thought, such as his argument that "Western democracy is not suitable for Korea." Regarding this, in his campaign speech a few days later, Park metaphorically argued that Yun was wearing suits from foreign countries that did not fit, but, rather than fix them, he was just content to continue wearing them; Park criticized this as "a figurehead democracy, a democracy with only a shell and no substance, a flunkeyism democracy founded on flunkeyism . . . a 'false democracy' through and through."[15] On the other hand, the democracy he was advocating was a proposal to "take the principles, thought, and political systems from foreign countries and adapt them to our constitution and physique in order to make a society that is suitable for us." Accordingly Park countered that, as suggested, his democracy may appear to be a "heterogeneous democracy" because "it may seem that the democracy that old politicians are thinking of is the same as [Park's] fundamentally in principles and rules," but "the attitude . . . toward receiving" is different (September 28, 1963, 1:529–30).

Four years later, in a sixth presidential-election campaign speech, Park pointed out that, through the accomplishments of the national democracy he had implemented—such as (nearly achieved) food self-sufficiency, an economy that was not dependent on foreign aid, economic development through increase in exports, and the dispatch of Korean troops to Vietnam—Korea had risen to a "leading position" in international society (April 15, 1967, 2:1004). Subsequently, Park argued that "the establishment of national subjectivity or self-reliance isn't just talk, it is only possible through productive action" and that "it cannot be found in principled ideologies remote from reality but in the 'workplace.'" Park also emphasized that "the primary goal of national democracy is *self-reliance*" and "*self-reliance* provides the foundation that will build national subjectivity and the permanent residence that democracy can be anchored in" (ibid. 2:1005; emphasis original).[16]

In this way Park argued for national democracy in two presidential campaign speeches.[17] Through this, several of the distinctive characteristics of national democracy can be identified: First, because at the very least liberal democracy maintained its general nature in the constitution of the Third Republic, as a constitutional government system, national democracy did not contain any special proposal related to the content of democracy. Thus Park's proposed national democracy remained only as an idea of the Koreanization of democracy. In other words, it does not show any of the special characteristics that would be witnessed in the "authoritarianism dressed up as democracy" of the Yusin regime. Second, the national democracy asserted during the 1963 and 1967 elections emphasized independence and self-reliance, but a subtle change can be seen in the point that is stressed. In 1963 Park opposed the argument that "we must embrace Western democracy as it is" and criticized it as "flunkeyism democracy." And though he emphasized that the principles and fundamentals of Western democracy should be respected, he also stressed an independent attitude, one that transforms and applies those principles in order to suit the Korean situation.[18] However, in 1967, emboldened by the economic success he had achieved thus far, Park connected national democracy more heavily with the procurement of material conditions in the name of economic self-reliance. Seen in this way, the national democracy advocated by Park in the 1963 election emphasized a "historical background" and "cultural traditions" intrinsically different from those of the West while highlighting the need for an "independent" attitude that would transform Western democracy in a manner suitable to the Korean context. The national democracy advocated by Park in the 1967 election can, however, be seen as emphasizing economic self-reliance, based on an awareness of Korea's lagging economic circumstances and the results of the economic development that had taken place so far. Of course, such an interpretation is not meant to argue that there was any fundamental change in Park's thought regarding national democracy, given that he stressed the need for economic development even in *Uri Minjogui Nagal Gil* and in *Gukgawa Hyeongmyeonggwa Na*. More than that, the change in the campaign agenda and situation of the times may explain the shift in emphasis during the time between the two elections.

Park Chung-hee's argument regarding national democracy corresponded with the direction of contemporary public opinion. In a 1961 study that surveyed 377 students from Korea University and analyzed the data, 83 percent of respondents said that "Western democracy is unsuitable" when asked, "What do you think about Western democracy?" More specifically, regarding the reason for this response, 40 percent answered that "Korea is not prepared to implement Western democracy," whereas 30 percent pointed out "sociocultural differences between the East and West," 7 percent noted the "dissonance of theory and reality," and the final 6 percent indicated the need for "strong regulation of excessive freedom" (Hong Seung-jik 1962, 121–22). Here, if "inadequate preparation" can be interpreted as the need for economic development including economic self-reliance and "sociocultural differences" as the need for an adapted form of Western democracy, then it is clear that Park's national democracy was relatively responsive to trends in public opinion.

Finally, although Park Chung-hee never explicitly argued the connection, it can be inferred that, for Park, national democracy based on independence and self-reliance was an ideology that ultimately pursued the "freedom and prosperity of the nation" through the accomplishment of the tasks of modernization of the fatherland and national regeneration.[19] Of course, the freedom of the nation included reunification by the defeat of communism that would liberate the North Korean brethren from the oppression of communists. Park believed that internally the "domestic economic conditions—that is, poverty, starvation, unemployment, and so on"—and externally the threat of invasion by communists posed grave threats to the freedom of the nation (Park Chung-hee 1962, 41). Accordingly, it can be interpreted that, although the main priority of national democracy was to ensure the survival of the nation, ultimately it was to secure the freedom and prosperity of the nation. In addition, declaring that "modern liberal democracy is the only system under which our nation can live and prosper," Park connected liberal democracy to the survival and prosperity of the nation (22).[20] In other words, just as many Koreans felt at the time, Park understood liberal democracy as well as economic development to be parts of the multidimensional tasks of nationalism.

However, the relationship between liberal democracy (and political democracy) and national democracy was not a smooth one. Although there were many undemocratic and antidemocratic elements in the operation of the constitution during the Third Republic, formally speaking (up until the declaration of a state of national emergency in December 1971) the constitutional government system maintained the basic frame of a liberal democracy. Of course, it is true that Park's national democracy and a political democracy centered on political parties and parliament made strange bedfellows. Accordingly, although Park's statements on political democracy were sometimes positive and at other times negative, generally speaking Park strengthened his criticism of political democracy as time went on.

During the Third Republic, Park actively referenced democracy as a principle and expressed his commitment to it in all three of his inaugural speeches. For example, on December 19, 1963, during his inaugural speech as South Korea's fifth president, he said, "I will take a leading role in creating a political climate featuring a multiparty system of lively competition and gentlemanly policy debate among parties in order to promote peaceful governmental turnover" and emphasized that "our endeavor for democratic competence and the internal solidarity of our nationalist camp that will be able to succeed in resisting and defeating communism . . . will lead us to the path to reunification" (December 19, 1963, 2:5–6).[21] Park also referenced political democracy in a generally positive way in his Constitution Day speeches during the Third Republic. Recalling constitutional history, Park stated in the early period of the Third Republic that the fact the constitutional system has not been democratically managed in the past was not a problem of the constitutional system itself; rather, he placed the blame on and criticized "politicians of the past" who violated the constitution for their own "convenience and gain," though he refrained from criticizing contemporary politicians or party politics (July 17, 1967, 3:13). While stressing the democratic management of the constitution, he also often requested the "protection of the constitution" and a "law-abiding" spirit from both politicians and ordinary citizens. After enforcing the third-term amendment, which would allow him to stay in the presidency beyond a second term, Park entered the seventh presidential race, barely beating out opposition party candidate Kim Dae-jung in April 1971. In that year's Constitution Day speech, Park spoke highly favorably of the party politics of the time, stating, "Ideals of the party politics that will support the sound management of the constitutional government are gradually taking deeper root" (July 17, 1971, 4:7).

In this way, whether sincere or rhetorical, Park repeatedly asserted his pledges regarding the implementation of democracy, but varying with the political situation he also frequently leveled criticism at the party politics of the time—in actuality, the political behavior of the opposition party. For example, in his January 1966 annual presidential address, he heavily criticized the reality of party politics, pointing to the intense confrontations between the ruling and opposition parties during the National Assembly ratification process of the 1965 normalization treaty between Korea and Japan. "How much," he asked, "have all of these political irregularities—individual slander, emotional backlash, unjustified division and conflict, extreme confrontation, all of which have turned their backs on tolerance and compromise and are a far cry from policies or ideas—caused us to waste our state power, time, and energy? How dark have they made our society?" (January 18, 1966, 2:591). Such attacks became gradually stronger until the end of the Third Republic, and after the 1972 declaration of the Yusin regime they would become all the more sweeping.

Park's critical attitude toward political democracy not only can be seen in his direct attacks on political parties and parliamentary politics but is also expressed by his reconceptualization of politics from the perspective of productivity or economic development. Of course, this was utilized even more aggressively in order to reject political democracy after the Yusin regime was introduced, under the pretext of the "cultivation of state power." For example, in his 1967 Constitution Day speech, Park admonished the return "to productive politics and the move away from good-for-nothing political strife" (July 17, 1967, 3:14). In his 1968 Constitution Day speech, unlike in the past, he omitted reference to the "protection of the constitution" and "law-abidingness," although he still emphasized that it was "not formal liberty and equality but substantial liberty and equality," that it was not "social justice only recorded in the provisions of the constitution" but "social justice enjoyed substantially," that was important. He further maintained that the new starting point for achieving all of this was "construction, increased production, and exports" (July 17, 1968, 3:249). Here the emphasis on "substantial liberty and equality" and "social justice," which appeared instead of "protection of the constitution" and "law-abidingness," implied the potential to violate a liberal democracy that seriously cherished procedure and form, as many arguments in support of substantial democracy had done historically.[22]

Korean-Style Democracy

Along with the establishment of the Yusin Constitution, Park proposed his final version of "authoritarianism dressed up as democracy." Through this Park denied liberal democracy overall, which would impede his own permanent rule, and, instead, offered the administrative democracy that had been proposed but had never materialized during the early phase of the military government.

To begin, Park laid the groundwork for the legitimacy of the Korean-style democracy that he would propose in the future by launching a frontal attack on political democracy, which had brought on political perversions and ills by prematurely emulating Western democracy. After being elected in the April 1971 presidential election for his third term thanks to the third-term amendment, on December 6 of the same year Park declared a state of national emergency under the pretext of a threat to national security and announced that he would be partially deferring citizens' rights, among them freedom of the press ("Special Statement regarding the Declaration of a State of National Emergency," December 6, 1971, 4:87). At the same time, through the special statement, he criticized "irresponsible security debates under the guise of freedom of the press" and the opposition party's "irresponsible security polemics for the sake of party interests or election strategy" even during the critical national-security crisis that was a matter of life and death for the nation, thereby creating a tense political situation (ibid., 4:88–89). In addition, in his 1972 Constitution Day speech, after giving a long-winded explanation relating unification and the political significance of the July 4 South–North Korea Joint Communiqué, Park sharply criticized the management of the constitutional system at the time: "Ultimately, haven't we . . . endured inefficiency in the name of representative parliamentary politics? In our indulgent insistence on freedom, haven't we called the establishment of social discipline a dictatorship? Haven't we unintentionally mistaken democracy for division and factional strife? We must reflect deeply on these questions" (July 17, 1972, 4:254).

Such remarks were ostensibly attacks aimed at the opposition party, students, or other opponents of his government, but in reality their implied meaning was an overall rejection of a representative parliamentary system, freedom of political opposition, and party politics, thereby completely denying the democratic constitutional system itself. Subsequently, Park stressed that "from now on the management of the democratic system must be developed in a more organized and efficient way, not in the dimension of external form but in the dimension of practical substance." Finally, "the path to a proper understanding of the spirit of the constitution is not merely the cry to protect the spirit of the constitution as a mere formality but going one step further and redoubling our practical efforts to carry out the substance of the constitutional system" ("Constitution Day Speech," July 17, 1972, 4:255). As a matter of course, such a statement would presage an ominous, extraordinary change in the constitution in the near future.[23]

In the end Park carried out a full-scale attack on the then-parliamentary politics, announcing the dissolution of the National Assembly and the suspension of the constitution, in his "Special Declaration" on October 17, 1972. "Now," he declared, "disorder and inefficiency still run rampant in our surroundings, and the political world is unable to get out of the conflicts of factional fighting and maneuvers. Not only that, it is becoming a trend to make great national tasks [e.g., peaceful unification, South-North talks] into politically motivated quarrels. When irresponsible parties are abandoning their sense of national mission and the representative organ falls victim to their political maneuvers, who, then, can expect them to achieve our cherished desire for peaceful unification? Who can believe they truly support South-North talks?" (4:298–99).

On the basis of such logic, Park carried out the Yusin (Revitalizing Reform) in October 1972, submitted and passed the Yusin Constitution through a national referendum on November 21, and took presidential office on December 27 under the Yusin Constitution. During this process, through the "Special Statement regarding the Announcement of Constitutional Revision Proposal" made public on October 27, Park began to advocate "Korean-style democracy." He said, "Regarding the Announcement of the Constitutional Revision Proposal, I hope in earnest that a Korean-style democracy that is the most suitable for our circumstances will take root and establish a proper constitutional order without further delay" (October 27, 1972, 4:306).

In the same statement, Park criticized the past "premature attempts to emulate the democracy of others as is" as having only caused political instability, "inefficiency and waste," and "consumption of state power," and then he stressed the need for a Korean-style democracy. "I believe that just as one must adjust clothes that don't fit one's body before wearing them, so must we creatively develop a democracy with a nationality, one that best matches our history, cultural traditions, and our reality, and we must maintain our confidence as we carry out this democracy" (October 27, 1972, 4:307).

Park's criticism of imitative democracy and advocacy for "democracy that suits our reality" had already been presented in *Uri Minjogui Nagal Gil* (Park 1962, e.g., 221–23, 231), and, because it was at the core of the national democracy that he had advocated previously, Park's justification logic of Korean-style democracy was hardly new. Accordingly, in his New Year's speech on January 1, 1973, immediately after the establishment of the Yusin Constitution, Park defended Korean-style democracy, claiming that, because "the freedom to establish political parties and guarantee of a multiparty system are clearly stated in the Yusin Constitution, our nation's basic order . . . is laying its roots in democracy," while warning that, bearing previous politics in mind, "nevertheless, disorder disguised as freedom and inefficiency disguised as democracy will not be allowed or tolerated as they were in the past" and criticizing the conduct of past politicians as "the ugly manners of anti-Yusin" (January 1, 1973, 5:13).

As briefly mentioned before, Park's tendency to gauge democracy or politics from the perspective of efficiency and productivity was always pronounced, but this tendency reached its peak during the Yusin regime. In his New Year's press conference of 1973, Park asserted that the basic political guideline set by the October Yusin order was that "all our actions must be directly coupled with production" in order to achieve the cultivation and organization of state power. In addition, he acidly criticized the "inefficient operation of the National Assembly," calling it the single greatest hindrance to the cultivation of state power and condemning it furthermore as "not merely guilty of being unsuccessful in cultivating state power but rather the main culprit of wasting and squandering of state power" (January 12, 1973, 5:21–22; refer also to "National Assembly Opening Session Address," March 12, 1973, 5:71–72). He went on to point out, "In developing countries, particularly countries with special conditions, such as being a divided nation like South Korea, the whole country is in a great uproar and the foundation of the nation quakes and degenerates in every election. We cannot afford to have such corrupt and overheated elections," and he criticized the past election system for having aggravated "regionalism" and "national division" ("New Year's Press Conference," January 12, 1973, 5:28). Through statements like these, Park increased his direct attacks on representative parliamentary politics, party politics, and elections, thoroughly denouncing political democracy.

In his 1975 Constitution Day address, through his criticism (of the opposition party's legal parliamentary activity) that "irresponsible words and deeds that trample on the constitutional government order and jeopardize state security are antidemocratic acts that reject and destroy democracy," Park in actuality attacked political democracy. At the same time he praised "Saemaeul leaders in the city and countryside silently working by the sweat of their brow . . . industrial warriors [workers] and businessmen, and . . . soldiers defending our countries," calling them "the true pillars of democracy who are working hard to foster the development of democracy in this land." He further emphasized that "the fields and the factories, offices and homes in which they are working hard" are the "true site of democratic practices" (July 17, 1975, 5:452). From that time on, Park emphasized the Saemaeul Movement (New Village Movement) more specifically in the implementation of Korean-style democracy. Through the Saemaeul Movement, Park admonished "the cultivation of firm solidarity with the leaders at the center" and making decisions on "village joint ventures" that are "based on a consensus of the residents." From this aspect, he repeatedly stressed the Saemaeul Movement as the "practicing site of Korean-style democracy" ("Admonition to Nationwide Saemaeul Leadership Congress," December 10, 1976, 6:120–21). Park proudly stated that, "in the process of pushing forward with the Saemaeul Movement, farmers came to understand the meaning of democracy and the proper way to practice it," explaining it as follows: "Since the Saemaeul Movement brings villagers together autonomously to join forces and develop the 'live well' movement, they must at first meet in a meeting hall, elect a leader, and debate on various things to create a plan and then implement it as a community. In addition, Saemaeul leaders must report back to the villagers about the status and budget of projects that were decided upon based on the villagers' opinions" ("Admonition to Nationwide Saemaeul Leadership Congress," December 9, 1977, 6:242).

Park's Korean-style democracy, institutionalized through the Yusin Constitution, sought legitimation in three ways. First, so his reasoning went, Korean-style democracy emerged as the result of the failure of political democracy, as has been previously mentioned. The purpose of political democracy is to establish the desirable political goals of a country and turn them into policy. To promote this purpose, it institutionalizes political competition through the establishment of political parties, elections, and parliament. In Korean reality, however, it only brings about waste, factional strife, and inefficiency, which use up state power, and thus it must be deferred indefinitely. Park criticized not only the Liberal Party government of the First Republic and the Democratic Party government of the Second Republic in the past but also the Democratic Republican Party government of his own Third Republic for "emulating Western democracy as is," and he argued that from this perspective the experiment of political democracy had ended in failure ("New Year's Press Conference," January 19, 1979, 16:44).

The second way Park sought to legitimize a Korean-style democracy was that, on the basis of such awareness and awakening, Korean-style democracy was the realization of Park's conception of national democracy in the form of a constitutional system, through an adaptation of Western democracy that was the "most well suited to the circumstances" and "history and cultural traditions" of Korea in order to maximize "all-out national security," "all-out national consensus," "cultivation of state power," and so on. The combination of the two aforementioned justifications resulted in infringement on popular sovereignty, damage to political parties and representative parliamentary politics, and weakening of the system of checks and balances in the Yusin Constitution: the expansion of the legal suspension of the guarantee of the people's basic rights; the expansion of the president's nearly unlimited power, such as through the abolishment of the presidential term limit, the implementation of indirect election, and the president's authority to dissolve the National Assembly and declare emergency measures; the sharp reduction of parliamentary power, such as the presidential appointment of one-third of the National Assembly members, abolition of the inspection of the executive government, and the shortening of National Assembly sessions; and damage to judicial independence. If national democracy and political democracy had uncomfortably coexisted in the past, during the Third Republic now, through the Yusin Constitution, the newly named Korean-style democracy had revealed an antagonistic relationship with political democracy and institutionalized de facto abrogation of political democracy.

And Park sought to legitimize Korean-style democracy in a third way. As can be seen from the use of the Saemaeul Movement as its example, Korean-style democracy meant not a political but an administrative democracy. Thus the people participated only in the effective execution of policies initiated by the government and were allowed to advance proposals to and criticism of governmental policies as needed so the government could rectify faulty policies. In other words, the plan regarding administrative democracy that Park had proposed during the military-government phase but had never implemented was later to be realized through the Yusin Constitution. From the perspective of the average citizen, Park's administrative democracy, which became more concrete via the Saemaeul Movement, intended to greatly improve the people's "political competence" and "self-governing ability." In sum, Korean-style democracy was Park's final version of democracy, a fusion of national democracy and administrative democracy, at the expense of political democracy, the main culprit of the squandering of state power. Thus negation and criticism of the Yusin regime was now considered "an antidemocratic act rejecting and destroying democracy" ("Address on Constitution Day," July 17, 1975, 5:452). Consequently, anyone who continued to argue for the level of freedoms experienced in the West was branded a "fanatic romanticist," ignorant of the way the world works, and a "fanatic democrat" ("Armed Forces Day Speech," October 1, 1974, 5:312; and then "New Year's Press Conference," January 14, 1975, 5:378).

CONCLUDING REMARKS

As has so far been examined in this discussion, certain commonalities and continuity exist between administrative, national, and Korean-style democracy. In particular, it can be said that Korean-style democracy, given the experience of the rule of the Third Republic, was the finalized version, a synthesis of both administrative and national democracy. To summarize the commonalities: More than anything else, Park Chung-hee first consistently opposed the direct transplant of Western democracy and argued for an alternative that suited the social, economic, and political circumstances of Korea as well as its historical background and cultural traditions. Second, Park adopted the stance that, because political democracy centered on political parties and elections and parliament caused the waste of state power, internal strife, and inefficiency, it had to be deferred, at least while North Korea continued to be a national-security threat and until the task of economic development and modernization of the fatherland was complete.[24] Park originally intended to carry out the military-government phase for a considerably longer period of time and wanted to implement administrative democracy and suspend political democracy. In the meantime, his plan seemed to aim to cultivate a group of sound leaders and improve the self-governing ability of the people. But, due to internal and external pressures, Park accepted the transfer of power to a civilian government faster than he had originally expected, and he appeared to hold a faint hope for political democracy during the subsequent Third Republic by relying on the Democratic Republican Party, which was ushered in as a group of sound leaders and the center of a generational shift. However, to Park, who viewed politics and democracy in terms of productivity as it concerned the task of modernization, it would become clear that political democracy was the culprit in the waste of state power, functioning as an obstacle to his permanent rule. The result was Korean-style democracy, the final version of the Koreanization of democracy, and the entrance of the Yusin regime based on the Yusin Constitution. Of course, it sounded a death knell for political democracy. Now all that remained was the physical collision of naked government power, which had arisen from the realm of the sovereign prerogative, and "street democracy," which had sprung from opposing activists. Third, Park believed that liberal democracy could only be realized at the level of Western democracy once economic self-reliance and prosperity, the result of successful modernization, reached the level where they could be enjoyed (Park Chung-hee 1962, 226).

Whereas these three elements are consistently discovered in Park's three concepts of democracy, concrete details about a form of democracy that would suit Korea's historical background, cultural tradition, and unique reality were never clearly proposed before the final version of Korean-style democracy. In particular, it was never made clear either in administrative democracy or national democracy, except that it would be skeptical of or hostile to political democracy and would stress "leadership dependent on innovative elites" (Park Chung-hee 1962, 212). It eventually appeared in the form of the Korean-style democracy of the Yusin Constitution that had emasculated political democracy, in the form of a government centered on a supreme leader who held all the power. But the administrative democracy that Park had proposed earlier at the cost of abandoning political democracy would find its concrete shape in the Saemaeul Movement, which started right before Yusin. From Park's perspective, the movement coincided precisely with the essence of the administrative democracy previously described as "a democracy . . . growing 'from the bottom up,' democracy awakened from below" (231).

Looking back, Korean-style democracy would be the culmination of Park's pristine plan regarding Korean politics, roughly designed in his book hurriedly written immediately after the coup. It was arrived at after ten years of his actual governance and the gradual systemization that took place with it. In *Gukgawa Hyeongmyeonggwa Na*, published ahead of the 1963 presidential election, Park, in reference to democracy, stressed the need for a "powerful guiding principle" over the importance of "party politics and parliament" and "democratic political power" and suggested that the guiding ideology needed by a patriotic leader was not "normative democracy" but "guided democracy" ushered in by a sole strong leader. "Even in democratic politics," he wrote, "one powerful guiding principle must be established. Needless to say, the backbone of democratic politics lies in party politics and parliament together with their own spiritual basis, ideology, platform policy, etc. But as it will be implemented . . . through the same conservative route, the need for consistent powerful guiding principle is greater than that of democratic political power" (Park Chung-hee 1963, 75–76). "In particular," he added, "on deciding how the direct importation of Western democracy will be applied to the Korean constitution and temperament, this guiding principle can also come through a patriotic ideology. Whether it will be guided democracy or normative democracy can also be chosen via the guiding ideology" (254).

Park's beliefs such as these would cast ominous clouds over the future of Korean democracy. Ultimately, Park's "guiding principle" or "guiding ideology" was realized through the Yusin Constitution, which made possible rule by a sole supreme leader. Defining the May 16 Revolution as a multidimensional revolution, Park called it the "revolution of establishing the Subjectivity Consciousness," "modernization revolution," "industrial revolution," "revolution initiating national regeneration," and so on. Then he also declared that it would not be finished "with the mere installation of the Third Republic" but, rather, was the "Nation's Permanent Revolution," to be passed down from generation to generation with no definite time limit until its aims were reached (Park Chung-hee 1963, 27–28). This declaration, when combined with "will to power," refers precisely to Park Chung-hee's permanent rule.

NOTES

1. Many political studies on the Park Chung-hee regime have addressed his political thought on democracy, but most of these are rather loose, lacking systematic analysis, because Park's antidemocratic rule is taken for granted. But Jeon In-gwon's essay "Park Chung-hee Minjujuuigwan: Yeonseolmuneul Jungsimeuro" (Park Chung-hee's View of Democracy: Focusing on His Speeches) is outstanding, analyzing Park's position on democracy in full. Examining Park's political thought on democracy from diverse perspectives, Jeon concludes that Park held an "instrumental view of democracy," which means that "democracy can be suspended for an indefinite period of time if it can function as an obstacle to the achievement of the happiness of the nation as a whole or certain other national goals" (2002, 154). I may agree with Jeon's conclusion on the whole, but his essay did not delve deeply enough into Park's discourse on democracy, failing to consider the dual political order of democracy and authoritarianism, structural characteristics brought about by the dialectic of nonsimultaneity elaborated on in chapter 2.

2. In the aftermath of the military coup d'état, Park tried to articulate his political creed systematically, justifying the coup in pamphlets and books he published. Two pamphlets were printed in 1961—*Jidojado* (The principle of leadership) and *Hyeongmyeonggwaeobwansureul Wihan Gungminui Gil* (National citizen's path for completing revolutionary tasks). As for books, in 1962 he published *Uri Minjogui Nagal Gil* (The path for our nation to take) and, just before the presidential election for the transfer of power to a civilian government in 1963, *Gukgawa Hyeongmyeonggwa Na* (The state, revolution, and I). The two pamphlets were published as a temporary expedient immediately after the military coup, and their format and content are rather crude and poor in comparison to the two books published later. *Uri Minjogui Nagal Gil* provided more theoretical and systematic insights into the Korean political situation at the time—as compared to *Gukgawa Hyeongmyeonggwa Na*, which was written in essay style—but it remained at the abstract level without offering any concrete policy proposals. By contrast, the latter suggested the outline and direction of concrete policies absent from the former by analyzing the Korean economic situation and supplying the achievement of the "revolutionary" government and the future objective of the revolution. In order to analyze Park's political thought, I reviewed other books published in his name during his presidency—such as *Minjogui Jeoryeok* (The latent power of the nation; 1971), *Minjokjungheungui Gil* (The way to the national regeneration; 1978), and so on—but they were embellished in a very elegant and academic style. So I mainly focused my analysis on the two early books and Park's speeches and statements issued during his presidency.

3. Park did not mention administrative democracy and national democracy as frequently as he did Korean-style democracy. He did not have enough time to implement administrative democracy because his position fluctuated between the prolongation of the military government and the transfer of power to a civilian government, and the duration of the military government turned out to be brief in the end. He mainly used the term *national democracy* in his campaign speeches of the 1960s. Nevertheless, considering that the Korean-style democracy Park had advocated in earnest since the

beginning of the Yusin regime was a synthesis of the other two, closely examining both styles helps us understand Park's view of democracy.

4. By contrast to the situation in Korea, it seems useful to recollect that anti- or nondemocratic regimes that appeared in nineteenth-century Europe before the ascendency of democracy as a universal idea did not need democratic embellishments to claim their legitimacy, a point I make in chapter 2 and address again later.

5. Seen from this perspective, the Korean-style democracy Park advocated later may be duly interpreted as the device ultimately brought about by dismantling and incapacitating the reins holding liberal democracy, as I examine later.

6. In the same speech Park cited a Chinese proverb: "When a tangerine tree in the South was transplanted to the North, it had become a trifoliate orange tree." Relying on this analogy of an edible tangerine and an inedible trifoliate orange, he suggested that, if Western democracy were to be transplanted to Korea and cultivated in the wrong way, it would surely become as inedible as a trifoliate orange tree.

7. Of course, this point is true of powerful Western nations to a certain extent, but it is all the more so of Korea.

8. With this in mind, Park may well have considered a communist system as an alternative. He dismissed it, however, as a nonstarter, pointing to the inevitability of communist dictatorship and economic failure, not to mention his own anticommunism (Park Chung-hee 1962, 228–29).

9. As shown in the discussion thus far, the fact that Park's sincere concern with the relationship between economic development and democracy began to appear immediately after the coup deserves our close attention, because it refutes the cursory assertion that Park advocated economic development only to justify his own dictatorship or the prolongation of his rule.

10. There are, however, some significant differences found among the three concepts, but some scholars who examine Park's view of democracy seem to disregard them as trivial or overlook them entirely. For example, Kang Jun-man (2004a) points out that "*administrative democracy* was a term interchangeable with *Koreanization of democracy* or *Korean-style democracy*" (204). Such an interpretation is valid in the sense that both administrative and Korean-style democracy expressed Park's concern with the Koreanization of democracy and both were related to the restriction of liberal democracy for the effective pursuit of the modernization. But it should also be noted that the former was proposed as a temporary measure during the military government, whereas the latter was institutionalized in the form of a constitutional system during the Yusin regime. Due to this fundamental variance, there were significant differences between the two, as I show later in this chapter. Cho Hyeon-yeon (2003) also examines Park's three concepts of democracy only in the sense that they rejected democracy in toto (315–20). Thus the significant differences among them are overlooked.

11. In his first official speech, "The Inauguration Address for the Chair of the Supreme Council for State Reconstruction," Park also pledged to devote himself to building "a genuine democratic welfare state" and to "rebuilding a genuine democratic republic" (July 3, 1961, 1:4).

12. In a way, it was almost natural that administrative democracy set the ordinary people as its object, given that party politics or congressional politics centered on professional politicians was suspended during the military government phase.

13. Commenting on the governance of the military government as "the death of politics," Kang Jun-man (2004a) states that "direct election of the head was repealed in all institutions of self-governing character such as agricultural cooperatives and farmland improvement cooperatives as well as local governments," and provincial mayors and governors were all replaced by the military (54–55).

14. It has been suggested that Park's idea of "national democracy" was indebted to Hwang Yong-ju, his classmate at the Daegu Teacher's School and chief editor at that time of the *Busan Daily Newspaper* (Kang Jun-man 2004a, 239). It is also interesting to note that the term *national democracy* had been used before by politicians of diverse ideological stripes: President Rhee Syngman had discussed national democracy in his administrative-policy speech before the National Assembly in September 1949. However, his sense of the term differs from Park's; Rhee said Korea "as a single and pure nation-state does not allow any privileges to individuals and groups and pursues a state in which all are equal" (quoted in Kim Hye-su 1995, 338). In this sense, Rhee's national democracy corresponds to his *ilminjui* (doctrine of the unitary nation). Paik Nam-un, a moderate socialist active in the aftermath of liberation, had once proposed *associative new democracy*, a kind of social democracy based on the wide alliance of classes, also labeling it *national democracy* (quoted in Seo Jung-seok 1991, 370).

15. In the same speech Park criticized Yun Posun's democracy as flunkeyism democracy, for Yun demonstrated by "hanging around the US embassy for no specific reason" ("Presidential Campaign Speech," September 28, 1963, 1:530).

16. In the same speech Park, in reaction to Yun's manifesto, focused on political matters regarding the constitution and party law, pledging himself to "achieve the complete self-reliance of the economy" by carrying out the second five-year plan for economic development (April 15, 1967, 2:1005). In his presidential campaign for the 1967 election, however, Park did not charge Yun Posun with advocating "flunkeyism democracy."

17. It is rather surprising that Park did not mention national democracy in his official addresses and writings except in presidential campaign speeches. In his presidential address to settle the incident of June 3, 1964, brought about by violent demonstrations opposing the impending normalization treaty between Korea and Japan, Park stressed national democracy from the perspective of self-reliance and not depending on foreign aid. He said, "We have to realize the day we become self-reliant. Isn't there a certain limit even in the aid from allied nations? . . . This is what is meant by national democracy" (June 26, 1964, 2:135). Park made this statement intending for the funds for economic cooperation—offered by Japan as a result of the normalization treaty—to be invested in the economic development then being promoted, because Korea could no longer rely on the United States, which gradually reduced its aid to Korea.

18. When the Park regime pushed the normalization treaty between Korea and Japan, many students and citizens were vehemently opposed to it, criticizing the diplomacy for humiliating Korea, even staging a funeral for national democracy. At that time opponents also seem to have understood national democracy primarily in terms of an "independent" attitude, as did Park. In this regard it appears that opposition activists took issue with the word *national* rather than with *democracy*.

19. In this regard, Park's political thought on democracy should be understood in connection with nationalism. His nationalism is fully examined in chapter 6.

20. Here it is important to note that liberal democracy is a dichotomous contrast to communism, which does not admit any other category. If a political regime is not communist, then it is a liberal democracy by default. In this way, in his inaugural address as seventh president, made on July 1, 1967, Park stressed the "fact that democracy can accomplish more efficient economic development than communism," inspired and encouraged by the economic development achieved by that time (3:4).

21. Due to space limitations I do not quote from other inaugural addresses. For more information on the sixth and seventh presidential inaugural speeches, refer to each address (July 1, 1967, 3:4–5; July 1, 1971, 4:4).

22. Here I do not undertake a detailed analysis of the Constitution Day speech given in 1968. But with the benefit of hindsight, such a subtle change from formal liberty and equality to substantial liberty and equality suggested significantly that some maneuver to initiate constitutional revision for a third term was going on behind the scenes.

23. The speech given on Constitution Day in 1972 seems to have been composed while bearing the impending October Yusin declaration in mind; I make a similar point with regard to the Constitution Day speech of 1968 in the preceding footnote.

24. Of course, this stance is deeply rooted in Park's view of politics or aversion to politics, in which politics is understood only in terms of productivity and efficiency, not in terms of negotiation and compromise between conflicting ideas and colliding interests.

Chapter 5

Antiliberal Conservatism for Modernization

The goal of this chapter is to shed light on the conservative and liberal (or antiliberal)[1] facets of Park Chung-hee's political thought, which has molded the frame of the modern Korean state. Because the conservative and antiliberal nature of his political thought is usually taken for granted, it has been only superficially handled when the character of the regime, its policies, and ruling ideologies during the Park Chung-hee era are addressed. Thus studies that carefully analyze Park's own political writings and various speeches for their conservative and antiliberal implications are actually rather scarce.[2] However, Park's political thought, which has thus far been conjectured roughly from the overall character of his regime, can be unveiled more completely through research on his political thought that analyzes his official discourses—writings, speeches, public statements, and so forth.[3] Bearing this in mind, in this chapter I attempt to examine the particular characteristics of Park's conservative thought by presenting it as "antiliberal conservatism for modernization." I first examine Park Chung-hee's state-centered (statist) political outlook before moving on to outline his conservative political thought contained in his policies of anticommunism, national security, and economic development. Then I attempt to shed light on Park's conservativism through the perspective of "modernization conservatism" by correlating it with the dialectic of nonsimultaneity. Next I examine the antiliberal aspects of Park's thought more concretely. Finally I summarize how Park Chung-hee's conservatism reflects nonsimultaneity and suggest how it is connected with the sanctification of nationalism.

THE MEANING OF POLITICS TO PARK CHUNG-HEE

In order to understand an individual's political thought, we must know how he or she thinks fundamentally about politics before concretely analyzing his or her beliefs or ideologies. In other words, it is first necessary to examine the individual's view of politics. After coming to power through a coup d'état in 1961, Park Chung-hee frequently commented on current politics while criticizing opposition politicians or figures and students in specific circumstances—for example, during the presidential campaign or the New Year's press conference. Besides, in his speeches on Constitution Day or his presidential inauguration he often made normative statements on democracy or politics that reflected the aims of such official events. Yet Park almost never expressed his own view of politics as a general proposition in his speeches or writings. However, on April 3, 1978, at the peak of the Yusin regime, Park made an exception by revealing his overall view of politics succinctly in the speech he gave at the Korea Military Academy graduation ceremony. "In short," he said, "I believe that the aim of politics and the true value of the political institution is to put the people's wisdom and capabilities together and to encourage and support their demonstration of productive capacity at its fullest in order to effectively resolve the country's pressing problems and to steadily actualize ambitious state goals. . . . the stark reality we are facing is such that we cannot possibly tolerate political maneuvers, whatever their pretext or reason, that hinder all-out national consensus and social stability or that attempt to divide state [national] opinion or waste state power" (April 3, 1978, 6:304).[4]

What is interesting in this speech is that the aim and institution of politics is described as serving the state's goals. Thus, to Park, the correct "view of the state" is "something demanded to precede politics" ("Air Force Academy Graduation Ceremony Address," February 22, 1963, 1:378).[5] Such thought, which considers the state as superior and/or prior to politics, directly conflicts with Western liberal thought—the basic premise of the social contract theory—which proposes that the reasons politics and the state exist are secondary, intended only to preserve individual life, liberty, and property. Accordingly, such political thought can be seen as strongly statist.[6] In addition, it is the proper function of politics—founded on democratic consensus in contemporary democracies—to seek to define and resolve the state's "pressing problems" and "ambitious state goals." But, to Park Chung-hee, such pressing problems and ambitious goals are presented as something urgent and self-evident, imposed by a harsh reality accompanied by crisis that leaves no room for choice, and politics presented merely as a means to help realize such tasks and goals. Although it can be said that it is also the task of politics to play a role in realizing certain goals, it is the recognition of such pressing problems and the establishment of ambitious goals that are indeed properly the major task of politics. But, just as the materialization of the Yusin Constitution and the rule of Park Chung-hee have amply shown us, when establishment of tasks and goals is excluded from the realm of politics under the pretext of an urgent crisis or, in other words, when setting tasks and goals of the state is no longer the object of democratic consensus but rather the product of the foreknowledge and determination of a supreme ruler, there is a greater likelihood that politics takes on the image of a sovereign dictatorship dependent on a transcendental leader.[7]

Park later went on to specifically elaborate on the government's goals and methods of implementation, stating, "It is only through all-out national security and the cultivation of state power that we can defend our country, guard the nation's right to survival, and consolidate peace and prosperity. This is the only shortcut to bring forward the peaceful unification of our fatherland" ("Korea Military Academy Graduation Ceremony Address," April 3, 1978, 6:305). In doing so, Park presented the government's goals, including the defense of the state and nation, "peace and prosperity," and "peaceful unification," while indicating that, on the basis of his individual judgment and interpretation, "all-out national security" and the "cultivation of state power" were the only means to realize these goals. However, as history has shown, all-out national security and the cultivation of state power as a means of implementation can result in the suffocation of democracy. In particular, when emphasizing productivity while pushing forward agendas of all-out national security and the cultivation of state power, political democracy, which aims to avert the abuse of arbitrary and dictatorial power through the free political competition of opposing parties, is written off as a high-cost, inefficient waste or luxury.[8] Such thought can be commonly found in statements made by Park Chung-hee defending his Yusin regime: "The Yusin Constitution aims to overcome crisis by maximizing the efficiency of overall state politics and organizing state power and to cultivate democracy in a fruitful way that suits our actual circumstances. However, in the midst of this, what must not be forgotten is to minimize political expenses, notably election costs, and to mobilize all resources for the purpose of cultivating state power. This is the basic purpose of the constitution" ("Press Conference," August 4, 1976, 6:74).

It was precisely in this context that Park Chung-hee made sweeping criticisms of the Third Republic of South Korea, which he himself had overseen, as well as the First and Second republics, during his New Year's press conference on January 19, 1979, describing all of them as "exceedingly unproductive, inefficient, or bringing about only confusion and disorder" (January 19, 1979, 16:44). From this perspective it is clear that Park's view of politics stands in stark contrast to Western liberalism or democracy. Bearing this in mind, we now examine Park's political thoughts through discourses related to conservatism and liberalism.

PARK CHUNG-HEE'S CONSERVATISM

As discussed in chapter 2, one notable ideological feature of the Korean political order before democratization was the dual political order, authoritarian and liberal democracy constituting two sides of the same coin. Thus *predemocratization conservatism* was defined as an ideology proposed in order to defend an authoritarian political order with concentrated power under the pretext that this power protected liberal democracy from the aggression and threat of communism and also maintained the national security (anticommunism) and political stability needed for economic development. Using this concept, Park Chung-hee's conservatism is parsed and interpreted on the basis of his assertions regarding national security (anticommunism) and economic development. Then I subsequently contemplate the unique characteristics of his style of conservatism, a concept called "conservatism for modernization," which was born of nonsimultaneity. The nonsimultaneity was dictated during the belated process of rapid modernization whereby Korea pushed forward.

Anticommunism and National Security

More than anything else, Park Chung-hee actively utilized and emphasized anticommunism and national security to justify his authoritarian system. The greatest force threatening national security was North Korea. Because North Korea had not only provoked the June 25 War but also executed armed provocations on many occasions afterward, national security naturally came to mean both anticommunism and anti–North Korea, with North Korea seen as the main target both internally and externally.

Right after carrying out a military coup d'état in May 1961, the coup forces, headed by Park Chung-hee, justified their actions by stating that the "fatherland" was in the midst of "moving from the brink of disaster to an endless crisis," adding that they "could no longer entrust the state and the nation to the current corrupt and incompetent regime and established politicians." In addition, in Article 1 of the Revolution Pledge, they declared that, above all else, they would "make anticommunism the first priority of state doctrine and strengthen and reorganize the readiness for anticommunism, which has up until now been nothing more than formalities and rhetoric" (Kim Sam-ung 1997, 256). In July 1961, during his first official address as a politician—that is, in "Inauguration Address for the Chair of the Supreme Council for State

Reconstruction"—Park Chung-hee stated that he would "block the aggressions of communism" (July 3, 1961, 1:4).

In particular, when Park declared a state of national emergency on December 6, 1971, a prelude to the later establishment of the Yusin regime in October 1972, he also justified it from the angle of a national-security crisis. Noting various internal and external security affairs—such as China's admission into the United Nations and its election as a permanent member of the Security Council in October 1971, discussions on the additional reduction of US Forces Korea, and North Korea's strengthened wartime mobilization system—Park argued, "The security of our Republic of Korea is currently facing a grave crisis. If democracy is so precious to us . . . in order to protect it, we must have a stiff resolve to voluntarily defer a part of the freedom that we enjoy when necessary and to cope with the crisis" ("Special Statement regarding the Declaration of a State of National Emergency," December 6, 1971, 4:90).[9] Of course, Park's national security–crisis discourse was less concerned with a shift in the balance of power and more focused on how that shift incited North Korea's intentions of armed provocation.

Thus a particular emphasis on national security is a distinct characteristic of South Korea's conservatism that differentiates it from modern Western conservatism. Of course, in the Cold War era, conservatives in the "Free World," including the United States, also stressed the threat of global expansion of communism and advanced anticommunist ideologies. However, for South Korea, the threat of North Korean communism was always imminent, as seen in the North's frequent armed provocations, such as the June 25 War and the North Korean dispatch of armed guerillas. In other words, to Park Chung-hee, North Korea was a threatening presence "making frantic efforts to raise tensions on the peninsula" that "instigated the June 25 aggressive war and was still looking for a chance to provoke another war with the aim of imposing its antinational heterogeneous thought and communist dictatorship" on South Korea ("National Foundation Day [literally, Heaven Opening Day] Congratulatory Address," October 3, 1976, 6:88).

As long as the threat of North Korea remained strong, the emphasis Park Chung-hee's conservatism placed on anticommunism and national security retained its validity and logical basis. There is a subtle similarity and difference, however, between Western and Korean conservatism in their respective stress on national security and anticommunism, although both share, undoubtedly, the fear and hatred of communism. It is true that Western conservatism stressed national security and carried out a strong foreign policy in order to deal with the Cold War and the spread of communism. In contrast, South Korean conservatism frequently mobilized anticommunism and national security as a means to suppress internal political dissidents as well as to deal with the threat of North Korea.[10] In addition, there is a notable difference between the two in political philosophy and policy orientation. Contemporary Western conservatism could not accept communism's espousal of "progress," the "ultimate perfectibility of human nature and human society," and economic "plans" carried out through government intervention (Ball and Dagger 2004, 104–5). In contrast, Korean conservatism represented by Park Chung-hee accepted the idea of progress and acknowledged the necessity of active governmental intervention in the economy and the utility of economic planning to a certain extent, given that it was conservatism for modernization from above; however, it was not clear then that it espoused the "ultimate perfectibility of human nature and human society."

Like all forms of conservatism, Park's conservatism emphasized the stability of domestic order through the "maintenance of law and order." In the West, considering that this is stressed due to the need for crime prevention and public order, it means that the primary goal of public security is the maintenance of civil order. However, in the case of Park Chung-hee, the maintenance of public order was more focused on guarding the Park government than on the civil order of everyday life. Thus it was frequently devoted to enforcing authoritarian rule and suppressing those who opposed the government. Hence the maintenance of law and order, even the problem of civil order, was frequently handled in the same way as national security in order to discipline students and citizens (*gungmin*), making them into docile subjects under authoritarian rule.[11]

This point can be verified by the fact that from 1970 to 1979 Park Chung-hee made convening the Central Meeting for Nationwide Public Order and Reservist Officials[12] a priority, second only to the annual New Year's press conference. During those meetings Park often reiterated the need for national-security preparedness against North Korea's aggressions and emphasized that national security was not merely an issue of defense but also directly related to public order (the stability of domestic politics), stressing that political unrest created by student protests and other such actions would lead to North Korean provocations. In this respect the Central Meeting held great significance as an event to emphasize and check not only national security but also the public order so as to guard the regime in the beginning of the year. Accordingly, at the Central Meeting on January 21, 1976, during the height of the Yusin era, Park announced[13] that he would deal with all unrest and confusion and even "decadent trends" as issues of national security. "Political unrest, social confusion, division in state opinion, lax social discipline, decadent trends, and other such antisocial irregularities are our weaknesses," he said. "From the perspective of national security, the resolute banishment and clear elimination of such problems is of utmost importance. . . . Accordingly, I have emphasized before that I will deal with such problems as if they were the affairs of national security" ("Central Meeting for Nationwide Public

Order and Reservist Officials," January 21, 1976, 6:34). In this way, the announcement that even so-called decadent trends like long hair and mini-skirts would be dealt with strictly as issues of national security meant that under the pretext of national security the everyday freedoms of the people could be severely suppressed.[14]

Moreover, an ideology of national security armed with anticommunism became firmly tied to authoritarianism through the routinization of the military culture that had begun to take root with the military's seizure of power. In response to the Blue House (*Cheongwadae*) raid in January 1968, a North Korean armed guerrilla attempt that was successful in infiltrating as far as the area surrounding the Blue House, the Homeland Reserve Forces were created later that year. In 1969 military-training classes for high school and university students were introduced to instill a "correct view of the state," a statist mentality, and to elevate national-security awareness. In 1975 the Student State Defense Corps, composed of students and school faculty and staff, was launched at various levels within high schools and universities. Thus, at the previously mentioned Central Meeting for Nationwide Public Order and Reservist Officials in January 1976, Park ordered a "'better safe than sorry' mentality via the united efforts of military, government, and civilian forces" such as the military, police, Homeland Reserve Forces, Student State Defense Corps, and Civil Defense Corps. In short, he requested "all-out national security as a way of everyday life" (January 21, 1976, 6:35). In this way, the routinization of security (i.e., making security part of daily life) was carried out, reminiscent of wartime.

The January 1968 Blue House raid by the North Korean armed guerillas also provided the political background for the first revision of the Resident Registration Act in 1968, which had been originally legislated in 1962. The second revision in 1970 is noteworthy because it expressly stated a goal of "strengthening readiness for anticommunism, with spies or impure elements quickly detected and tracked down"; the third revision in 1975 stated a goal of "strengthening national security readiness" and "establishing a foundation of all-out war preparedness" (Hong Seong-tae 2008, 95–96). In this way, through the Resident Registration Act, under the pretext of administrative convenience and national security, *gungmin* (citizens) were caught in the web of a "society under total surveillance" (85). The Saemaeul Movement, which had been in full force since 1970, was also touted as "ostensibly [intended] to improve the economic livelihood of peasants through 'income increase' and the 'modernization of rural villages,'" but by combining it with discourse such as "the cultivation of state power," "the path of patriotism," and "the path of all-out security," it was also used to strengthen security awareness (Koh Won 2008, 28).[15] Thus, whereas the military culture of Korean society was first inculcated around the political and economic arenas—not only the deeply pervasive military culture of the Korean Central Intelligence Agency, Democratic Republican Party, and government bureaucrats but also the pushing of economic-development agendas and export increases through methods reminiscent of wartime operations—it gradually spread to schools and the general public. Thus Korean society as a whole gathered momentum toward the regimented life of the military.[16]

Economic Development

In Park Chung-hee's brand of conservatism, economic development retained a multidimensional imperative. It was a means not only to achieve economic self-reliance and affluence (a welfare society) but also to function as a necessary precondition for independent national defense and the cultivation of democratic capability. At the beginning of his rule Park first accepted and put into practice the "economy first" slogan, originally put forward by the Second Republic. In *Gukgawa Hyeongmyeonggwa Na* (The state, the revolution, and I), Park advanced *"minjok jeil juui-wa gyeongje useon juui"* (nation first and economy above all else; Park Chung-hee 1963, 255), and during the Third Republic he condensed "economy first" even further, frequently using the words "exports first" (e.g., "Third Export Day Appreciation," November 30, 1966, 2:855; "Fifteenth Export Day Appreciation," November 30, 1978, 6:371).[17] However, after the Yusin regime, he started outright emphasizing "national security first" (e.g., "New Year's Press Conference," January 15, 1976, 6:8; "Administrative Policy Speech on the 1977 Annual Budget Submission," October 4, 1976, 6:94). Of course the mantras of "exports first" and "national security first" were not meant to replace each other but to work in tandem.

Actually, it could be said that, more than anything else, economic development was the overall driving force sustaining Park Chung-hee's regime. During the Park regime, reports of dazzling economic results from increased exports and economic growth usually adorned the front pages and economics sections of daily newspapers, capturing the attention of the entire nation in much the way today's professional sports do. In addition, in many speeches, such as the annual presidential addresses, New Year's and regular press conferences, administrative-policy speeches on the annual budget submission, Export Day, and various ground-breaking and ribbon-cutting ceremonies, Park enumerated specific figures and economic achievements at great length in order to show off the results of economic development, then presented detailed descriptions of economic-development goals yet to be attained. In this way he sought to maximize support for the government. It was this "development first" (or "developmentalism") mantra that was the most effective ideological resource for creating and sustaining popular support for his authoritarian regime.[18] The entire nation responded with ardent devotion to Park Chung-hee's policies—not least one summarized as "live well"—as Korean society became swept up in the fever of economic development. By integrating "development first" with the anticommunism of Rhee Syngman, Park was able to compensate for his conservative authoritarian rule, which stressed political stability, through offering the "carrot" of economic development (Kang Jung In 2009b, 73; Choi Jang-jip and Lee Seong-hyeong 1991, 219).[19]

Although the goal of economic development was, more than anything else, "the immediate resolution of the poverty that was on the brink of despair and starvation" as revealed in the May 16 Revolution Pledge, it was also connected to successful anticommunist reunification in that the goal was to "cultivate the capacity to defeat communism for the sake of reunification" (Kim Sam-ung 1997, 256). For Park, economic development was in fact top priority, and in his "New Year's Message to the People [*Gungmin*]" on January 1, 1962, during the military government, he stressed, "The utmost goal that we are confronted with is industrial development for economic reconstruction" (1:157). That same year, in his "Ulsan Industrial District Establishment and Groundbreaking Ceremony Speech," he justified the coup d'état by saying, "The real intention of the May 16 Revolution . . . was not solely to deliver the people out of poverty but also to rise up, out of a noble sense of duty, to achieve economic reconstruction to prepare eternal national prosperity and welfare for our future generations" (February 3, 1962, 1:177–78). During a time when Korea was struggling under poverty, the Korean people deeply identified with the Park regime's commitment to the goal to "live well" under its "economy first" mantra, which became an important pretext that allowed the coup d'état to draw vast support.[20] Accordingly, as Kim Dong-chun points out, during the 1960s "a sort of populist alliance" formed between "the Park regime and peasants," born of the combination of "developmentalist logic" and "the people's desire to escape from poverty" (Kim Dong-chun 1994, 233; 1996a, 287).

In addition, economic development was intimately connected to anticommunism. In *Uri Minjogui Nagal Gil* (The path for our nation to take), Park stressed that poverty was "a path of infiltration for communism" (1962, 35; refer also to 32, 223) and that economic development was an effective preventative against such infiltration. Although the strategy for economic development in the 1960s did have a general aspect of competition with the rest of the world, it was also waged as a "strategy to defeat communism" by winning "victory in economic competition" against North Korea. Thus, to Park Chung-hee, anticommunism unaccompanied by the "cultivation of [state] capacity" through economic development was merely "anticommunism in words"; in other words, as he criticized in his Revolution Pledge, it was nothing more than "formalities and rhetoric" ("Seventh Anniversary Ceremony Speech to Anticommunist Students Day," November 23, 1963, 1:573).

Economic development was an issue directly connected to both national defense and unification strategies. In a 1966 statement, Park emphasized that "the construction of a self-reliant economy" along with the work of "modernization of the fatherland" was "another important task in defeating communism," every bit as effective as armed struggle in the fight against communist aggression ("Twelfth Anniversary Speech to Freedom Day," January 23, 1966, 2:596–97). During his New Year's press conference on January 9, 1970, Park also stated that "national defense equals economic construction, economic construction equals national defense. In other words, defense and construction are synonymous" (3:670). It was in such a context that economic development constituted one axis of the reunification discourse. Consequently, in 1966, during his "Sixteenth Anniversary of the June 25 War Statement," Park stated that "the work of modernization of the fatherland and the construction of a self-reliant economy are indeed an enterprising project for reunification and progressive efforts toward reunification" and stressed that, "once again, we must be sure to remember that the reunification of the national territory[21] will only be possible after the intermediate goal of self-reliance and modernization has been achieved" (June 25, 1966, 2:712). Through this speech Park Chung-hee firmly reiterated his "construction first, then unification" doctrine.[22]

Conservatism for Modernization: A Contradiction in Terms?

At the beginning of the nineteenth century, the primary mission of European conservatism was opposing modernization, such as the Industrial Revolution on the one hand and the Enlightenment and liberalism of the French Revolution on the other, while defending a feudal agricultural society and the aristocratic order. Withdrawing its original mission, however, this Western conservatism later shifted to primarily oppose socialism or state intervention in the economy with the rise of socialism after 1848 (even more so after the outbreak of the Russian Revolution in 1917) and then to oppose the emergence of the principle of revised capitalism. In addition, by setting the defense of individual freedom and limited government as its key tasks, this conservatism eventually transformed into a contemporary conservatism that partly accommodated the results of modernization and converged with classical liberalism (Ball and Dagger 2004, 96–112; Kang Jung In 2009b, 40–43).

In contrast, the conservative forces in South Korea that came to power after liberation first pushed for industrialization and made liberalism (or liberal democracy) the ideology that justified their political position. They did so in order to accomplish "modernization from above" that was imposed by nonsimultaneity. In this regard, whereas Confucian *wijeongcheoksa* (literally meaning "defend orthodoxy and reject heterodoxy") in the late nineteenth-century Joseon of Korea exhibited similarities to European conservatism in the early nineteenth century with respect to modernization, South Korea's conservative forces after liberation also came to take on a form similar to that of contemporary Western conservatism.

After World War II, as conservative forces of newly independent countries pushed for modernization from the top down, this conservatism for modernization was a national survival strategy as part of the task to "catch up with the West."[23] Accordingly, although conservatism for modernization may be a contradiction in terms within the context of modern Western political thought, in newly independent societies like South Korea it cannot help but emerge as a historical imperative and an important attribute of right-wing nationalists. Furthermore, unlike contemporary Western conservatism, which opposes the state's active intervention in the economy in order to protect individual freedom, Korean conservatism for modernization pushed for state-led, top-down economic development. Accordingly, it took the state's active and broad intervention in the market for granted; it led and accepted the government's direct and indirect restriction of economic freedoms. Just as authoritarian rule based on anticommunism and national security suppressed individual political and social freedoms, so did state-led economic development considerably restrict the economic freedom of average citizens as well as private businesses.

In addition, whereas Western conservatism—especially the British variety represented by Edmund Burke—accommodated gradual social change, respecting time-honored traditions, religion, history, and authority, Park Chung-hee's conservatism for modernization combined with nationalism stressed the need for radical social change in order to overcome the contemporary predicament and crisis. Furthermore, Park's conservatism for modernization was similar in form to the progressive thought of the West in the nineteenth century, as seen in its rose-colored view of the future—such as the realization of a highly industrialized society and an affluent social-welfare society—created through radical transformation under the name "modernization of the fatherland." At the same time, this future, combined with nationalism, also projected a restorative vision through rhetorical phrases that conjured up the glory of an idealized past—for example, "the Revival of the Nation"; "Dangun, the Sacred Father"; "Valor and Spirit of Goguryeo"; "Spirit of Hwarang" of Silla; King Sejong, inventor of hangul (the Korean alphabet); among other such exaltations. In other words, conservatism for modernization embraced both a progressive outlook and a restorative vision.[24]

Similarly, through the progressive character accompanying conservatism for modernization, typical progressive logic and rhetoric emphasizing change and innovation can be easily found in Park's speeches. For example, in a graduation speech at Seoul National University in 1967, Park stressed to graduating students, "Victory lies in living in the future it is moving forward with hope and courage. Victory is what is gained at the cost of banishing vestiges of a decadent past" (February 27, 1967, 2:959).[25] In another speech, in 1969, Park characterized the circumstances of the day as "a process of constant change, where everything that is traditional, reactionary, and shabby will be expeditiously modernized, reformed, and renewed" ("Message at the Fifth Anniversary Celebration of the Foundation of the Journalists Association of Korea," August 18, 1969, 3:540).

At the same time, however, through his consistent emphasis on political stability in order to attain the glorious goal of modernization, Park argued for the conservation of the existing political order. At the "Sixth Presidential Inaugural Address" on July 1, 1967, Park declared, "We have already launched a truly groundbreaking historic task in our national history," praising the country for making "great advances in creating a shining industrial nation in Asia through *balanced economic growth*," while emphasizing that "political stability is a prerequisite of economic development" (3:4; emphasis original). Accordingly, "social unrest and confusion" came to symbolize a threat that would "inevitably create a loss of motion and a delay in results" in the "task of modernization" that was to bring about national glory ("Twelfth National Defense Graduate School Commencement Speech," July 10, 1967, 3:10).

In addition, when criticizing the "radical aspect" of student-led antigovernment protests for democratization, Park rejected the students' requests for reform with the typical logic of conservatism: "From the students' point of view, our social reality, or maybe everything in the world, looks absurd . . . they may [want] to demonstrate in order to turn everything upside down, but . . . the structure of society is very complicated with diverse interests getting tangled and twisted. The students must understand that things are not as easy as they may think they are in their simple minds" ("New Year's Press Conference," January 18, 1974, 5:240).

Park Chung-hee defended his logic using an increase in the price of rice as an example. According to Park, an increase in rice prices would in fact bring an increase in the wages of workers, but this would cause a rise in the prices of industrial products, which in the end would cause farmers to suffer economic loss (January 18, 1974, 5:240–41). This point of view was very similar to the "ecological view of society" advanced by British conservative Burke in order to oppose drastic changes to the existing order. According to Burke, the overall implementation of new policies or changes over a short period of time leads to changes that cannot be foreseen or controlled and upsets the ecological equilibrium. This is because, given the chain reaction that follows such attempts, the scale of change is more widespread than intended or anticipated. Thus there is a risk that the subsequently generated detrimental side effects can outweigh the originally intended benefits (Kang Jung In 2007, 482–83).[26]

PARK CHUNG-HEE'S ANTILIBERAL THOUGHT

Meeting with the opportunity for exogenous modernization due to the full-scale intrusion of modern Western civilization in the late nineteenth century, Koreans could not avoid the task of "Western modernization" for the sake of the survival of their nation and state.[27] However, not only Korea's strong tradition of Confucianism but also its severe historical experience since the late nineteenth century, in which the life and death of the nation or the state were at stake—the country's experience of losing national sovereignty and colonization during the Japanese imperial period, the fascism and statist education imposed by Japan, Korea's division after liberation, the severe internecine June 25 War, and the like—made it difficult to wholly integrate a Western liberalism that gave priority to individual freedom over the state, nation, or society.[28] Due to such experiences, Park Chung-hee as a politician would have also been unable to wholly internalize liberal ideology. Moreover, it is clear that his long career as a soldier who had to be readily willing to give up his own life for the cause of the nation and the state must also have made it difficult for Park personally to accept liberalism. Accordingly, Western individualistic liberalism was a distant ideology to Park. As a result, the main characteristics of Park's thoughts on liberalism can be summarized as Cold War liberalism, which set communism as its main enemy; "national liberalism," which prioritized the liberty of the nation over that of the individual; and the denigration of individual rights.

Although Park defined *liberation* as "the freedom of the nation" in his congratulatory speech on National Liberation Day in 1969, he also mentioned that Koreans had "come to realize that liberation doesn't exactly bring about freedom," stressing that "national security and national stability" constitute "our supreme task," and as "our supreme imperative . . . if this is not guaranteed" not only "the meaning of liberation" but also "the value of freedom and the hope of peace will all be in vain." By emphasizing the need to "eradicate the invasion of communism above all else in order to make liberation, freedom, and peace our own," he made it clear that the main enemy of freedom was now North Korean communists after liberation and the division of the peninsula (August 15, 1969, 3:537, 539) because communists were a group whose "basic tenets negate the sanctity of human dignity and repudiate freedom" ("Speech at the Sixth Meeting of Anticommunist Asian Christians," September 30, 1970, 3:832). In addition, by requesting "an iron-willed solidarity and fraternity" and "total mobilization of peoples who love liberty" in order "to overthrow communism and defend liberalism," Park made it clear that the main enemy of liberty was communism, not only in Korea but around the world, in his "Message to the Fourth General Assembly of the International Anticommunism Association" in 1970 (September 16, 1970, 3:824). Such a statement verified Park Chung-hee's liberalism as Cold War liberalism. In this respect, the criticism is valid that Park's and Korean conservatives' Cold War liberalism, through crackdowns on citizens' basic freedoms and rights, betrayed the integrity of liberalism proper more than it pursued its substance (Kim Dong-chun 1996a, 285–86).

However, if we are allowed to disregard criticism of the perpetrators on the basis of political ethics and consider the ideological structure of contemporary Korean politics, the reality that Cold War liberalism thwarted classical liberalism in Korea can be understood as having been partially caused by nonsimultaneity. In England and France, the birthplace of classical liberalism, the main targets liberalism struggled against were "religious conformity," "ascriptive status," and "political absolutism" (absolute monarchy) imposed by ancient European regimes, as mentioned previously in chapter 2 (Ball and Dagger 2004, 50–60). However, at the time of Korea's liberation, religious conformity (the all-encompassing reign of Confucianism), ascriptive status (system of noblemen [*yangban*], commoners, and slaves), and autocratic monarchy—hereafter the "three main enemies of freedom"—were, in all reality, overthrown during the process of reform in the late Joseon dynasty and Japanese colonial rule and its ensuing defeat. The Japanese imperial reign in Korea, another form of political absolutism, collapsed in liberated Korea as well. Thus, immediately after liberation, due to the threat of a communist revolution (including the establishment of a communist system in North Korea) and the spread of the Cold War system, the fact that Korean conservatives and liberals identified a communism asserting a proletarian dictatorship (another variety of political absolutism) as the main threat to freedom seemed to correspond with their creed as well as the circumstances of the times. In other words, after liberation the task imposed on Korean liberalism was not a struggle against the classic three main enemies of freedom but a struggle against communism. However, the liberalism as ruling ideology in Korea was not equipped with the progressive momentum Western liberalism had acquired in its struggle against the three main enemies through its own revolutionary fervor in the eighteenth and nineteenth centuries. Accordingly, as examined in chapter 2, Korean liberalism as ruling ideology fell into a prematurely reactionary ideology due to the threat of an imminent communist revolution, making anticommunism its first priority and violating or ignoring citizens' freedom and rights.[29] In this regard the official liberalism of the South Korean government was confronted with a fundamental self-contradiction. Its anticommunism was not "anticommunism for freedom," in the true sense of the phrase. Rather, it was "anticommunism for its own sake," in order to purge political opposition forces—in other words, to suppress political freedom.

Another characteristic of Park's thoughts on freedom, as can be gathered from his frequent mention of "freedom of the nation" in his public speeches, was that the main agent for the enjoyment of freedom was not the individual but rather a collectivity such as the state and the nation, of which the individual was a part.[30] This is seen by the terminology Park frequently used—for example, "free *people*," "free *Asia*," "free *people of the world*," "free *allies*" (emphasis added). According to Park's logic, the individual can enjoy personal freedom only when the collective entity to which the individual belongs enjoys collective freedom (i.e., independence and autonomy from outside forces) first.[31]

Viewed from the history of thought, it was not only Park Chung-hee who believed the main agent of freedom was a collective entity such as the nation, the state, or the race. Diverse ideologies that dominated the late nineteenth century, such as nationalism, racism, social Darwinism, social-organism theory, and imperialism, were focused on the collective survival of the race or nation and established the collectivity (e.g., nation, ethnicity, race), rather than the individual, as the basic unit for political struggle, conceptualizing freedom in the collective dimension (Jeon Bok-hui 1996; Schmid 2002; Shin Gi-Wook 2009). Yan Fu (嚴復; 1854–1921), Chinese enlightenment thinker active during the late nineteenth and early twentieth centuries, represented this tendency as well. He introduced to China the writings of a diverse set of Western thinkers, such as Charles Darwin, Thomas Huxley, Herbert Spencer, Adam Smith, John Stuart Mill, and Charles de Montesquieu. However, unlike the Western liberal thinkers he studied, Yan Fu distinguished between the "freedom of nation-society" and the "freedom of the individual" and stressed the priority of the former over the latter (Schwartz 1964, 171–72). He said, "When we view the situation of China, we realize that the liberty of the individual is not yet a matter of first urgency. It is rather the matter of maintaining ourselves against the aggression of other nations which will brook no delay. The freedom of the nation-society is more urgent than the liberty of the individual" (Yan Fu, quoted in ibid., 172).

This can also be seen in the early development stage of British liberalism. Hobbes's *Leviathan* is a case in point. Through his political philosophy, Hobbes unwittingly provided the first seeds of liberalism in the theoretical process of justifying the absolute state in terms of a social contract that was based on radical and atomistic individualism. Hobbes conceptualized liberty not as "liberty . . . of private men" but as "liberty of the commonwealth" or "the right of the public" and argued that the "state" or the "commonwealth" that is "not dependent on one another . . . has an absolute liberty, to do what it shall judge, that is to say, what that man, or assembly that representeth it, shall judge most conducing to their benefit" (Hobbes 1962, xxi, 162–63). Here the liberty that Hobbes affirmatively references and grants value to is not "that any particular men had the liberty to resist their own representative, but that their representative had the liberty to resist, or to invade other people" (xxi, 162).[32] In this regard the freedom of the commonwealth advanced by Hobbes has common aspects with the freedom of the nation espoused by Park.

In addition, Park distinguished between greater and lesser freedoms in line with the distinction between individual and national freedoms. In his 1974 National Forces Day speech, Park called the Yusin Constitution "a system that protects our freedom from communist aggressors" and argued that "the only way to avoid losing our greater freedom is by having the wisdom to know that lesser freedom must be sacrificed or moderated in order to protect greater freedom" (October 1, 1974, 5:312). Thus the lesser freedom of the individual or a small group could become a disturbance that threatens the greater freedom of the nation or the state. Park also negatively referenced personal freedom in his commemorative speech on the anniversary of the Universal Declaration of Human Rights in 1962. "Our precious freedom," he said, "which can be considered greater than human life itself, must not be made into a disgrace of intolerant self-centeredness. We must adjust and exercise freedom in order to coincide with the improvement of the national interests and the welfare of public society and nurture our skills to do this" (December 10, 1962, 1:338). It is evident that to Park this was not the kind of freedom that excludes the state's interference or restriction of rights—in other words, the individualistic freedom of the modern West that allowed individuals to act as they wished as long as they did not harm others—but rather was a freedom meant to serve the interests of the state.

To Park—who justified his prioritization of state security and the survival of the nation in the name of the greater freedom—freedom was not a right accorded by natural law but a concept closer to legal positivism, allowed only within the bounds of maintaining the order and stability of the entire community and within the limits of positive law.[33] From this perspective, Park argued, "it is not necessary to restore 'freedom' or 'democracy' to the point that it drives society into confusion," and "to what degree freedom is allowed and to what degree it must be restricted must be based on the particular circumstances of that country."[34] In the same vein, Park also brought up "historical reality, environment of the times, and several social characteristics" ("Special Address on Holding a National Referendum," January 22, 1975, 5:400–401; "New Year's Press Conference," January 14, 1975, 5:377). Ultimately, Park believed, "There can be no democracy without a state, and there can be no freedom without the guarantee of the right to national survival."[35] Thus selfishness was conceptualized not in the private and personal realm but from the public and collectivist viewpoint of the state and the nation as "selfishness that had no regard for the state and the nation" ("Admonition to Central Meeting for Nationwide Public Order and Reservist Officials," January 21, 1975, 5:396; "New Year's Press Conference," January 15, 1976, 6:29).[36] In sum, Park was hostile toward freedom of the abstract individual—or, in other words, Western liberalism.[37]

In this context, Park denounced those opposed to the Yusin regime, which protected the greater freedom. "They are constantly shouting about so-called freedom and democracy," he said, "but in reality, they want to demolish the cultivation of state power and legal order that provided the very backdrop for such freedom and democracy to take root. They talk as if they are working for the people [*gungmin*], but in fact all of their actions are contrary to the interests of the people [*gungmin*]" ("Address at Unification and Security Report Meeting by the National Conference for Unification," December 16, 1974, 5:349). In other words, because the Park regime's political opponents, connected to North Korean communists, were a threat to the survival and freedom of the South Korean system, they were not the *gungmin* whose human rights must be protected but criminals guilty of "treason" who must be eradicated.

Thus, during his New Year's press conference on January 15, 1976, Park spoke regarding North Korea's call for the release of "democratic and patriotic figures" as a condition of South-North talks: "I don't know what kind of people these democratic and patriotic figures are, and I don't know if they are seen as democratic and patriotic figures to communists, but to us they are seen as criminals who have committed the great crime of treason by betraying their state. How can we release . . . communists, that is, spies and those who have cooperated with communism?" (6:23–24).

In his New Year's press conference of January 14, 1975, addressing the criticism of the torture of Democratic Youth and Student League (*Mincheong-hakryeon*) members as a violation of human rights, Park called it a case of "the ringleaders being imprisoned and brought to trial for their conspiracy to rebel and overthrow the current government" and avoided responding to allegations of torture. In the process, Park claimed, "freedom and rights are not absolute. They are guaranteed within the constitution and the limits of the law." Regarding the opposition forces who argued that "freedom and rights are natural, absolute, and inviolable, and even the constitution or law cannot restrict them," Park responded sharply, "That is wrong. . . . Even though the freedom to criticize the government is guaranteed by our country's law, the freedom to overthrow the government through violence is not guaranteed" (5:379).[38]

Even so, as Korea's constitutional government stipulated liberal democracy, Park could not arbitrarily sidestep the guarantee of human rights as emphasized by individualist liberalism. It was on the anniversary of the Universal Declaration of Human Rights (December 10) that this problem was most sensitively felt, and Park had to reveal his official stance. Perhaps due to this, after coming into power, Park gave a commemorative speech or words of appreciation on its anniversary every year from 1962 to 1970.[39]

The speeches given by Park on the anniversary exhibit a typical structure. First he referenced the Universal Declaration of Human Rights as the solemn statement of the noble dignity of humanity and respect for natural freedom and rights, while addressing the history of the struggles to win human rights and the value of their guarantee.[40] Then he stressed the responsibility and obligation that accompanies the rights and freedom guaranteed in the declaration and emphasized this with his understanding that the "rule of law" to guarantee human rights usually refers to the obligation of public officials and citizens to abide by the law.[41] However, Park Chung-hee kept silent on the truth of his government's violations of citizens' rights and instead stressed the threat of endless armed provocations by North Korea. At the same time he criticized the deprivation of the people's basic rights and freedoms in the North Korean communist regime and communism in general, describing the people as suffering like slaves. In addition, he stated that the South Korean government was working hard to address pressing issues like liberation from poverty and economic prosperity so that human rights could become fully realized in that nation. Accordingly, he called for the active participation of the people in the economic growth and modernization of the fatherland.[42] In sum, Park argued that the guarantee of human rights was being more sincerely realized in the liberal democratic system of the South than in the North and resolved the need for reunification in order to secure the liberation of North Korean brethren. Through this rhetorical device he masked the dissatisfaction of ordinary South Koreans regarding their own human-rights situation by urging active participation of the people in the efforts of the government to do everything in their power to stimulate economic growth, modernization, and, finally, reunification.

It is interesting that after Park declared a state of national emergency in 1971 and installed the Yusin Constitution in 1972 he stopped giving a commemorative speech or words of appreciation on the anniversary of the Universal Declaration of Human Rights. Instead during these years he often issued speeches or statements at the National Saemaeul Leaders Convention, held around that time, and from 1975 to 1976 he actually hosted it on December 10, the declaration's very anniversary. Perhaps Park shied away from giving a commemorative speech when his own Yusin regime directly infringed on liberal democratic constitutional law. Or it is likely that Park had become fed up with the phrase *human rights* because it had become a powerful weapon of opposition forces and the US Carter administration in their criticism of the Yusin regime. In any case, it can be said that, by avoiding showing even minimal concern regarding human rights, Park tacitly acknowledged that the Yusin regime, which had been established to guarantee his permanent rule, was "antiliberalist."

CONCLUDING REMARKS

So far Park Chung-hee's conservatism has been discussed from the perspective of "antiliberal conservatism for modernization." In chapters 2 and 3 nonsimultaneity and sanctification are outlined as the two most outstanding characteristics of the ideological topography of Korean contemporary politics. Such characteristics can also be observed in Park Chung-hee's conservatism. First, one of the notable characteristics of Korean conservatism—particularly that of Park Chung-hee, in which authoritarian order is not justified and built upon for its own sake but under the pretext of defending liberal democracy—can be understood as the complex and contradictory phenomenon created by the dialectic of nonsimultaneity. It is an outcome of the collision between the imposition of world historical time that presented liberal democracy as the universal model to Korea and the resistance of Korean historical time that pushed for authoritarian order. In addition, unlike nineteenth-century European conservatives who strongly opposed capitalist industrialization, the core of modernization, Park Chung-hee's conservatism was a future-oriented conservatism for modernization (seen as an oxymoron in Western history) that rapidly pushed its capitalist industrialization agenda as a part of its modernization attempt to catch up with the West during the latter half of the twentieth century. In other words, from a Western perspective Park's conservatism, which can be seen as a complex and contradictory combination of conservative and progressive elements, may well be interpreted as having been caused by the dialectic of nonsimultaneity.[43] Moreover, as examined in chapter 4, Park's conservatism for modernization attempted to restore the loss of its legitimacy by dressing itself up as an appeal for democracy. However, in this process Park's conservatism, combined with a democracy discourse and its proposal of the future blueprint—"national reunification" and "affluent welfare state"—completed its vision of the sanctification of nationalism. This subject is fully discussed in chapter 6, which examines Park Chung-hee's nationalist discourse.

NOTES

1. One may well wonder if we can find liberalism in Park Chung-hee's political thought at all. But Park's views of liberalism can be reconstructed through his

negative statement of it, which is revealed in the process of examining his political discourse. The relationship between conservative and antiliberal elements on the one hand and nationalism on the other in Park's thought are addressed in chapter 6.

2. Jeon In-gwon's work is exceptional in this regard. Through his detailed analysis of Park's books and speeches, Jeon investigates Park's political thought from various perspectives such as "elitism," "statism," "reservation about democracy or instrumental view of democracy," "power politics (*realpolitik*)," and so on (2006, 326–32). In contrast, this book adopts a strategy to approach Park's political thought from universal categories of modern Western political ideologies such as conservatism, liberalism, nationalism, and democracy. In addition, my interpretation of Park's view of liberty is different from Jeon's, as is shown later in this chapter.

3. Of course, there are many works that discuss anticommunism and developmentalism (or economy first) as part of the ruling ideology or dominant discourse during Park's reign (e.g., Choi Jang-jip and Lee Seong-hyeong 1991; Cho Hui-yeon 2003b; Kim Jeong-hun and Cho Hui-yeon 2003; Lee Kwang-il 2003). It should be noted, however, that ideational elements deduced from the nature of the regime and its policies or the ruling ideology do not directly translate into Park's personal political thought. In this sense, studies that approach Park's conservatism in a systematic and comprehensive way are rather rare.

4. Park's political thought, which ceaselessly stresses "the stark reality we are facing," can be thought of as political thought conjuring up crisis and emergency. We delve into this subject in chapter 6.

5. Park's view of politics is strongly state-centered in the sense that the state precedes politics, rejecting the pluralist conception of politics that acknowledges the pervasive presence of politics and power in a variety of human associations including the state.

6. See Jeon In-gwon 2006 (257–60) for the statist aspect of Park's thought.

7. Carl Schmitt's theory of sovereign dictatorship is discussed more fully in chapter 6.

8. Of course Park made many statements defending political-party and parliamentary politics, in ritual or in principle, when giving speeches and addresses on official occasions—like Constitution Day, the presidential inauguration ceremony, and the opening session of the National Assembly. These statements were made more frequently during the Third Republic than during the Yusin regime, which incapacitated the politics of political parties and parliament. However, as examined in chapter 4, he maintained throughout his rule a belief that Western democracy is not suited to Korean political situations.

9. Park made a similar statement at the following year's New Year's press conference, on January 11, 1972 (4:133).

10. Of course it was intended to suppress not only political opponents but also the labor movement, which had a potentially strong socialist orientation.

11. Allegedly, in December 1970, in his inaugural address as chief of the KCIA, Lee Hu-rak announced, "The Korean Central Intelligence Agency (KCIA) is the bastion of state security. The state security is the security of the president. To protect and defend the president is in itself to protect and defend the state. We are in the vanguard

of protecting and defending President Park" (quoted in Jungangilboteukbyeolchwi-jaetim 1998, 28). Here it is interesting to confirm that public security to defend Park's authoritarian regime domestically was the same as the state security: "state security = regime security = Park's personal security."

12. The original name of this meeting was, from 1970 to 1972, the Central Meeting for Public Order and Reservist Officials, but it was renamed the Central Meeting for Nationwide Public Order and Reservist Officials in 1973. Pyongyang dispatched armed guerillas to South Korea twice in 1968. In order to provide for such contingencies, the Homeland Reserve Forces were created that year, and the government started holding the annual Central Meeting at the beginning of 1970.

13. In the "Special Statement on National Security and the Current Situation," issued on April 29, 1975, Park attributed the communization of Vietnam and Cambodia to the "political instability and unrest" resulting from their "division of state opinion and disunity within the people" (5:425).

14. To Park, long hair and miniskirts were symbols of decadent trends of foreign origin. See Kang Jun-man 2002 (110–16) regarding Park's hatred of long hair and the political implication of the crackdown on these trends.

15. National ethics, which had been adopted into the high school curriculum since 1963 and was enforced as one of the liberal arts requirements at the college level in the 1970s, contained anticommunism education as its main element. National-history education, which was strengthened with the cause of establishing the national subjectivity and thus included the history of "overcoming state crises" as its important subject matter, contributed to promoting security concerns (Jang Young-min 2008).

16. Kim Jeong-hun and Cho Hui-yeon (2003) define the whole of South Korean society as a "society disciplined by anticommunism." They further argue that the Park regime had "completely reorganized South Korean civil society in a military mode and imposed military culture upon it." Noting this "militarization and regimentation" of Korean society, they call Korean society during the Park regime a "society regimented by anticommunism" (130).

17. Park designated 1963 as the "Year of Export" and November 30 as "Export Day." Then he began to cite business people who made great contributions to export. Kang Jun-man notes that the "exports first" doctrine was a "kind of faith" in the Park regime (2004a, 277) and estimates that Park was a "powerful and competent general commander of exports" (2004b, 13).

18. For more on the concepts of development and developmentalism and their origin in social sciences, see Douglas Lummis 1996 (58–60).

19. When Choi Jang-jip and Lee Seong-hyeong (1991) discuss the dominant ideologies of the Park regime, they point out that, "once anticommunism and authoritarianism were grafted upon developmentalism, dominant ideologies shifted from a passive and defensive posture to an active and offensive one" (218–19).

20. Such phrases as "live well," "let's live well," and "we are determined to live well" appeared frequently in Park's speeches, not only during the period of the Third Republic but also during the Yusin regime.

21. During Rhee's and Park's reigns North Korea was regarded a rebel illegally occupying the northern part of the Korean Peninsula. So the phrase "unification of the

national territory" was frequently used, but "national (re)unification" was rarely used in the mainstream.

22. Park, in his press conference in 1966 on the third anniversary of his inauguration, stated that "the proposal that our government will discuss earnestly the matter of unification in the late 1970s" means "that we will be able to take the matter on full-scale and boldly in the late 1970s after we succeed in building our state power for ten years henceforth" and stressed that "in order to deal with the matter of reunification successfully . . . we have to secure a status and capacity far more advantageous and superior to the Northern puppet and then engage the matter" (December 17, 1966, 2:886–87). However, Park's doctrine of "construction first, then unification" has been criticized for being a de facto strategy to suspend the unification matter and preempt and suppress the free discussion of it, as shown in chapter 3. Park's unification policy is addressed more fully in chapter 6.

23. This point is elaborated in chapter 3.

24. Benedict Anderson (1985) and Anthony Smith (1999) have already pointed to this dualistic aspect in the nationalism of many newly independent states in the postwar world.

25. A similar remark is found in Park's speech of March 30, 1967 (2:982–83).

26. In *The Rhetoric of Reaction* (1991), Albert Hirschman makes an interesting classification of the rhetoric of reaction into three theses: "futility, jeopardy, perversity." Park's logic here approaches the jeopardy thesis.

27. The antiliberal nature of Park's political thought is addressed further when Park's nationalism and statism are examined in chapter 6.

28. Kim Dong-chun (1996a) makes a persuasive point about the poverty of liberalism and the predominance of nationalism in contemporary Korean political thought constituting different sides of the same coin (298, 302). There is, however, a subtle disagreement over whether the poverty of liberalism has brought about the predominance of nationalism or the preemptive strengthening of nationalism has caused the poverty of liberalism. Although this disagreement is not well recognized, it is a subject worth close examination. Overall, Kim Dong-chun holds the former position, but I join Park Myeong-lim (1996a) and Shin Gi-Wook (2009) in holding the latter.

29. In this context it seems useful to note that Sheldon Wolin (2004) distinguishes the tradition of democratic radicalism from that of liberalism intermingled in the history of modern Western political thought and then denies the conventional interpretation of liberalism as subversive ideology armed with revolutionary fervor. Wolin further reinterprets liberalism as the "philosophy of sobriety" reflecting "timidity" and "prudence," typical attributes of the middle class (263–68). If we follow this new interpretation, it becomes easier to understand the premature turn after liberation to reactionism by the propertied class of South Korea, including leading and ordinary members of the conservative Korea Democratic Party, who threw themselves into the arms of anticommunism due to their horror of communism. In this regard we may find greater similarity between the European bourgeoisie in the nineteenth century and the Korean propertied class in the late twentieth century than their conventional contrast.

30. Park (1962) considered domestic and international situations threats to national freedom. The former notably included "the domestic economic situation such as

poverty, famine, and unemployment" and the latter, "the aggression of communist imperialism masterminding the Northern puppet" (41).

31. At the same time, Park (1962) pointed out in a book published immediately after the coup that this logic applied only to postcolonial countries such as South Korea (40).

32. Thus Hobbes makes the following statement: "There is written on the turrets of the city of Lucca in great characters at this day, the word LIBERTAS; yet, no man can thence infer that a particular man has more liberty or immunity from the service of the commonwealth there than in Constantinople. Whether a commonwealth be monarchical or popular, the freedom is still the same" (Hobbes 1962, xxi, 162). Of course, we should not overlook that Hobbes bestowed radical and atomistic freedom on individuals in the state of nature.

33. Here Park's concept of freedom almost coincides with what Hobbes defines as the liberty of subjects. To Hobbes, "the Liberty of Subjects" does not mean "an exemption from laws." It means "that in all kinds of actions by the laws praetermitted, men have the liberty, of doing what their own reasons shall suggest, for the most profitable to themselves" (Hobbes 1962, xxi, 161).

34. In this context the Yusin Constitution placed a legal suspension on most individual rights and, furthermore, eliminated the comprehensive clause stipulated in the constitution of the Third Republic that prohibited the violation of the essential elements of basic rights under any circumstances (Article 32, Clause 2). As a result, the guarantee of basic rights shifted from the natural-law tradition to legal positivism. Moreover, the Yusin Constitution stipulated the presidential authority to declare an emergency decree that would make possible the temporary suspension of people's (*gungmin*) liberties and rights. Thus, as was shown in the political history of the Yusin regime, the liberty and freedom of the people fell into a defenseless state, being exposed to the arbitrary exercise of power by the regime.

35. Criticizing political opponents who asserted the freedom of the press during the Yusin regime, Park employed similar rhetoric ("New Year's Press Conference," January 19, 1979, 16:48).

36. Thus Park's concept of freedom—which insisted that individual freedom serve the common good of the state and the nation and criticized "selfishness that had no regard for the state and the nation"—parts company with Hobbes's, which allows individual selfishness "in all kinds of actions by the laws praetermitted," as quoted previously in note 33.

37. Immediately after President Rhee resigned after the fallout of the student-led April Revolution, Park reportedly said privately in reaction to the argument that postwar Japan's successful economic reconstruction was made possible by the efforts of Japanese liberals, "Liberals? What can we make of liberals? It is the spirit of nationalists that has made today's Japan. We have to learn their spirit" (quoted in Cho Gab-je 1998, 187).

38. In appreciation addresses or commemorative speeches given on the anniversary of the Universal Declaration of Human Rights until 1970, Park frequently referenced human rights as inalienable natural rights in accordance with the spirit of the declaration. However, as indicated earlier, his frame for human rights changed from

natural law to legal positivism in his speeches and addresses given after the installation of the Yusin Constitution.

39. Excepting 1964, when he did not give a speech on the anniversary as he was paying a visit to West Germany at that time.

40. This kind of declaratory remark by Park, which seemed to defend human rights in the natural-law tradition, did not contradict the restrictions of freedom and rights by the positive law. This was also true of Hobbes, who conceived of the state of nature and civil society as discontinuous moments.

41. Here Park emphasizes the "rule of law" mainly in terms of the obligation of public officials and citizens to observe the law. According to modern constitutionalism, however, the "rule of law" as opposed to the "rule by men [humans]" or "rule by law" is not primarily intended to emphasize the law-abidingness of the people but to focus primarily on the prevention of the violation of human rights by rulers. People's obligation to obey the law is what the rulers have invariably and historically stressed.

42. Here the summarized contents are distilled from Park's commemorative speeches given in 1967 (3:97–98), 1968 (3:385–86), and 1969 (3:643–44).

43. Noting this contradictory aspect, Jeon Jae-ho (2000) characterizes Park's political thought as "reactionary modernist."

Chapter 6

Discourses on Nationalism

Park Chung-hee's nationalism is the subject most proliferating in the research of his political thought. Given the purpose of this chapter, what attracts our attention in the studies of Park's nationalism are those that focus on the "nationalist" character of his political thought, which is usually equated with the nature of his regime, from a normative perspective, applying the researchers' own concept of nationalism to the research. In this regard Jeon Jae-ho (1997) categorizes the trend in research on Park's nationalism into three approaches: the first approach characterizes and accepts Park's political thought as nationalism; the second interprets it as shifting from nationalism in the beginning to antinationalism later; and the third regards it categorically as "antinationalism" or "the absence of nationalism" (4–12).[1] Examining not only the political character of the Park regime (with a special focus on the May 16 military coup d'état and the Yusin system) but also political ideologies revealed in Park's speeches and books and the policies his regime implemented—such as the Korea-Japan Normalization Treaty, industrial and economic policies, anticommunism and North Korean policies, and traditional-culture-promotion policies—these studies have passed normative judgment as to whether they are really nationalist.[2]

However, as Michel Foucault's theory of discourse in his 1980 book *Power/Knowledge* has shown so persuasively, the *problematique* (i.e., whether the Park regime or Park Chung-hee as a political leader was genuinely nationalistic) is misleading and obscuring at best. Clinging to a true/false dichotomy, the *problematique* has the discursive effect of leading us to overlook the crucial fact that nationalism in Korean politics has constituted the realm of the most intense discursive struggles between ruling and oppositional forces.[3] Thus drawing upon Foucault's insight, this chapter examines Park's discourse on nationalism with the premise that the question as to whether his nationalism was true or false is less important than whether it was effective in practice. When Park's discourse on nationalism was effective—organizing and regulating relations of power successfully—it produced a "regime of truth":

> The important thing here . . . is that truth isn't outside power, or lacking in power. . . . Truth is a thing of this world: It is produced only by virtue of multiple forms of constraint. And it induces regular effects of power. Each society has its regime of truth, its "general politics" of truth; that is, the types of discourse which it accepts and makes function as true; the mechanisms and instances which enable one to distinguish true and false statements; the means by which each is sanctioned; the techniques and procedures accorded value in the acquisition of truth; the status of those who are charged with saying what counts as true. (Foucault 1980, 131)[4]

If we step aside from the normative question of whether Park Chung-hee was a "true" nationalist and then pay close attention to the actualized reality, it is not difficult to confirm that, among Korean presidents, Park produced nationalist discourses most ardently and circulated them most widely. In contrast to preceding political leaders, Park took advantage of nationalist discourses vigorously, making them the most dominant in Korean politics. He actively incorporated anticommunism, economic development (or modernization), statism, and national or Korean-style democracy into nationalism, and he marginalized or excluded from it procedural democracy, economic democracy, South-North talks, and unification problems. In this way, the Park regime set up economic development and state security (or anticommunism) as the foremost objectives of nationalism and excluded or marginalized the unification discourse that had been promoted vigorously and propagated widely by progressive forces during the Second Republic (1960–1961) and was also considered essential to nationalism by the general populace (Jeon Jae-ho 1997, 23). We might well estimate that the Park regime was successful in this task regardless of whether or not we agree with it.

In this way nationalist discourse constituted the core of the dominant discourse that the Park regime produced and utilized to secure popular support for the regime and to maximize popular mobilization for economic development. However, a serious academic account of Park's nationalism that systematically analyzes his discourses on nation and nationalism, which were scattered throughout his books and speeches, seems to be rather rare.[5] In order to close this gap in the preceding works on Park's nationalism, this chapter intends to systematically reconstruct his discourses on nationalism and articulate their characteristics more clearly by conducting an elaborate analysis of his books and speeches.

To do this, first, the implication of the nonsimultaneity dialectic for nationalism in Korea is explored. Then, Park's nationalism is characterized as "state/statist nationalism" based on the indissoluble bond of the nation and the state. Third, there is an investigation into how anticommunism (national security) and economic development, two important pillars of Park's conservatism, are related to his nationalism. Fourth, his unification discourse is analyzed in connection with nationalism. Finally, it is noted that Park's nationalist discourse did not reign supreme in Korean politics and that it was subject to severe attack (criticism) from opposition forces in government or movement politics. In this sense, it is shown that nationalism was the site of most intense discursive struggles and Park's nationalism was a double-edged sword.

NONSIMULTANEITY AND KOREAN NATIONALISM

If modernization (or economic development) is considered to be the core of Park Chung-hee's discourse on nationalism, the following statement by Choi Jang-jip (1996) grasps the intimate relationship between the nonsimultaneity dialectic and the nationalist aspiration in a telling way:

> When capitalism, as a system of production and exchange, is organized at a global level, the units that constitute this system in economic and political terms are national states. This indicates that a structure of spatial inequality has been created as a consequence of the regional variance between the center and the periphery in the developmental process of the world capitalist system. . . . Using the analogy of a wave, Gellner once defined the rise of nationalism as a series of movements in response to the wave of capitalist modernization as it swept into different countries with varying degrees of temporal delay. From this perspective, nationalism can be seen as a struggle on the part of late-developing peripheral capitalist states to rise to central status and, at the same time, as the ideology that undergirds this struggle. . . . As long as the nation-state remains the basic unit of world capitalist competition, it is inevitable that nationalism remain the dominant ideology. (197)

According to this viewpoint, modernization, as pursued by latecomer countries in order to catch up with early comers, is a spatial movement aimed at moving from the periphery to the center, premised on the "unequal space" created by the global capitalist system. It is also a temporal historical process that attempts to overcome nonsimultaneity produced by the discrepancy between the world and local historical times. Nationalism in latecomer countries, then, has been fundamentally characterized by their dualistic attempt to cope with spatial inequality in the form of the rupture between center and periphery, on the one hand, and nonsimultaneity created by the uneven coexistence of world and local historical times, on the other. As the insights offered by Anthony Smith (2000), Ernest Gellner (1995), and Partha Chatterjee (1986) demonstrate, in other words, nationalism in latecomer countries has been an ideology used as part of a collective effort to resolve the insecurity and contradictions brought about by nonsimultaneity.

It is useful to compare the experience of Western early comers with that of Korea more specifically. England and France completed the tasks of nationalism in a relatively smooth and sequential way from the building of a unified nation-state through industrialization to democracy under conditions in which territorial integrity and the protonation were formed stably in dynastic states. In contrast, most newly independent states in the non-Western world failed in autonomous modernization efforts, fell into a colonial state, and gained independence only after the end of World War II. Thus they were confronted with more compressed multidimensional tasks, such as building a nation-state including national unification or integration, industrialization (modernization), democratization, and the like, as the goal of nationalism. However, they were ill-equipped to carry out these tasks simultaneously from the beginning for various reasons. There also arose intense conflicts over prioritizing multiple tasks among contending nationalists who espoused different ideologies at the same time, as well as inevitable collisions of diverse kinds when carrying out individual tasks. Besides, rightist and leftist ideologies such as liberalism and socialism, respectively, appeared almost at the same time and competed intensely with one another to win and preempt nationalism, which would sanctify their blueprint of a future state envisaged by their own ideological designs. In this way ideological conflicts between leftists and rightists have been intensified even within nationalism, as examined in chapter 3.

STATE NATIONALISM GUIDED BY AN INFALLIBLE LEADER

The most notable feature found in Park Chung-hee's nationalist discourses is state nationalism based on the indissoluble bond between the state and the nation. This reached its climax in state nationalism guided by an infallible leader with the advent of the Yusin regime, which enabled him to stay in power permanently.

Historical and Personal Background

In his congratulatory address on the forty-seventh anniversary of the March First Movement in 1966, Park Chung-hee defined the spirit of that movement as a "symbol" of the "national soul" that announced all over the world that "the autonomous subjectivity, independence and prosperity of the nation, and world peace are our nation's . . . cherished wish" (March 1, 1966, 2:261). This statement fits well with the common definition of *nationalism* as "the ideology and movement seeking the unification, independence, and development" of a nation (Maruyama 1997, 323). Most Western scholars tend to understand nationalism as a modern phenomenon. For example, as cited earlier in chapter 3, Ernest Gellner (1983) defines *nationalism* as "a political principle, which holds that the political and the national unit should be congruent" (1). In contrast to this, most Koreans tend to believe that such congruence was naturally achieved in premodern times, so they take for granted the primordial existence of the nation.[6] In addition, as a result of this belief, when Koreans lost their state sovereignty to Japanese imperialism in the early twentieth century, the trauma incurred from the loss of the natural congruence was such a great shock that their attachment to the state as well as the nation became all the more desperate.[7] Moreover, due to the division of Korea into South and North Korea, the national wish for restoring congruence foundered once again. At the same time, as the regimes in South and North were engaged in a deadly struggle to win the status of legitimate representative of national history, the attachment to the nation by the contending regimes (i.e., "nation complex") became all the more intensified among Koreans.

Thus the emergence and formation of state nationalism based on the indissoluble bond between the state and the nation can be explained in the following way: First, Koreans had acquired a deep nationalism, a long-held pride in an unprecedented single and pure nation based on a single ethnicity inherited from Dangun, legendary founder of Old Joseon (Gojoseon). This national consciousness was wounded as a result of modern traumatic experiences like the loss of sovereignty to Japanese imperialism, the colonial experience, the national division, and the June 25 War. In particular, during Japanese colonial rule Korea suffered the shock of losing its "natural congruence of the state and the nation" for the first time in its history, becoming a "nation without a state." This has morbidly impassioned Koreans about nationalism. Second, statism in Korea was strengthened by strong attachment to the state once lost to Japanese imperialism—a fascist view of the state imposed and internalized by Japanese militarism—and by the statism in a divided state that insisted on representing the whole nation exclusive of the North Korean regime. When wounded nationalism and overblown statism are combined as in Korea, it does not seem surprising to witness the emergence of a Korean brand of state nationalism,[8] which would be more pronounced later during the reign of Park Chung-hee.

In addition to such historical factors, Park Chung-hee's nationalist discourse embodied state nationalism more intensely due to his personal background. Of course, Park must have also internalized national history into his own life by experiencing a personally painful time as a member of a stateless nation during Japanese colonial rule and unprecedented national ordeals such as the national division and the June 25 War. Moreover, due to his lifelong experience as a soldier, which began with his education in military academies both during Japanese colonial rule and in South Korea, he internalized a deeply statist mentality and discipline. Therefore he can be understood as one of those who embodied state nationalism most extremely. State nationalism in Korea, brewed from the indissoluble coagulation of the state and nation, both of which were conceived of as monolithic and sacred, was further strengthened by Park Chung-hee. Thus the state nationalism he embodied came to acquire an enormous weight and invincible sacredness that would deny—even transcend—the autonomy of individuals and civil society.

Park's Discourses on Nation and Nationalism: National Conscience and the General Will

Koreans have imagined the nation as a single monolithic entity transcending the sum total of individual members since the late nineteenth century, absent of the experience of the individualist liberal revolution that took place in Western Europe (Schmid 2002). Such terms as *national soul, national spirit, national vital force*, and the like had been coined and widely circulated, especially during Japanese colonial rule, to encourage the morale of the nation deprived of the state. These concepts, however, have unconsciously forced Koreans to imagine the nation as a single personality, which does not admit the distinctiveness and individuality of each national member. In this light, Park Chung-hee also said in his New Year's address in 1962 that "a nation has a permanent life" (January 1, 1962, 1:158). Thus he frequently represented the nation as a single personality by using phrases such as "the conscience of the nation" and "national conscience."[9]

If a nation were supposed to have an intuitive conscience that did not admit a pluralist conception and ambiguous realm, it would be quite evident that, just as a person could not have two consciences at the same time, those who are insensitive to or opposed to the national conscience were ipso facto to be branded "antination(al)" or "nonnation(al)." When Park discussed the harmony and conflict between individual interest and the interest of the whole in his book *Uri Minjogui Nagal Gil* (The path for our nation to take; 1962), his definition inevitably harbored very collectivist and statist implications:

> But the individual interest and the interest of the whole are more likely to oppose each other than harmonize. The "principle of equity," that is, social justice, is restored when such opposition and conflict are properly recon-ciled. When the interest of the whole and individual interest are found to be opposed and conflictual, the congruence should be struck out by sacrificing

and regulating the individual. When the individual interest and the interest of the whole are found to be opposed and conflictual, exploring and discovering the congruence between the two by controlling and checking the self is what is called "good sense." When this is viewed from the national perspective, it may well be "national conscience." Social justice that enables our nation as a whole to prosper will be realized when good sense is restored and national conscience resurrected. (29)

Park's national conscience seems to share a lot with the *general will* Rousseau coined and stressed in *The Social Contract*. Just as national conscience is always right, so is Rousseau's general will (Rousseau 1967, II, iii, 30–32). Just as the national conscience is a concept evident and intuitively clear to every Korean, the general will is something very "clear and luminous" and thus easy to perceive by an uncorrupted citizen (ibid., IV, i, 109). Just as the national conscience is directly linked to the realization of social justice, the general will is directed toward equality, common interest, justice, and equity (ibid., II, i, 27–28; II, iii, 30–32; II, iv, 33). Just as the general will is indivisible and indestructible (ibid., II, ii, 28–30; IV, i, 109–11), so too the national conscience. Just as the Korean nation could not be destroyed, no matter how severe Japanese colonial rule might have been, neither could the national conscience be destroyed. Moreover, just as Park stressed that individual Koreans had to discover congruence through their sacrifice and self-control in accordance with the national conscience when the interest of the whole and that of an individual are in opposition, for Rousseau each individual has to put "in common his person and his whole power under the supreme direction of the general will" (ibid., I, vi, 18–19). In other words, just as Rousseau's citizen in *The Social Contract* has to constantly internalize the indestructible and indivisible general will and guide his individual will in accordance with it, so the Korean people have to internalize the national conscience and regulate their action in accordance with it, following the creed of nationalism to pursue the independence, unification, and prosperity of the nation.

However, it cannot be denied that there is an unbridgeable gulf between Park's national conscience and Rousseau's general will. Whereas the general will manifests itself through citizens' direct participation in legislative activity in Rousseau's ideal polity, Park's national conscience is not to be discovered and legislated through such participation. Rather, it would be identified and guided by a supreme political leader under dictatorships such as the Park regime. Yet, as we witness historically the case when the general will was utilized to justify the Jacobin dictatorship during the French Revolution, it is apparent the general will could also be abused in the same way. Thus it seems plausible to interpret that it also contained a totalitarian or collectivist character to a certain extent, as some of Rousseau's commentators have pointed out.

Statist Discourse: The System of "Total Unity as a Whole" in Accord with the Military Model

In addition to having a strong collectivist conception of the nation, Park Chung-hee was also the incarnation of the statist mentality.[10] His lifelong military career functioned as a decisive background for cultivating and strengthening statist thinking. In a speech given at the ceremony of his discharge from military service in 1963, which would enable him to participate in the upcoming civilian politics, Park defined the mission of a soldier. "The death of a soldier even transcending his own death in an extreme life-and-death situation," he said, "is the culmination of the spirit of sacrifice willing to throw out his small self—as if it were bits of straw—for the sake of justice and truth" and thus the "glorious and sacred mission only a soldier can bear" (August 30, 1963, 1:489). This definition of the mission combined with his statist thinking led to the justification of the military coup in his own way, as Park asserted in the same speech that "the value of the state based on this sacred death is to be confirmed only as long as human rights are guaranteed in justice and truth, but the revolution is inevitable once the state, the supposed embodiment of such values, is on the brink of ruin, even before realizing such values" (ibid.). This speech shows clearly Park's justification of his coup, how a soldier armed with statist thinking could overthrow the government (or the state) in an extreme situation. At the same time, it reveals the quintessence of the statist thought in Park as a soldier by defining the soldier as willing to throw out his "small self" (life) "as if it were bits of straw," for the state, the embodiment of "justice and truth."

When Park was asked at his New Year's press conference in 1970 what was meant by "spiritual modernization" as opposed to "material modernization," he stressed the establishment of "sound morals as *gungmin*" and "social ethics" and then pointed to the internalization of statism as the essence of spiritual modernization: "We usually say that such behavior as paying loyalty and service to the state, and in particular sacrificing oneself to work for the state, is the most beautiful and exemplary action among human activities, and that such behavior is as good as living by the great cause" (January 9, 1970, 3:686). Accordingly, Park continued to say that we called "our individual I the 'small self'" (*soa*) and "the State as enlarged and extended I the 'big self'" (*daea*), defining "our nation" as "the 'big self' as enlarged I" like the state. In this way he confirmed that the nation and the state as the "big self" were inseparable and interchangeable (ibid.). He then elaborated on his reply: "The fatherland and the nation in our phrases such as modernization of the fatherland and national regeneration mean that the "big self" as enlarged I refers to the fatherland and the nation. This also means that our willing participation in and service for the modernization of the fatherland and national regeneration is not something we do for others but something we do for ourselves, something we do for posterity. We have to acquire firmly our awareness of joint responsibility and common destiny" (ibid., 3:688).

The expression of such statist mentality as embodied in Park as a career soldier had been a frequent refrain whenever he admonished soldiers regarding the sacrificial spirit for the state and the nation and eulogized or mourned their deaths in his presidential instructions at the graduation ceremonies of military academies (including naval and air force), as well as when giving presidential statements on the anniversaries of the June 25 War.[11] Therefore it was utterly impossible to conceptualize the state as the outcome of a voluntary contract that individuals holding various ideas, values, and interests conclude to preserve their own lives, liberty, and property—that is, to conceptualize the state pluralistically and instrumentally.

Hence, reflecting Park's militaristic and statist mentality, many words and phrases stressing unity (solidarity), mobilization, and obedience in perfect order and thereby reminiscent of totalitarianism were poured out in his speeches addressed to the general populace, all the more so after 1971, when he declared a state emergency. Favorite words such as *gungrontongil* (unity of state opinion), which enabled him to suppress the expression of diverse opinions as *gungronbunyeol* (division of state opinion), are representative. In addition, words with the prefix *chong-* (all-out), which has the connotation of military mobilization, appeared increasingly in phrases such as *chongjingun* (all-out military advance), *chongdongwon* (all-out mobilization), *chongmaejin* (all-out engagement), and *chonggwolgi* (all-out stand-up). In addition, words prefixed by *chonghwa-* (all-out harmony) or *chongnyeok-* (all-out effort) decorated many speeches at various occasions: *chongnyeokanbo* (security by all-out effort), *chonghwayusin* (revitalizing reform by all-out harmony), *gungminchonghwa* (all-out harmony of *gungmin*), *chonghwahoguk* (protection of the state by all-out harmony), *minbonchonghwa* (people-centered all-out harmony), *chonghwadangyeol* (unity by all-out harmony), *chonghwajeonjin* (advance by all-out harmony), *chongnyeokcheje* (the system by all-out effort), *chonghwaui daehaengjin* (grand march by all-out harmony), and so on. As a notable example, in his New Year's message in 1974 Park Chung-hee mentioned *"chonghwayusin,"* *"gungminchonghwa,"* and *"chongnyeokanbotaese"* (security posture by all-out effort), and finally, the *"chonghwacheje"* (the system by all-out harmony), as he called the comprehensive version of the Yusin system (January 1, 1974, 5:193–95). As a matter of course, the usage of such words should be interpreted as announcing Park's will to not admit any kind of dissent and opposition to his government and its policies. Then it was rather natural that Park, who held such a statist mentality, abhorred elections, representative politics, and party politics that sought to institutionalize political conflicts on the basis of democratic principles, as we examine in chapter 4.

As an extension of such thinking by Park, the state and the *gungmin* were in fact identified with the military. So, even in nonmilitary affairs and policies, teachers, public servants, business persons, college students, workers, peasants, and the *gungmin* in general were often called "soldier," "army," or "warrior" missioned with industry, export, construction, production, modernization of the fatherland, building of a self-reliant economy, making history, national regeneration, national unification, reconstruction of the fatherland, and the like. Indeed, it was meaningless for Park to distinguish between civilian affairs and national-defense areas, for he frequently identified the "building of a self-reliant economy and modernization of the fatherland" with "national security" (January 23, 1966, 2:596–97; January 9, 1970, 3:670). Thus the statist mentality of the solider would of course apply to the everyday life of the *gungmin*. The Park regime expanded, arranged, and applied this statist spirit to make it the general guideline of *gungmin* life. The final outcome was the Charter of National Education proclaimed in December 1968, which began with the famous sentence "We are born in this land with the historical mission for national regeneration."[12]

According to this statist thinking, public servants who committed irregularity and corruption were often condemned as "state traitors." In his New Year's press conference held in 1969, Park declared, "In this great [era] when we are launching the historic task of national regeneration . . . those who commit irregularities or corrupt their conscience" are "traitors to the state" (January 10, 1969, 3:430). Of course such public servants might well be decried as "antinational" as well as "antistate." For Park to say that a corrupt public servant should not only be condemned for committing individual wrongdoing (misconduct) but also be defined as a traitor to the state dramatically indicates how incompatible statism is with liberalism.

Indissoluble Bond of the State and Nation Led by a Supreme Leader (*Yeongdoja*)

In Park Chung-hee's speeches the state and the nation, both of which were indivisible and monolithic, appeared frequently as a pair in various combinations,[13] such that state nationalism based on the indissoluble bond between the state and nation became a more impenetrable entity. Here what is meant by "appeared . . . as a pair" is that the two words were not only juxtaposed directly but also in paired phrases, each word accompanied by various modifiers and predicates: "modernization of the fatherland" and "national regeneration"; "the development of the fatherland" and "the glory of the nation [*minjok*]"; "unification of the state territory" and "national regeneration"; "right view of the state [*gukga*] and correct national consciousness"; "saving the nation [*gyere*] . . . defending the country [*nara*]"; "devoting a noble life to the fatherland for the sake of the nation [*gyere*]"; "nation [*gyere*] more than an individual, state [*gukga*] more than a group"; "guard the state territory and protect the nation [*minjok*]"; and so on. Even the phrase "state nation" appeared often, even four times in a short speech (October 3, 1963, 1:537–38).

Because Park was armed with such strong state nationalism, he was not satisfied with the common moral conception of selfishness (egoism) as seeking only one's own interest while disregarding others and redefined it, expanding public mores to include the state and nation as "others." Hence, as I briefly mention in chapter 5 as well, *selfishness* was redefined as seeking only one's own interest "in disregard of the state and the nation" (January 15, 1976, 6:29). He further politicized selfishness by denouncing that if "the extreme selfishness [of thinking that] it is all right for me to eat well and to live well [regardless of] what happens to others, and [that] this is also freedom," became a prevalent ethos, it would do harm to "unity and all-out harmony of the *gungmin*" (January 12, 1973, 5:23). Of course, throughout his rule following the military coup, Park criticized the selfishness of politicians, business persons, workers, and college students and stressed the mission and patriotism for the state and nation. The reason he listed the tightening of "discipline of the *gungmin*" as one of the objectives of the Yusin system in 1972 should be understood in this context (ibid.).

Behind Park's politicized critique of selfishness lay his emphasis on the spirit of sacrifice or the military spirit demanding the willingness to give up one's life for the state and the nation. In this context Park mourned and eulogized soldiers and civilians who lost their lives in the June 25 War, using the juxtaposed phrase to equate the state with the nation and calling them "the soldiers in the national army and patriotic brethren" who "saved the nation [*gyere*] by throwing away their lives and defended the state by devoting their lives" (June 25, 1966, 2:711). Furthermore, Park retroactively applied state nationalism to the period of the Joseon dynasty, defining exemplary ancestors of the nation as those figures "who thought lightly of their own personal sacrifices or lives as if they were a feather for the sake of state, for the sake of nation, and cheerfully ran the risk of their lives for the great cause" (April 11, 1967, 2:999).

Park had expressed his state-nationalist thinking consistently since his seizure of power, and it reached its peak at the establishment of the Yusin system in October 1972. Soon after, at the New Year's press conference in 1973, he stressed that "the nation and the state" have "eternal life," "the glory and development of the nation without the state is unthinkable," and "the state is the nation's guardian." Furthermore, he even discarded his previous distinctions between the "big self" and the "small self" and insisted that "'country' and 'I' are not different things but one and the same," thereby demanding "thorough commitment to the state" (January 12, 1973, 5:20).

Even before the proclamation of the Yusin Constitution, Park had shown a hint of dangerous thought, viewing the president himself as the only leader who could mediate the indissoluble link between the state and the nation. At his presidential campaign speech in 1967, he defended the Korea-Japan Normalization Treaty and the dispatch of the Korean army to Vietnam, declaring that "it is the responsibility of the president, who had to make the final decision over the critical issues the destiny of the state and nation depend upon" (April 23, 1967, 2:1052). When Park issued a special statement, declaring a state of national (state) emergency in December 1971, he claimed that the responsibility of and duty for state security were vested solely in the president himself: "State security is what takes most precedence over any other duties of the president. . . . Therefore, the estimate of the impending danger to state security is vested solely in me as the president. The responsibility for devising a proper, timely countermeasure following the estimate of the danger belongs also to my primary responsibility for state security" (December 6, 1971, 4:90). Although issues regarding state security were described solely as the president's duty and "primary responsibility"—that is, framed in terms of duty and responsibility—this statement stressed in fact that those issues were the "exclusive prerogative" of the president, which does not admit any free criticisms and diverse opinions by politicians or the general *gungmin*.

In regard to this, we need to recollect the political situation of England under absolute kingship and Yulgok Yi I's proposal for "the build-up of a hundred thousand soldiers" in the Joseon dynasty. Just before the outbreak of the English Civil War, Charles I (reigned 1625–1649) tried to levy "Ship Money" upon the English people in the name of a security threat posed by the Netherlands. Facing "considerable opposition to this tax," he "claimed both that any sovereign must have the power to raise military forces for the defense of the realm and that it [the Crown] must be the sole judge of whether a threat to the realm existed" (Tuck 1989, 23).[14] However, in a famous legal case in 1637 in which parliamentary leader John Hampden was charged for not paying the tax, the opposition denied the second point, "arguing that public opinion, particularly when represented in a Parliament, could also be the judge of whether a threat existed—and manifestly England's security was not endangered by the Dutch" (23–24). This case shows clearly that the claim of the Crown regarding the security threat did not reign supreme even under absolute monarchy, although Hampden lost the case in the end. It is a baffling paradox, however, to observe that Park made such a claim that his exclusive and absolute authority regarding state security affairs was equivalent to that of an absolute monarch—even more so in an ostensibly democratic country.

Almost at the end of the aforementioned special statement, Park reminded the country of Yulgok Yi I's late-sixteenth-century warning to build up a hundred thousand soldiers to protect against the threat of the impending Japanese invasion, admonishing, "We should not repeat errors and follies of our ancestor by not listening to his warning" (December 6, 1971, 4:90). As this case suggests, the king in the Joseon dynasty, who was commonly regarded as a variety of Oriental despot by modern Western thinkers, should listen to the warnings regarding state security issued by his ministers, who were then able to raise their opposition to the king's judgment of state security affairs. Then, just as the ministers and/or subjects were able to raise a critical voice against the king's judgment of state security in premodern monarchies East and West, so should general citizens as well as opposition politicians have been allowed to raise a critical voice to Park's declaration of a state of national emergency in contemporary politics, all the more so in an ostensibly liberal democratic system. However, he never allowed this, as confirmed in emergency decrees frequently declared on the pretext of national security during the Yusin regime as well as in this special statement.

The indissoluble bond between the state and the nation would require the personified power that should embody them. This was ultimately institutionalized by the establishment of the Yusin Constitution and the elevation of the president to the status of supreme leader. Kal Bong-geun (1976), professor of constitutional law deeply involved in designing and drafting the Yusin Constitution, pointed to the flaws of the constitution of the Third Republic based on the classical presidential system, by asserting that the centripetal point of the *gungminchonghwa* (all-out harmony of the people), which must be urgently realized to fulfill the national task of unification, should lie with the head of state, but the classical presidential system often failed to maximize efficiency due to mutual checks and balances according to the logic of the separation of powers. Then he explained that the "new constitution personified the power of the head of the state . . . and elevated the constitutional status of the president," so the president was "able to secure the status of the national [*gungmin*] arbitrator and furthermore the status of a 'supreme leader' [*yeongdoja*] who could guarantee the perpetuation of the state" (272).

As a result, as to the proper interpretation of the form of government the Yusin Constitution adopted, Park Il-gyeong (1972), professor of constitutional law, proposed a "presidential system led by a supreme leader [*yeongdojeok daetongryeongje*]" (1), which had then become the mainstream interpretation among professors of constitutional law. In accordance with this, "the status of the guardian of the state" was stipulated in Article 43, Clause 2, of the Yusin Constitution: "President as the guardian of the State shall have the responsibility and duty to safeguard the independence, territorial integrity, and continuity of the State and the Constitution." Thus the president as the guardian of the state had the authority to declare an emergency decree and martial law (Articles 53 and 54). The Yusin Constitution was the first complete case that stipulated a "sovereign dictatorship" explicitly in the constitution.

Carl Schmitt (1996) originally proposed a theory of sovereign dicta-torship—on the basis of his interpretation of presidential power to issue emergency decrees under the Weimar Constitution—that would lead to the justification of Hitler's seizure of power. Schmitt's sovereign dictatorship can be interpreted as a kind of constitutional dictatorship that combined con-stitutional legitimacy and the idea of dictatorship through the creation of a permanent dictatorial organ based on the constituent power of the people. In a state of emergency or a state of exception, it would serve the cause to defend the inevitability of political (sovereign) decisions that would free the execu-tive from any legal restraints to its power, such as parliamentary approval and rigorous bureaucratic procedures, that would normally apply (Choi Hyeong-ik 2008, 248–49, 255). According to Schmitt, "sovereign dictatorship" had to take the form of personified power as a representative of the constituent power in an actual situation who could issue an emergency decree in accordance with or even by replacing the constitution. Its typical example was Article 48 of the Weimar Constitution, which gave the president power to issue an emergency decree—including the use of armed force and/or suspension of civil rights and even the constitution—to restore law and order in the event of a serious threat to public safety or national security. However, although the constituent power of the people, which Schmitt stressed as the essential political mechanism for democratic legitimacy in a sovereign dictatorship, had never operated in the Weimar Republic, Schmitt did not take issue with this problem and escaped into the nebulous idea of political theology (ibid., 257).[15] In regard to this point, Choi Hyeong-ik argues that the most notable innovation of the Yusin Constitution lay in the creation of the National Conference for Unification to cope with this political dilemma. According to Choi's interpretation, the National Conference as the standing organ of sovereign mandate or supreme sovereign was distinct from the National Assembly but was created in tandem with it. It was created to work as the permanent institutionalization of constit-uent power, which was absent from the Weimar Constitution (257, 261–63).

Choi Hyeong-ik draws our special attention to the phrase "the historical mission of the peaceful unification of the fatherland" in the preamble of the Yusin Constitution to show the strong influence of Schmitt's sovereign dictatorship. According to him, the Yusin Constitution set up the "unifica-tion of the fatherland" as the objective of the state, articulated the relation-ship between friend and enemy, and stressed itself as the result of political determination in a state of exception. Thus elements hindering the unification of the fatherland were ipso facto considered "the enemy" (Choi Hyeong-ik 2008, 258–59). The most typical element of the sovereign dictatorship was the presidential emergency decree, which was the application of Schmitt's extraordinary decree. It also belonged to the type of presidential emergency power that is stipulated in the constitution of the Fifth Republic of France.

It should be noted, however, that the Yusin Constitution stipulated that the president's power to issue emergency decrees could be exercised unlimitedly without any ex ante/ex post control, for it stipulated that the emergency decree was not subject to judicial review and that the president could issue a decree not only when national security or public safety is threatened seriously but also when such threat is felt to be imminent (Article 53).[16]

Park Chung-hee issued the President's Special Announcement on October 17, 1972, which declared the dissolution of the National Assembly, suspension of the effect of some articles in the constitution, and the drafting of a revised constitution. As a result, the new Yusin Constitution was established. In the announcement, Park presented the détente in international order such as the Nixon doctrine, the Sino–US rapprochement, the impending withdrawal of US troops from Korea, and so on, as creating a crisis in national security. He then criticized the domestic political controversies over the South-North talks that had been going on since the South–North Korea Joint Communiqué for being conflicts ensuing from reckless and irresponsible "factional struggles and political maneuvers" and denounced the National Assembly as a critical stumbling block on the way to "the peaceful unification of the cherished national aspiration." Confronted with this extraordinary state or crisis situation, he further maintained that he was obliged to take extraordinary measures to carry out a drastic reform of the system including the constitution, laws, and decrees that were made for the Cold War in general and the South–North Korean confrontation in particular and therefore no longer fit the rapidly changing international situation and the recently ongoing South-North talks (October 17, 1972, 4:297–99).

Almost at the end of this special announcement, Park said, "As for myself, I have already devoted everything to the altar of the unification of the fatherland and national regeneration for a long time" (ibid., 4:301). This brings to mind a phrase in the book he published during the military government, *Gukgawa Hyeongmyeonggwa Na* (The state, the revolution, and I; 1963): "I, the current I since the time of May 16, have been forced to run the risk of my life before the fatherland, the nation, and the history" (25). At the time of the coup, Park had also defined that juncture as a time of total crisis, an extraordinary situation, when the survival of the state and the nation was at great stake. Thus he insisted that his own revolution was the "last opportunity for national regeneration" (27). Hence the critique that the security crisis at the time of enacting the Yusin Constitution was rather weaker than before (Ma Sang-yun 2003) would be advanced plausibly to refute Park's argument contained in the special announcement. However, it is important to remember, in Jeon In-gwon's (2006) words, that contemporary Korean history had been confronted with a "series of perpetual ordeals and crises," or a "permanent emergency" as seen from Park's perspective (254–57).

When we recall some of Park's phrases cited earlier from his speeches—
"The state is the nation's guardian," and "the 'country' and 'I' are not different things, but one and the same," and so on—the Yusin system may
well be interpreted as the official formulation of the trinitarian combination
of "the state = the nation = I"[17] and its actual (and exclusive) application
to Park Chung-hee himself, the supreme leader. In this way Park was able
to reign supreme at the pinnacle of power as the incarnation and the leader
of the nation and the state. In a way, the titles of the two books published
by Park in the aftermath of the military coup—*Uri Minjogui Nagal Gil* and
Gukgawa Hyeongmyeonggwa Na—ominously alluded to the advent of the
Yusin system, a completed version of state nationalism guided by a supreme
leader. After all, the trinitarian synthesis "I [Park Chung-hee] lead the road
for the nation and the state to take" was completed through a series of two
revolutions—that is, the May 16 coup and the Yusin (palace) coup—and the
inseparable mediating loop of that combination (i.e., the Yusin system). However, it would also share the same destiny as Park's rise and fall.

PARK CHUNG-HEE'S CONSERVATISM AND NATIONALISM

As reviewed fully in chapter 5, anticommunism (national security) and
economic development are presented most often as the primary pillars of
conservatism to support and legitimate Park Chung-hee's authoritarianism.
The anticommunism and economic development that Park stressed ultimately
reinforced their legitimacy by appealing to nationalism, as examined in
chapter 3. In this sense Park's conservatism shared the feature of nationalist discourses from above by the rightists. Given that anticommunism and
economic development in Park's thought are examined fully in chapter 5 and
their relationship to nationalism is reviewed in chapter 3, here the discussion
briefly focuses on their relation to Park's nationalist discourses.

Anticommunism and National Security

Anticommunism and national security, which were stressed constantly by
Park Chung-hee, contained elements of both statism and nationalism. In
particular, anticommunism against North Korean communists bore strong
nationalist characteristics. Nevertheless, when the state was presented as
the guardian of the nation, it was rather natural that the nationalist halo was
bestowed upon state security.[18]

Above all, North Korea was branded "antination" by Park Chung-hee as
well as Rhee Syngman. Park defined the Korean nation as consisting of a
single homogeneous ethnic group with the same blood lineage. This thought

appeared frequently in his speeches whenever he stressed unification while criticizing North Korea. Park urged "conscience" or "guilty conscience," often stating in a admonishing tone that he did not want to give up "the slightest hope and expectation" from North Korean communists as human beings, adding "still less from the same nation sharing the same bloodline from the same ancestor!" (October 1, 1970, 3:839). At the same time, the North Korean communists who often trampled "the slightest hope and expectation" were regarded as "antination" or "nonnation."

Overall, he suggested three reasons the North Korean communists were regarded as antination: First, the "North Korean puppets who stretched out their hands for communization of the whole Korean Peninsula by hook or by crook, acting as the agent of the Soviet Communist Party," were the entity "without nation or the state"[19]—that is, antination or nonnation and devoid of subjectivity as a nation (November 7, 1961, 1:86). Second, they were antinational as "aggressors," for they had not been content with only "provoking an all-out war in this peaceful land, massacring numerous brethren, driving a nail into the conscience of the nation, and burning our beautiful mountains and plains to the ground," but also, even after the war, they "persistently pursued aggressive policies for communist takeover through military force and violence, continuously making frantic efforts to prepare a war of national traitors" (June 25, 1969, 3:515; February 26, 1976, 6:41; April 12, 1977, 6:180). Third, and finally, "North Korean communists" were antinational because they "denied our national history, eliminated our own cultural tradition, and were possessed by fanatical alien thought as to be tenaciously intent upon disrupting our orthodox national history" (February 26, 1976, 6:40). Developing this type of logical progression, Park also made anticommunism a nationalist task, as Rhee Syngman had done.

Just as a brutal criminal who has committed unforgivable atrocities against humans is antihuman (against humanity) ethically, although he or she is also a human being by biology, North Korean communists were granted by Park Chung-hee the dual status of being a member of the nation ethnically but a member of the antination politically. In this sense the political definition of the nation overdetermined its biological definition. However, this kind of anticommunist nationalism that excluded communists from the nation was a conditional one: Once North Korean communists gave up antinational acts and repented their antinational guilt, then they would recover their status as a national member.[20] In other words, the characterization of North Korean communists as antinational was not something unchangeable and absolute as a biological attribute but contained a resolutive condition stipulating that once North Korean communists "restore their national conscience," stop committing antinational activities, and cooperate with the peaceful unification of the fatherland—for example, taking measures to allow the reunion of divided families in South and North Korea to "relieve their sufferings"—they would recover their status as members of the nation (August 15, 1972, 4:264). Park expressed this in his Liberation Day speech of 1972: "I am pleading with North Korean brethren. We are a community of destiny that shares the same language, same history, and the same blood, although separated between the South and the North. Although ideologies may change, the nation is permanent.[21] Let's resolutely make a historical turning point to restore ourselves as the Korean nation and resuscitate national conscience in the North as soon as possible" (August 15, 1972, 4:264). This statement suggests the possibility that nationalist logic based on ethnicity could ultimately overwhelm ideological differences. It is this dualist conception contained in this statement stipulating the conditional and temporary definition of the "antination" and the permanent and blood-based definition of the "same nation" that provides the space for the South-North dialogue or negotiation without causing contradictions.

Economic Development (Modernization)

Park Chung-hee set up "modernization" as the "historical task" of Korean nationalism and stressed economic development as the core of modernization (Park Chung-hee 1962, 128). Then he suggested as the task of modernization, first, that "the nation be liberated from the semifeudal and semicolonial vestiges." He then maintained that "the nationalism of the backward countries is 'the voice of the poor world' and their will to survive" and that "nationalist passions had erupted in all nations of the past whenever they made the leap from traditional society to modern society." To make that happen, he declared the urgent need for "the realization" that modernization is "not possible without forming the mood for modernization"—that is, an awakening for modernization (128). He proposed "the accomplishment of economic self-reliance by emancipating the nation from poverty" as the second task (129).[22] Furthermore, Park stressed economic development as a precondition for democracy,[23] arguing that "it is poverty, famine, and low income that pose the most threatening challenge to the modern liberal democracy our nation claims to advocate" (32).

Elsewhere Park set up the "building of an independent economy" as the objective of economic development and argued that it would be the fruit of the nation to bear only when all the *gungmin* were united as one body, put forth maximum effort and patience, and devoted all their blood, sweat, and passion. To achieve this objective, he sought to mobilize the entire *gungmin* according to their status and role: "A professor provides a good theory, a politician guides the *gungmin* with a good policy, a scholar creates a philosophy of national revival, those in culture and the arts encourage the drive for construction, all business people and industrialists devote themselves to their businesses and industries, respectively, peasants and workers shed their sweat, students renew themselves with a frugal spirit, soldiers are imposing with a solemn posture, all public servants act as genuine servers. Only then will we be able to achieve 'the miracle of the Han River'" (Park 1963, 265). As history would show later, Park evidently failed to achieve the "Koreanization of democracy" among his nationalist tasks. However, he devoted himself most assiduously to the task of "emancipating the nation from poverty" (i.e., the task of economic development) and bore its fruit in the end with notable success.

The urgent demand for modernization facing the Korean nation was felt not only by Park Chung-hee but also by most of the intellectuals of the time. When Park Chung-hee staged a coup d'état in May 1961, Chang Chun-ha, editor-in-chief at *Sasanggye* (World of Ideas), a critical monthly news magazine, actually supported the coup in the June issue published immediately after it in the editorial "Foreword: 5/16 Revolution and the Proper Course for the Nation." In the editorial he stated that "just as the April 19th revolution . . . was a democratic revolution, so the May 16th revolution was a nationalist military revolution to demolish corruption, incompetence, disorder, and communist maneuvers and set the direction of the state straight," although he did not fail to mention that power should be restored to the civilian politicians as soon as possible (Chang Chun-ha 1961, 34). In an article contributed to the November 1961 issue of *Sasanggye*, Yang Ho-min also asserted that "a series of values such as freedom, human rights, democracy, and the like may remain empty rhetoric after all, without overcoming economic poverty by . . . industrial revolution" and suggested economic development as the most urgent task (Yang Ho-min 1961, 48).

Other writers who contributed their articles to *Sasanggye* made the same argument to this effect, thereby leading and reinforcing the prevailing opinions of the times. Like Park Chung-hee, most of the intellectuals also agreed to measuring economic development by gross (aggregate) figures. Lee Chang-ryeol asserted in an article published in 1963 that it was not until "per capita GNP would be increased to one hundred or two hundred dollars as soon as possible" and would then continue to level up that the "development" of an "independent economy" could be expected (Lee Chang-ryeol 1963, 113). However, Park's developmental policy was later condemned for being an antinationalist growth strategy. Economic development under the Park regime relied heavily on enormous foreign debts (or loans), such that it was criticized for increasing the dependency of the national economy on foreign countries. Nevertheless, most intellectuals at the time shared the prevailing opinion that "mobilization of overseas capital was necessary for development," while asserting the building of an independent economy at the same time (Kim Bo-hyeon 2003, 359). Kim Bo-hyeon summarizes the prevailing opinion of the intellectuals: "As a matter of fact, they thought that as many of the resources as possible must be mobilized, regardless of whether they are domestic or foreign capitals. They did not think that it was impossible to achieve economic self-reliance while relying upon foreign capitals, nor do they mean that relying upon foreign capitals should lead to neglecting the mobilization of domestic capitals" (360).[24]

At a congratulatory speech on Liberation Day in 1964, Park stated that "all the instability and chaos facing Korea today" are "ultimately attributable to poverty to the greatest extent" and "the sound development of democracy, building of the welfare state, and the cultivation of state power for the unification by defeating the communist North depend upon the success or failure of economic construction in the end" (August 15, 1964, 2:162). Likewise, economic development was a necessary precondition not only to achieving economic self-reliance and economic affluence (the welfare society) but also to cultivating state power and democratic capacity and attaining unification. Thus it was a panacea necessary to fulfill various tasks of nationalism seeking the independence, prosperity, and unification of the nation. In his statement to commemorate the sixteenth anniversary of the June 25 War in 1966, with regard to the relationship between economic development and the unification, Park announced "the modernization of the fatherland and building of a self-reliant economy" as "the forward-looking plan for unification and progressive effort for unification" and stressed, "I want to make clear once more that unification of the national territory is possible only after achieving the intermediate goals of self-reliance and modernization" (June 25, 1966, 2:712).[25] Through this statement, he declared firmly his doctrine of "construction first, then unification."

PARK CHUNG-HEE'S DISCOURSES ON UNIFICATION AND NATIONALISM

Regardless of the thorny question as to whether the nation or nationalism is a "modern" entity or phenomenon,[26] most Koreans tend to believe strongly that the congruence between the political and the national unit had long existed as an unquestionable historical fact. Thus, to the Koreans who abruptly experienced the national division and subsequently the internecine June 25 War, the rebirth of South and North Korea as a single nation-state through reunification was, all the more, the foremost and urgent task of nationalism.

However, because the objectives of nationalism, such as economic development, modernization, democracy, and national unification, could collide with one another and not be solved all at once, the urgency and importance of each objective should be weighed and given priority accordingly. Diverse political groups had to confront one another over this matter. In contrast to Chang Chun-ha and other unification-oriented nationalists who insisted that the unification be the supreme and most urgent task, Park assigned unification to the last task in the temporal sequence, while admitting that it was the supreme task. Contrary to the commonly held notion, Park also acknowledged democracy and democratization as a task of nationalism. In addition to his stress on the Koreanization of democracy as a task of nationalism, he explicitly admitted the importance of liberal democracy as a national task, as is shown in the phrase "Korean nationalism . . . should be developed in the direction to improve and indigenize ideas and institutions of our liberal democracy" (February 26, 1971, 3:961).[27] He also firmly believed that the South Korean system, which had to be defended in confrontation with North Korea, was a democratic system. At the same time, as he acknowledged that the South Korean system was immature in democracy, he often made statements such as "The sacred task of unification . . . is not to be realized until our economic prosperity and *democratic capacity* become firm" (July 17, 1966, 2:729; emphasis added).[28] Apart from "building a self-reliant economy and the task of modernization" and "the cultivation of democratic capacity," he added the "improvement of [South Korea's] international status" and the strengthening of international cooperation as preconditions for unification (July 25, 1966, 2:734–35).[29] In this way the unification problem is set as the ultimate task, one that cannot be tackled on a full scale until the accomplishment of economic development, strong democratic capacity, and strengthened international status. Thus it may be carried out successfully by "the latter half of the 1970s when we are able to command mastery over North Korea in all aspects" (June 25, 1966, 2:712).

As a method of unification, Park advocated peaceful unification as opposed to unification by military means such as Rhee Syngman's "unification by marching forward to the North," stating that "it is our earnest desire to avoid the method of a bloody internecine war by any means, no matter that the unification of the national territory is the cherished desire of the nation and the supreme objective of the state (October 1, 1969, 3:575).[30] Then he proposed the settlement of peace as the precondition for peaceful unification (August 15, 1975, 5:460). As to the specific method for peaceful unification, the Park regime also announced peaceful unification through a free general election both in South and North proportional to the population under UN monitoring. However, considering that there was little possibility that North Korea would accept such a proposal, Park seemed to set the peaceful recovery or absorption of North by South as an alternative strategy, stating that the unification would be realized when "our economy, our freedom, and our democracy overflow to the North," after the South secures its absolute superiority to the

North in terms of economic power and democracy in the long run (January 17, 1967, 2:926). In short, to Park Chung-hee as well as most Koreans, a self-reliant economy, the modernization of the fatherland, independent national defense capability, liberal democracy including Korean-style democracy, and unification should all be accomplished at any cost for the sake of national independence, unification, and prosperity.[31] It was natural, then, that implementing each of these tasks was considered nationalistic.

CONCLUDING REMARKS

Thus far Park Chung-hee's nationalist discourse has been analyzed and characterized as statist nationalism guided by a supreme leader. At the same time, it has been stressed that not only his conservative discourse such as anticommunism (national security) and economic development but also his discourse on democracy and unification were elements of nationalism. In this respect Park's discourse on nationalism can be interpreted as that of conservative nationalism from above representing the right-wing position in South Korea.

In the preceding chapter Park's conservatism is defined as "modernizing conservatism," an oxymoronic phrase in the nineteenth-century Western experience. To a modernizing conservative like Park as well as to a progressive, the present was seen "as the beginning of the future" to launch a radical and strenuous struggle to win glorious goals without setbacks in the future, whereas Western conservatives see the present as the "latest point reached by the past in a continuous, seamless growth" with the preservation and expansion of time-honored tradition, religion, history, and authority (Nisbet 1986, 25). Accordingly, at a congratulatory speech given on the anniversary of Liberation Day in 1970, Park presented a lofty vision of the future of Korea, so that his nationalist discourse combined with modernizing conservatism took on the guise of a sacred utopia. "In the year 2000 . . . our fatherland will have been transformed into the following proud form: a strong nation-state that will have achieved the unification of the national territory a long time before; an advanced and affluent welfare state in which all the *gungmin* will share in prosperity together; and a dignified state that will participate in and contribute to the mainstream of the world history with confidence" (August 15, 1970, 3:811).[32]

However, opposing political forces critical of or resisting the Park regime branded most policies of the regime "antinational" as well as "antidemocratic" in the end. First of all, they advanced a critique that his discourses on anti-communism and unification contributed to the reproduction and perpetuation of the national division or the strengthening of "statism in a divided state," so that they obstructed genuine unification efforts from below and delayed unification in the end. Second, they offered criticism that his economic development for building a self-reliant economy completely disregarded the welfare of the *minjung* and autonomous subjectivity of the nation through the worsening economic inequality and the subordinate economy dependent on foreign capital. They also condemned Park's discourses on democracy, for the "liberal democracy" he advocated was nothing more than a fiction that was actually used to suppress the freedom of individual members of the nation, whereas anticommunism, national security, and Korean-style democracy were weapons and rhetoric mobilized only to justify his dictatorship. Therefore the Park regime had to share the stigma of "antinational" with Japanese imperialism and was often compared with the latter. Thus opposing forces condemned the Park regime in the name of the nation when they opposed the normalization treaty between Korea and Japan, attacked the fraudulent general election of 1967, and protested against the Yusin system.[33]

In this context it is significant to note that important democratic struggles broke out with an announcement or statement on March 1, a symbolic anniversary of Korean nationalism resisting Japanese imperial rule. Although the spirit of the March First Movement in 1919 includes democracy (or republicanism) as well as nationalism, the announcements issued on that anniversary, which protested Park's dictatorship, showed dramatically that the ultimate legitimacy of the democratizing movements was to be found in nationalism. For instance, when the National (*Gungmin*) Congress for Restoring Democracy issued the March 1, 1975, statement "Message to the *Gungmin*: In Commemoration of the 56th Anniversary of the March First Movement and in Regard to the Manifesto of Democratic *Gungmin*'s Charter," they asserted that "the independence and autonomy our ancestors so cherished" had been violated by the comprador Park regime, which had imported the Japanese capitals, and that "basic freedoms of the *gungmin* our ancestors shouted so desperately had been trampled down relentlessly not by a foreign nation but by the dictatorial regime of the same nation." Through this assertion, they declared openly that the antinational and antidemocratic Park regime was the target of the overthrow by insurgent nationalism. Moreover, the announcements and manifestos issued by democratic forces often included not only the message calling for democracy but also core phrases related to nationalism such as *guguk*[34] (saving the state)—for example, emergency resolution for *guguk*, *guguk* struggle, *guguk* announcement, *guguk* march, *guguk* prayer meeting, and democratic *guguk*.[35] Reminding the Korean public of Japanese colonial rule explicitly or implicitly when Koreans struggled to recover the independent state and national freedom, these manifestos urged the *gungmin* to struggle against Park's dictatorship. In this way the ruling elite was condemned not only as antidemocratic but also as antinational. In sum, democratic forces developed their antigovernmental struggles in the name of "saving the state" in order to appeal to the entire *gungmin* and maximize their mobilization. This reveals not only that democracy was one of the important nationalist tasks but also, at the same time, confirms that the ultimate legitimacy of the democratic struggle lay in nationalism.

Seen from this perspective, Park Chung-hee's discourses on nationalism epitomized by "modernization of the fatherland" and "national regeneration" did not reign supreme in contemporary Korean politics, for insurgent discourses produced by opposing forces to attack and criticize the Park regime found the locus and appeal of their legitimacy in nationalism as well. Thus nationalism as the ultimate source of legitimacy was not something the Park regime could monopolize. Nationalism was a double-edged sword the opponents to the Park regime could also wield against the regime effectively. Thus nationalism turned out to be the site of intense discursive struggles both the regime and its opponents engaged in fiercely.

NOTES

1. See that same section of the work for a more detailed review of these three approaches, including the respective individual scholars who apply them in their research. Jeon examines Park Chung-hee's discourse on nationalism through discursive analysis while keeping some distance from the existing research trend. I adopt his approach in this chapter as well.

2. Of course, this trend originates partly from the sanctification of nationalism in the Korean ideological topography.

3. This effect has been also directly related to the sanctification of nationalism.

4. Thus, depending on different discursive effects—for example, Palestinians fighting to regain land in the West Bank from Israel used to be described either as freedom fighters or as terrorists—this may well apply to the assassination incident carried out by An Jung-geun, a Korean independence activist, who shot Itō Hirobumi to death in 1909 to protest Itō's leading role in annexing Korea, as well as to the crash of US airplanes by Arab "terrorists" on September 11, 2001.

5. The works of Jeon Jae-ho (1997) and Kim Jeong-hun (2000) are rather exceptional in this respect. Recently Kim Bo-hyeon (2006) analyzed Park's economic-development policies in relation to nationalism.

6. Most Korean historians also adopt this primordial and objective understanding of the Korean nation. For the recent trend to oppose this understanding and adopt a modern and subjective understanding of the Korean nation, see Schmid 2002 and Park Dong-cheon 2008.

7. The Sino-Korean phrase *gukpasanhajae* (國破山河在 in Chinese characters), which was widely used during the Japanese colonial period, suggests the loss of the state and the persistence of the nation. Here *gukpa*, which literally means "the state destroyed," refers to the loss of the state, whereas *sanhajae*, which literally means "mountains and rivers still existing," refers to the continual existence of the nation.

The male heroes who appeared in many novels written during the colonial period were often fatherless, which also signified the loss of authority and state.

8. Here my concept of state nationalism is different from Friedrich Meinecke's concept of "political/state nations." Meinecke makes a distinction between "cultural nations" (*Kulturnationen*) and "political nations" (*Staatsnationen*). The former refer to "nations that are primarily based on some jointly experienced cultural heritage," such as "a standard language, a common literature, and a common religion," whereas the latter refer to "nations that are primarily based on the unifying force of a common political history and constitution" (Meinecke 1970, 10). Germany belongs to the former, whereas France and England belong to the latter. However, Meinecke acknowledges that "a cultural nation can be a political nation as well, and we often do not know whether political ties or the ties of religion and church are the stronger in holding it together" (11). According to this scheme, the Korean nationalism that rose in earnest in the late nineteenth century has retained both attributes at the same time. In addition Park Chung-hee's state nationalism has strong characteristics of totalitarianism. But it is different from such ultranationalism as German Nazism, Italian Fascism, or Japanese militarism. Whereas the latter is related to national superiority and/or racism, Park's state nationalism is related to the national inferiority complex coming from the loss of sovereignty to Japanese imperialism and the subsequent colonial experience and legacy, as well as other particular Korean historical experiences mentioned in the main text. Criticizing the prevalence of this kind of nationalism among Korean historians, Carter Eckert wrote the chapter essay "Epilogue: Exorcising Hegel's Ghosts; Toward a Postnationalist Historiography of Korea" (1999). See also Bruce Cumings 2007.

9. Park Chung-hee often used phrases like "national conscience" or "conscience of the nation" when criticizing corrupt civil servants or opposition politicians, when condemning the North Korean regime, and when exhorting university students and members of the National Conference for Unification. Of course, these phrases were not monopolized by Park; they were used widely by opposition forces, including students. Chang Chun-ha, one of Park's most vehement critics, also used them. In his famous article "The Way of the Nationalist," Chang identified the "way for the nationalist to take" with "living one's life in accordance with the national conscience" (Chang Chun-ha 1985, 50). In addition, he defined "those who really wished for unification" as those determined to live by "national conscience," and he enumerated people "in this land who can live only with the realization of unification" and "*minjung* who have their everyday life destroyed due to the division" as "national consciences" (40). Moon Ik-hwan (1985), who wrote the preface to a book dedicated posthumously to Chang that also included a collection of Chang's writings, commemorated the memory of Chang as the incarnation of "national conscience" (3). In this regard it should be noted that the negative aspect of national conscience that conceived conscience collectively was also shared by the resisting elements.

10. Here I use *statism* to refer to the belief in the primacy of the state over the rights of the individual. Thus the state has an ethical value transcending that of individual members, such that individuals have an obligation to serve and sacrifice for the state. See Jeon In-gwon 2006 (257–65) for a more detailed analysis of Park's statist thinking.

11. See, for example, "Admonition to the Graduation Ceremony of the Korean Military Academy" (February 13, 1967, 2:954) and "The Statement on the June 25 Rebellion [War]" (June 25, 1967, 2:1110).

12. We need to remember, of course, that the nation was equated to the state not only by Park but also by most Koreans.

13. The commonly used pairs are, among others, "the state and the nation," "fatherland and *gyere*" (a pure Korean word for *nation*), "*aegukaejok*" (loving the state and loving the nation), "*gugukgujok*" (saving the state and saving the nation), "the state and *gyere*," and "the country and the nation."

14. The social-contract theory formulated later by Thomas Hobbes in *Leviathan* also advanced the argument in defense of Charles I by allowing the sovereign ruler to exercise power in security matters without regard for public opinion: "*to the end he may use the strength and means of them* [individual members] *all, as he shall think expedient, for their peace and common defence*" (Hobbes 1962, xvii, 132; emphasis original).

15. See Lee Hae-young 2004 and Choi Hyeong-ik 2008 for a more detailed analysis of Schmitt's political theology.

16. According to the Yusin Constitution, "When the National Assembly passes the resolution recommending the lifting of the emergency decree with the concurrent vote of a majority of the total members of the National Assembly, the President shall comply unless there are any particular reasons" (Article 53, Clause 6). However, it should be noted that this was actually an almost-impossible scenario, given that the president recommended and appointed one-third of the total members of the National Assembly.

17. Here it is worth recalling the equation "state security = regime security = Park's personal security," which I formulated by citing Lee Hu-rak's inaugural address as head of the KCIA in late 1970 (see chapter 5, note 11).

18. With regard to this, it is plausible to criticize the Park regime as a system with statist characteristics in the guise of nationalism. Kim Bo-hyeon (2006) refutes this kind of critique, arguing that "the realistic bearer or carrier of the nation cannot but be the state" (37).

19. It is intriguing to note that this phrase brings to mind the *wijeongcheoksa* group, the Confucian fundamentalists in late nineteenth-century Korea who defined the Western "barbarians" as those "without the father and the king." If here we replace "the father" with "the nation," which stands for the continuity of the blood, and "the king" with the symbol that represents the state, then North Korean communists will correspond to those "without the father and the king." Because Confucianism attaches the greatest import to proper human relationships—notably including those between kings and subjects and parents and children—North Korean communists will fundamentally become an immoral entity "lacking proper humanity."

20. In this context it is important to remember that both Rhee Syngman and Park Chung-hee distinguished between North Korean communists and North Korean brethren (ordinary residents) and then in their public speeches branded only the former as "antination" while embracing the latter as the same nation. For instance, Park Chung-hee explicitly said that "all North Korean brethren are naturally members of the great *han* [Korean] nation" ("Congratulatory Speech on Liberation Day," August 15, 1972,

4:264). Of course, such a distinction was based on the interpretation that most North Koreans complied with the communist regime by force rather than actively supporting it by voluntary consent. Such a rhetorical interpretation would imply the legitimacy of the South Korean regime.

21. This sentence in the quotation reminds us of Kim Gu's (1997) famous statement that, whereas ideologies and beliefs are transient, only "the nation based on blood lineage" is "permanent" (370–71).

22. For the third task of modernization, Park listed "the reconstruction of sound democracy" (Park 1962, 129). This task is examined fully in chapter 4, which addresses his ideas of democracy.

23. As I discuss in the following, most intellectuals of the time also suggested economic development as the only solution to overcoming poverty and the prerequisite for political democracy (Kim Bo-hyeon 2006, 372).

24. See pages 359–64 of this same article for a detailed analysis of this point. Later many scholars distinguished between import-substituting and export-led industrialization and often categorized the former as the nationalist strategy, branding the latter comprador and antinationalist. Writers of the journal *Sasanggye* (World of Ideas) were also divided on this point, but the majority supported the latter, according to Kim Bo-hyeon's review (364–67). In this way the "export-first" policy advocated by Park Chung-hee was evaluated positively.

25. Here we need to take note of the subtle implication of "unification of the national territory" against the historical background of its use. North Korean communists were commonly regarded as antinational rebels by the Rhee Syngman and Park Chung-hee governments, for, the thinking went, they occupied the northern part of the peninsula illegally by force and oppressed the freedoms of the North Korean brethren. Therefore North Korean communists could not be a partner for unification but rather its object, although South Korean governments might tentatively engage in talks or negotiations with them. So such phrases as "unification of the national territory" and "recovery of the national territory" were frequently used instead of "national unification," although they are not used any longer.

26. However, most Western theorists of nationalism such as Ernest Gellner and Eric Hobsbawm tend to conceive of the nation as a modern entity. For example, according to Hobsbawm (1990), the nation "belongs exclusively to a particular, and historically recent, period. It is a social entity only insofar as it relates to a certain kind of modern territorial state, the 'nation-state,' and it is pointless to discuss nation and nationality except insofar as both relate to it" (9–10). Then Hobsbawm says, emphatically, "for the purposes of analysis nationalism comes before nations. Nations do not make states and nationalisms but the other way round" (10).

27. Park also mentioned the "construction of self-reliant economy" and the cultivation of "democratic capacity" as intermediate goals on the road to unification in another address given in the same year (August 15, 1966, 2:751).

28. It is suggestive, however, that the cultivation of democratic capacity did not appear in Park's public speeches after the installment of the Yusin regime as often as it had before. Instead he used more comprehensive phrases, like the "cultivation of state power."

29. As can be seen from his word choice, Park sometimes made a distinction between modernization and economic development, other times lumping them together almost as if they were synonymous. In a speech he used the "modernization of the fatherland" as a comprehensive concept to refer to long-term social change including "not only economic construction but also political democratization, and rationalization of the society" ("Presidential New Year's Address," January 17, 1967, 2:925). But he sometimes used "economic prosperity" as a condensed expression of modernization.

30. Of course, after the South–North Korea Joint Communiqué of July 4, 1972, Park announced his doctrine of peaceful unification more concretely by making the "June 23rd Announcement for a Diplomatic Policy for Peaceful Unification" in 1973, proposing a "mutual nonaggression pact between South and North Korea" at the New Year's press conference in 1974, and declaring "three basic principles for peaceful unification" at the congratulatory speech on Liberation Day (August 15) in 1974.

31. Park declared that the Korean-style democracy the Yusin regime claimed to embody was part of liberal democracy (October 1, 1979, 16:152).

32. Park presented a vision similar to this in his congratulatory speech on Liberation Day (August 15) in 1979, two months before his assassination (16:147). As a matter of fact, Park proclaimed the Charter of National Education in December 1968. Its first sentence—"We are born in this land with the historical mission for national regeneration"—suggests the quintessence of the sanctification of nationalism and indicates that nationalism imparts to individuals the ultimate meaning of life. Of course, as examined in chapter 3, most Korean historians who interpret Korean history only in terms of liberation, independence, and unification of the nation and by following nation-centered historiography are not free from this sanctification.

33. For example, protesters opposing the normalization treaty between Korea and Japan condemned "the humiliating treaty between Korea and Japan," focusing more on its "antinational" character than its "antidemocratic" features when they issued the famous pamphlet "Let's Hold a Funeral for National Democracy." They vehemently criticized the fictiveness of the national democracy by drawing upon various logical and rhetorical progressions centered on nationalism, such as "national conscience" (Kim Sam-ung 1984, 41–42). In addition, when students at Seoul National University banded together to say, "We Condemn the Fraudulent Election on June 8" in 1967, they were criticizing it for being antidemocratic but at the same time said, "We shall send the running dogs for the fraudulent election to the scaffold in the name of the nation without any hesitation," while also calling on the "national spirit" (60). In this way they made it clear that an antidemocratic act equaled an antinational act.

34. Although *guguk* is literally related to the state, it has a strong nationalist implication, because the state is the guardian of the nation to the general *gungmin* as well as to Park Chung-hee.

35. Of course *guguk* is also one of Park Chung-hee's favorite words. He once called the May 16th military coup d'état the "*guguk* movement for national renewal" (May 16, 1967, 2:1097). He used the word *guguk* frequently to praise historical figures and heroes who took the lead to overcome national crises and to stage the national-independence movement. In particular, Admiral Yi Sun-sin, who expelled

the Japanese invasion in Joseon Korea, was the most exemplary "hero of the *guguk*" (April 28, 1968, 3:217). Park also defined the Yusin system as the "true road to *guguk* the overwhelming majority of the *gungmin* cherish" and *gungmin*'s support for it as the "expression of the *guguk* will" (February 16, 1976, 5:29; January 15, 1976, 5:29). In this respect, *guguk* is a word representing nationalism to both Park Chung-hee and his opponents.

Part III

CONTEMPORARY KOREAN POLITICAL THOUGHT SINCE DEMOCRATIZATION

Chapter 7

Conclusion

Trends in Korean Political Ideology since Democratization

In part 1 I describe the evolution and characteristics of contemporary political ideology in Korea. After outlining the ideological evolution from immediately after liberation to the present, I highlight nonsimultaneity and sanctification as the two most conspicuous characteristics of the Korean ideological landscape prior to democratization in 1987. I identify nonsimultaneity as a structural condition resulting from the temporal and spatial gap between Korea, a peripheral latecomer country, and central early-comer Western states. Sanctification, meanwhile, is understood to be a substantial characteristic formed by a combination of the structural condition of nonsimultaneity and Korea's own particular historical experiences since the late nineteenth century. In part 2 I examine the political thought of Park Chung-hee, a figure who exerted huge influence on contemporary Korean politics and who also remains highly controversial when it comes to the interpretation of the country's contemporary history in terms of three major ideologies: liberalism (actually, liberal democracy), conservatism, and nationalism. At the same time, I attempt to assess how nonsimultaneity and sanctification were interwoven with Park's thought. Of course, this examination is not conducted under the naive assumption that his thought would reflect the two characteristics in their entirety and thus be the best exemplification of them. It is merely done in the belief that Park's political thought, be it his own personal thought or that which represented the thought of right-wingers at the time, could not have entirely escaped the influence of these defining characteristics and in fact can only have manifested itself to a certain extent as their carrier. In this final chapter I discuss how nonsimultaneity and sanctification have changed over the three decades since democratization in 1987. I then examine the changes undergone by political thought represented by Park Chung-hee over the same period and what we can expect of its legacy in years to come.

My assertions in this chapter are that Korean politics has now, at a basic level, completed the tasks of modernization and democratization and has joined the ongoing globalization and informationization coevally. As a result, nonsimultaneity is loosening, if not disintegrating altogether, as a structural feature of Korea's ideological landscape. This, in turn, has led to a gradual but comprehensive weakening of the sanctification of nationalism. This weakening is found in its most salient form in the paradoxical phenomenon whereby the nationalist passion that accompanied modernization and democratization in South Korea has clearly decreased with regard to unification since the achievement of the former two objectives. Moreover, South Korea has become an open society since then; the globalization and informationization that have accompanied and also led to this change have been strongly influential in the weakening of not only "unification-oriented nationalism" but also nationalism in general. With regard to this, I briefly introduce contemporary criticism of the sanctification of nationalism on the part of Korean academics and the emergence of so-called postnationalism. Of course, the factors sustaining sanctification cannot be ignored either: These include the continuous, mutually antagonistic division of the Korean Peninsula, the persistent belief among some progressive circles that the United States is to blame for Korea's division, the question of reunification, and unresolved issues relating to the historical interpretation of Japan's annexation of Korea and the dictatorial South Korean regimes. It appears that such factors will continue to exert a strong influence on resistant nationalism for some time to come.[1] The nationalist clashes that have recently occurred among South Korea, China, and Japan as part of Northeast Asian territorial and historical disputes, moreover, retain the potential to boost nationalism in the future.

This is why I make a clear distinction between the strengthening of nationalism and its sanctification. Korean nationalism may acquire new strength in the near future for internal or external reasons, as suggested above, but I believe it will not be able to sustain the same strong sanctity it used to enjoy in the past, due to the success of industrialization and democratization, the establishment of a clearly superior position of South over North Korea, and the social opening that has occurred after globalization and informationization. In other words, the weakening of the sanctification of nationalism will be confirmed when nationalism's powerful overdetermination of the other ideologies loses the strength it once had and the overpowering presence of one element over other elements in nationalism has weakened.

I also predict that the political thought of Park Chung-hee, which has both represented and shaped conservative right-wing ideology in Korea, is set for inevitable decline in the long term, due not only to the weakening of nonsimultaneity and sanctification but also to the democratization of Korean society as a whole. The anticommunism that has formed through the continuation of the national division and its powerful legacy, however, looks set to remain strong for the time being—in forms such as *banbuk* (opposition to North Korea) and accusations among South Korean politicians of being *jongbuk* (blindly following North Korea). In this chapter, then, I elaborate on each of these issues.

SIMULTANEITY OF THE NONSIMULTANEOUS

In chapter 2 I modify the concept of "simultaneity of the nonsimultaneous," as outlined by Ernst Bloch, to create the concept of the overwhelming of one region by another due to discrepancies between global (world) historical time and local/national (namely, Korean) historical time and to the latter's resistance to the former and the mutation resulting from their interaction. I then apply this modified concept to various aspects of Korea's ideological terrain. Now, however, my assessment is that the stabilization of democracy brings about a gradual convergence of Korean and Western ideological terrains, a phenomenon that is leading in turn to a gradual weakening of nonsimultaneity. In order to explain this, I begin by describing and examining various aspects resulting from the mutual interaction of global and local (Korean) historical time in contemporary Korean politics. I then give a general description of the weakening of nonsimultaneity in terms of political ideology. Finally, I make the observation that the dialectic of nonsimultaneity is not a phenomenon confined to non-Western latecomer countries but was witnessed in contemporary Europe following the end of the Cold War in the late twentieth century as well as in Nazi Germany of the 1930s, and I examine its implications.

Various Aspects of the Interaction between Global and Local Historical Time

Looking back over the seventy years since Korean liberation, it is possible to introduce and briefly describe several forms of interaction between global and local, state-specific historical time. These include the progressive overwhelming of Korean local time by global historical time, the conservative overwhelming of local Korean time by global historical time, the successful resistance to global historical time by local Korean time, and the gradual disappearance of nonsimultaneity or convergence of these two hitherto discrepant time frames. Let us now examine these four types of interaction.

First, the emergence of liberal democratic and communist regimes in South and North Korea, respectively, in the process of national division can be identified as an example of global historical time progressively overwhelming

local Korean time. The order proclaimed in South Korea's founding constitution at the time was fundamentally a capitalist, democratic political order
oriented toward a mixed economy. But when we consider the socioeconomic
conditions of the time—of local Korean time, in other words—both democracy and capitalism were systems that should have been implemented only
after much drastic transformation of South Korean politics and society.[2] The
communist system introduced in North Korea after liberation, too, was more a
teleological introduction resulting from progressive overwhelming by global
historical time (as defined by Marxism-Leninism) than the result of any
endogenous dynamic according to the local time of North Korean society.[3]

This is not to say, however, that pulling by global historical time happened
solely due to the unilateral actions of the American military government in
South Korea or the Soviet occupying forces in North Korea. In South Korea
conservative right-wingers took advantage of liberal progress as part of their
quest to contain certain radical-left and nationalist forces in order to block
a possible socialist revolution more radical in nature than capitalist liberal
democracy. It should be noted that the liberal and patriotic enlightenment
movements that took place in late nineteenth-century Joseon Korea, too, were
oriented toward liberalism and constitutional monarchy. In addition, the ideological development process led by the Shanghai-based Provisional Government of the Republic of Korea and other radical groups of the independence
movement during the Japanese colonial period converged also on a consensus
of a mixed economy and a democratic system, as suggested by Jo So-ang's
famous "Three Equals" doctrine.[4] The political and economic systems introduced by the founding constitution of the Republic of Korea, therefore, were
not completely unfamiliar to Korea's modern ideological tradition. It is clear,
moreover, that these internal developments in Korean politics were reflected
in the drafting of the country's founding constitution.[5] In the case of North
Korea, too, Kim Il-sung and other left-wingers in the Manchu area who also
had long been engaged in communist guerrilla warfare for independence can
be regarded as having jumped on the bandwagon of socialist global historical
time while removing certain right-wing nationalists.

Because the progress of global historical time is not, of course, linear, there
have also been cases in which it has overwhelmed local Korean time in a
conservative fashion. Such examples are easy to locate in the impact made on
Korea's ideological terrain by the decline of the doctrine of the welfare state
and the global spread of neoliberalism that have occurred since the 1980s—
particularly since the collapse of socialist regimes and consequent end of the
Cold War. In terms of the "schedule" of democratic development set by the
West, it can at least be said that democracy was fully consolidated by the end
of the Kim Young-sam administration in 1997 and should have begun a phase
of deepening. This deepening required increased democratic participation

and the progress of socioeconomic equality, an essential prerequisite to which was the introduction and development of a social-welfare system. But the neoliberalism that arrived in Korea in full force from the time of Kim's administration in accordance with global historical time, and the discourse on "national competitive power" that derived from it, removed the deepening of democracy from the political agenda and placed conservative pressure on local Korean time. Moreover, the Kim Dae-jung government, which came into office in 1998, was forced to fully accept the drastic neoliberal structural adjustment forced on Korea by the International Monetary Fund in the process of overcoming the financial crisis that occurred in 1997, at the end of the Kim Young-sam administration, despite the absence of a well-established welfare program. In other words, neoliberalism,[6] a phenomenon that appeared as part of global historical time, was fully adopted by Korean society, thus bypassing the so-called welfare-state stage and directly giving rise to a neoliberal order.

Of course, the changes in Korean politics resulting from the acceptance of neoliberalism are not solely the products of unilateral pressure from global historical time. It is true that, in the case of Korea, long-term state-led economic development had often produced unnecessary state-imposed control and regulation that restricted the freedom of markets and businesses. The resulting rampant government-business collusion, corruption, and lack of transparency in economic activity were reducing the efficiency of the Korean economy and the country's international credit standing. Reducing state interference and regulation while achieving economic transparency and boosting market-based competition, therefore, was to some extent needed in order to make Korea an advanced economy. This means that the introduction of neoliberalism, from the perspective of local Korean time, was, paradoxically, a progressive event to a certain extent. Indeed, some New Right–affiliated intellectuals and other conservative scholars, politicians, and economists did take advantage of arguments such as these to promote the adoption and spread of neoliberalism.

Nonetheless it is clear that the hasty deregulation of labor markets in the absence of a welfare system brought about a sharp increase in socioeconomic inequality. The Kim Dae-jung government responded to the growing rich-poor divide and consequent eruption of social conflict as a result of the radical structural reforms by creating and expanding parts of the welfare system, such as introducing the national basic-livelihood security system, reinforcing the national pension system, and reforming the national medical-insurance service. In this regard Korea can be seen as having taken a path in the opposite direction from the introduction of neoliberalism by reinforcing its social-welfare system in order to mitigate the damage inflicted. Sonn Ho-cheol (2011) describes this phenomenon with wry wit: "While welfare states in the

West 'retreated' due to neoliberalism, Korea began with no welfare state and is now 'advancing' toward becoming a neoliberal welfare state" (667–68).

When it comes to democracy, comparing the trajectory of early-comer Western nations with that of Korea reveals an interesting contrast: Whereas the former followed a progression of oligarchic liberalism, liberal democracy, welfare-statist liberal democracy (or social democracy), and finally neoliberalism, Korea omitted the welfare-state stage to produce a progression of Cold War–era anticommunist liberal democracy (or authoritarianism), liberal democracy, and neoliberalism (along with welfare-system expansion).[7] In Western countries, attempts by neoliberals to drastically reduce welfare benefits were met with strong resistance due to balanced distribution of power among social classes (compared with Korea, at least), and the welfare systems, still well established, helped mitigate the damage inflicted by neoliberalism. In Korea, however, where the social-welfare system was meager to start with and the working class was at a greater disadvantage when it came to the social distribution of power, damage resulting from the hasty introduction of neoliberalism inevitably produced a shock far stronger than that sustained in the West.

Contemporary Korean political history, however, is not one of always being overwhelmed by global historical time. There have also been times when Korea successfully resisted pressure from global historical time while asserting or adhering to its own local time frame. Examples of this include the rapid emergence and expansion of left-wing and radical nationalist thought in the 1980s as Korea witnessed the Gwangju Democratization Movement of 1980 and the ensuing establishment of the military regime under Chun Doo-hwan that suppressed it relentlessly, and the continuing conflict between South and North Korea even after the general collapse of the global Cold War order.

First, the left-wing ideology and unification-oriented radical nationalism that erupted in South Korea in the 1980s were, more than anything else, divorced from global historical time in the sense that it constituted a retrospective reappearance of left-wing and radical nationalist ideologies stifled in the process of national division in the "liberated space." As is well known, the liberated space offered left-wingers and unification-oriented nationalists temporary freedom for radical political action. But these same figures were thoroughly suppressed or eliminated in the course of successive events such as the establishment of the Cold War global order and of mutually antagonistic states in South and North Korea, the June 25 War, and the installation of increasingly stronger anticommunist dictatorial regimes in the South.

As examined while discussing the sanctification of nationalism in chapter 3, however, the emergence of the Chun Doo-hwan regime in 1980 served as a catalyst for the appearance of radical revolutionary movements in the ensuing decade. When we recall, however, the fact that socialist revolutions historically have occurred in the early stages of capitalism, before industrialization had made extensive progress; that policies of reform and openness in communist states, such as perestroika in the Soviet Union, ultimately led to the collapse of the socialist bloc; and that China's policies of reform and opening after 1978 actually moved toward the abandonment of socialism as an alternative to capitalism, the resurgence of radical nationalist liberation and revolutionary socialist movements in Korea can be regarded as a retrospective event divorced from global historical time. The view of South Korean radicals was, however, that the United States had been constantly involved in the dictatorial regimes in their country and the perpetuation of Korean division and that Korea's economic structure and the United States' role must be reassessed in order for democratization and unification to take place. Whereas such claims may have been feasible in terms of local Korean time, the search for solutions in the form of radical national liberation or socialist revolution appears, as history itself later showed, to have been an anachronism and out of sync with global historical time.[8]

Second, the ongoing conflict on the Korean Peninsula between two hostile states that are part of the same nation, despite the collapse of the Cold War order, illustrates stubborn resistance to global historical time by local Korean time.[9] Of course, the thaw in inter-Korean relations that occurred as a result of conciliatory policies toward the North on the part of the Kim Dae-jung and Roh Moo-hyun regimes once appeared to imply a convergence between global and local Korean historical time. Yet these conciliatory policies actually led to an increase in conflict within South Korea itself, and North Korea's ongoing nuclear-missile development and tests also created new inter-Korean tensions. The return of conservatives to power in the South, in the form of the Lee Myung-bak and Park Geun-hye governments, together with North Korea's belligerent provocations vis-à-vis the South and the perpetuation of its hereditary dictatorship (or "family socialism") through the transition of power to a third generation of the Kim family, have led to the continuation of the South-North conflict. In this respect relations between South and North remain unable to melt the Cold War time frame. This continued national division, moreover, acts as a powerful impediment to the weakening of the sanctification of nationalism, as is discussed later, while resolutely preventing the exit of long-entrenched anticommunism.

In addition to the overwhelming of one region's frame by another, or resistance to such pressure, another phenomenon often witnessed during the clash between global and local/national historical time is the convergence of the two different time frames through the dissolution of nonsimultaneity. Phenomena witnessed since the 1980s—such as Korea's pioneering journey to becoming an information society—its stable continuation of democracy, its entry into the ranks of advanced economies by joining organizations such as the Organisation for Economic Co-operation and Development and the World Trade Organization and actively signing various free-trade agreements, its acceptance of neoliberalism, its synchronization with the rest of the world in terms of consumer culture, and the advent of a multicultural society due to factors such as an influx of migrant workers and foreign spouses illustrate that much of what happens today in society is occurring at a point of convergence of global and local Korean historical time. In other words, these two time frames are converging at an ever-growing number of points, allowing Korean citizens to participate actively in and enjoy the global historical time frame.[10]

Above all, such phenomena are due to the globalization and informationization that have been in progress since the late twentieth century, that is, international and revolutionary changes that have weakened or entirely brought down temporal and spatial barriers. Nonetheless the local/national time-based factors that have produced remarkable success in the catch-up mode of development labeled "modernization" in Korea since the 1960s cannot be ignored. Starting in 1995, with the conviction gained from democratization and economic development, the Kim Young-sam government made *segyehwa* (globalization) one of its goals and implemented specific policies in order to promote it. This served as a dramatic signal that the convergence of global and local time had begun in Korea. *Segye* (世界), one of the most commonly used Sino-Korean words for "world," consists of two characters: *se* (世) means "time" (or "era"), whereas *gye* (界) refers to "space" ("place"). Thus *segye* means that the world is a place of residence for people sharing the same time and space.[11] Consequently, if the modernization pursued in Korea referred to change aimed at moving from the global historical past and periphery to present and center—change aimed at overcoming nonsimultaneity, in other words—*segyehwa* implies the understanding that this change has been successfully completed and that Korea is now aligned with the world in terms of time and space (as led by the West, of course). This change in consciousness is once again confirmed by the contrast between Park Chung-hee's proud claim in 1970, encouraged by the rapid economic growth of the 1960s, that the country had gone from being "Korea in Asia" to "Korea in the world" (December 17, 1970, 3:885) and Lee Myung-bak's promise forty years later to "make a Korea of towering stature in the world" while promoting a discourse of "advancement to the leading nations" (*seonjinhwa*) in his Liberation Day speech on August 15, 2009 (Lee Myung-bak 2009).

The Weakening of the Dialectic of Nonsimultaneity after Democratization

As mentioned briefly at the end of chapter 2, changes witnessed in the ideological terrain of contemporary Korean politics since 1987 have demonstrated the gradual weakening of the dialectic of nonsimultaneity, due to the dissolution of the dual political order of authoritarianism and liberal democracy. In terms of the party system, for almost three decades since democratization in 1987 the Korean political order seems to have converged and synchronized with that of the United States—where progressive-liberal and conservative-liberal parties (the Democratic Party and the Republican Party, respectively) constitute a two-party system—rather than with that of most Western European countries—which comprise a social democratic party and a conservative party. The current Korean two-party system, in which the notable presence of a third progressive party is relatively encouraging given past patterns of suppression, began to take its basic shape once the Kim Dae-jung government came to power (1998–2002), which achieved a peaceful power transfer through an election for the first time in Korean history, and continued with the subsequent Roh Moo-hyun government (2003–2007).

A basic outline of the current Korean party system is as follows: In the 2004 general election, under the Roh Moo-hyun government, Korean politics witnessed an unusual event. The Yeollinuridang (Uri Party), the ruling progressive-liberal party, gained a majority of seats (152 seats) for the first time, whereas the Hannaradang (Grand National Party), the conservative-liberal former ruling party, which had been the largest party since democratization, was relegated to the status of the second party, securing only 121 seats. The two-party system in which these major parties competed for power was consolidated. At the same time, a degree of ideological diversity, which would distinguish the Korean party system from that of the United States, was added when the social democratic Minjunodongdang (Democratic Labor Party) gained ten seats and rose to the third party while the conservative Jayuminjuyeonhap (Liberal Democratic Union) secured only four. The 2012 general election basically produced a two-party landscape. The conservative-liberal ruling Saenuridang (New World Party), successor to the Hannaradang, won a majority of 152 seats, whereas the progressive-liberal opposition, Tonghapminjudang (United Democratic Party), successor to the Yeollinuridang, secured 127 seats, maintaining its status as the second party. Ideological diversity was also sustained when the social democratic Tonghapjinbodang (United Progressive Party), successor to the Minjunodongdang, gained thirteen seats and the conservative Jayuseonjindang (Liberty Forward Party), successor to the Jayuminjuyeonhap, secured only four.[12] The ideological differences between Korean parties are not always as coherently or sharply articulated as those between parties in advanced Western democracies. Nonetheless, Korean parties still display discernible differences and characteristics in their professed ideologies and party platforms. Considering this party system in conjunction with the possibility (now a familiar scene) of peaceful transfer of power through democratic election, it may be said that the discrepancy between Western and Korean democracy has been weakened remarkably.

Thus the current political situation raises an interesting question as to the prospect of Korean politics in the twenty-first century: how will the ongoing convergence and differentiation of diverse political ideologies take shape? Supposing that the four major modern ideologies continue to constitute the ideological topography in the near future, two different prospects are feasible, as was suggested earlier. One is that Korean politics will evolve according to the American or Japanese model, in which progressive-liberal and conservative-liberal parties constitute a two-party system, and the other is to follow the Western European model, in which a social democratic party and a conservative party generally constitute a two-party system. Considering from the present vantage point a particularly Korean factor that Koreans are generally weak in class consciousness in politics due to a long legacy of divisive regionalism and strong anticommunism, and noting the general global trend that world politics has been undergoing overall conservatization due to the collapse of former socialist regimes and the upsurge of neoliberalism, the former prospect seems more likely to be realized than the latter.

Simultaneity of the Nonsimultaneous Ever-Present in Modernity?

Finally, I conclude this discussion by pointing out the limited utility of the dialectic of nonsimultaneity, used in order to bring the ideological differences between Korea and Western Europe into sharp relief. Fredric Jameson, who rose to become the foremost Marxist theoretician of postmodernism with the 1991 publication of *Postmodernism, or, the Cultural Logic of Late Capitalism*, characterizes modernism as "uniquely corresponding to an uneven moment of social development" or "the coexistence of realities from radically different moments of history," thereby resorting to "what Ernst Bloch called 'simultaneity of the nonsimultaneous'" (Jameson 1991, 307). It seems rather striking that Jameson has changed his position from that of defending "Lukács' notion of the all-embracing totality of capitalism against critics such as Bloch" to that of raising "Bloch's dialectic of nonsimultaneity to the fundamental matrix of (high) modernism" (Durst 2002, 171). While defining *nonsimultaneity* as "a historical situation marked by an often confused constellation of coexisting economic structures and sociocultural formations from different epochs," David C. Durst, in his attempt to explain Jameson's surprising conversion, points to the "stark realities of nonsimultaneity in former communist countries undergoing the painful process" of "uneven capitalist modernization" since the fall of the Berlin Wall—that is, the embarrassing "return of the capitalist modern in parts of Europe" in the age of "postmodern Western Europe" (ibid., 171).

Although Jameson's conversion to the dialectic of nonsimultaneity and Durst's defense of it appear plausible, I cannot help but think that they are still Western-centric in their interpretation of modernity. By focusing on the complex nature of its ideological terrain, my examination of the Korean experience of modernization has amply shown that capitalist modernization on a global scale, including that in most non-Western nations, has certainly been experienced not in terms of "Lukács' notion of the all-embracing totality of capitalism" but in terms of Bloch's "simultaneity of the nonsimultaneous," characterized by simultaneous existence of asynchronous time zones and their uneven development. The dialectic of nonsimultaneity may thus be interpreted as a common variable that applies not only to many non-Western nations belatedly undergoing modernization but also to some Western nations undertaking retroactive capitalist modernization. The difference between the two, then, in the dialectic of nonsimultaneity may not be one of kind but one of degree.[13] In fact it may be understood in continuum, not in dichotomy. Following this interpretation it could be stated that Western intellectuals like Jameson have belatedly witnessed nonsimultaneity, which non-Western societies have been experiencing as a part of everyday life, through the collapse of communist regimes and their subsequently uneven transitions to capitalism.

THE SANCTIFICATION OF NATIONALISM IN DECLINE

Nationalism has enjoyed the foremost status among various ideologies in South Korea. From this position of supremacy, nationalism has functioned as an ultimate source of legitimacy, bestowing legitimacy upon other ideologies or reinforcing their legitimacy. Moreover, among the various tasks of nationalism, it is unification that has occupied a position of overwhelming dominance and importance over other tasks such as modernization and democratization. In chapter 3 I label this ideological characteristic the "sanctification of nationalism" and examine it in detail. But from the perspective of the present, almost three decades after Korea's democratization, it appears that nationalist passion is gradually cooling and the desire for unification as part of the nationalist agenda is also slowly waning, leading in turn to a weakening of sanctification. I begin, here, with a detailed discussion of the weakening of unification-oriented nationalism before offering a brief diagnosis of the overall decline in nationalist passion resulting from the worldwide change brought about by globalization and informationization. I then briefly discuss the recent criticism in Korean academic circles of the sanctification that has occurred in conjunction with these actual changes and the emergence of so-called postnationalism.

"Modernization from above" and "democratization from below" were passionately driven in South Korea due to their combination with nationalist desire, but nationalism reached the peak of its sanctification when combined with the desire for unification.[14] In 1947, watching as the fate of his country veered toward division, and determined to prevent it, Kim Gu (1997) sanctified nationalism by comparing the ideological conflict between left and right to a "temporary storm" on the "eternal sea" of a nation bound by blood. "We must not forget that today's so-called left and right wings are no more than a temporary storm on the eternal sea of our blood," he said. "In this way, all the ideologies flow and ebb; thus, all beliefs shift up and down. Only the nation as bound by blood will persist on the earth as a body entwined with a net of common destiny of permanent vicissitudes" (370–71). Almost fifty years later, proposing a summit meeting to North Korean president Kim Il-sung "anytime, anywhere" during his inauguration speech in 1993, President Kim Young-sam echoed Kim Gu's statement by proclaiming the nation to be of greater value than any other alliance or ideology. "No ally is more important than our own nation," said Kim. "No ideology or thought can bring greater happiness than the nation" (Kim Young-sam 1993).

Park Chung-hee, frequently criticized by unification nationalists as a "divided statist" (a statist adhering to the separate South Korean state), made modernization the top priority of nationalism but emphasized that unification was the supreme task and often described it as the "sacred project," thereby reinforcing the sanctification of unification-oriented nationalism and getting on the bandwagon at the same time. As I mention while discussing Park Chung-hee's nationalist discourse in chapter 6, his gradualist doctrine of unification held that unification, the supreme task of the nation, was something that could only be realized once South Korea had achieved the tasks of economic development and democracy successfully, thereby reaching a position of overall predominance over North Korea.

Following Park's plan, many South Koreans would have once perceived the mid-1990s, when an imminent collapse of the North Korean regime was predicted, as a golden opportunity for unification. The government of South Korea under Roh Tae-woo, with its confidence boosted by the successful hosting of the 1988 Olympic Games, actively sought to engage diplomatically with North Korea while establishing diplomatic ties with China as well as other former communist states, such as Eastern European nations and the Soviet Union. Both Koreas joined the United Nations simultaneously in 1991. In December of that year both states signed the Agreement on Reconciliation, Nonaggression, and Exchange and Cooperation between South and North Korea (the so-called Basic Agreement between South and North), which created the atmosphere of a thaw. The Kim Young-sam government emphasized the nation in its inaugural presidential address (as quoted earlier), sent long-term unconverted political prisoner Lee In-mo back to North Korea unconditionally, and made moves toward a summit meeting with Kim Il-sung. But North Korea's withdrawal from the nuclear Nonproliferation Treaty and suspected development of nuclear weapons in 1993 brought tensions on the Korean Peninsula to a head once again. Moreover, the sudden death of Kim Il-sung in July 1994 and the ensuing fierce debate in South Korea over whether it should send a condolence delegation to his funeral placed even greater strain on bilateral relations. At the time, North Korea was driven into a relatively isolated position due to the collapse of socialist regimes and faced a serious economic crisis; a succession of natural disasters in the mid-1990s then pushed the country further into economic hardship and famine. This caused expectations of an imminent collapse of North Korea and absorptive unification by South Korea to spread rapidly through South Korean society (Jeon Jae-ho 2012, 96). The Kim Jong-il regime, however, managed to regain stability, making it clear that such expectations were nothing more than wishful thinking.

As discussed herein, South Korea, which had achieved the nationalist tasks of economic development and democratization by the end of the twentieth century—a rare feat for a non-Western state other than Japan—now found itself in the 1990s facing unification as the ultimate and "top priority" task for nationalism. When, in the mid-1990s, passion of unification movements in civil society ran higher than ever and was accompanied by a temporary thaw in inter-Korean relations, it appeared that the sanctification of unification-oriented nationalism had reached a peak. Looking back from the present over the three decades since democratization, however, it becomes ironically apparent that this point in time when unification emerged as the nation's top priority also marked the beginning of a gradual downward curve in hopes and expectations for unification. This gradual weakening of unification-oriented nationalism has been accompanied by a decline in the sanctification of nationalism.

The cause for this weakening of unification-oriented nationalism can be found, above all, in the fact that unification, unlike modernization and democratization in the past, has not been accompanied by strong nationalist passion on the part of the general public. Immediately after national division and the June 25 War, unification-oriented nationalism ran strong among the general public. But as the conflict between South and North continued and the prospect of unification appeared increasingly dim, the fervor for unification diminished. Unification movements reached a high point under the government of the short-lived Second Republic (1960–1961), but the Park Chung-hee government that replaced it soon set about suppressing such movements while calling for a modernization nationalism that put economic development first in order to eradicate extreme poverty. The Park regime took a leading role in sanctifying modernization nationalism while mobilizing the *gung-min* as "pillars of development" and "warriors of export" in accordance with its developmental export-first policies. From then on, democratic activists opposing the authoritarian regimes of Park Chung-hee and Chun Doo-hwan branded their rules antinationalist due to the way they rode roughshod over the sovereignty of the people (the nation, in other words). Such activists declared and launched a nationalist holy war for democratization, similar to that waged by Korean independence fighters during the Japanese occupation. This movement reached a climax with the June Struggle for democracy in 1987, when the desire of all Koreans for democratization successfully erupted on the back of nationalism. Citizens' associations that led the democracy movement—such as the United Association for Democracy, Unification, and Minjung Movement and the Headquarter of the National Movement for Winning a Democratic Constitution—understood democratization and national unification as inseparable. Identifying national division as the biggest obstacle to democratization, they proclaimed the expulsion of foreign powers and Korean dictators and the establishment of an autonomous, democratic government to be the first step toward unification (Ha Sang-bok and Kim Su-ja 2009, 236–37).

Though the twin currents of modernization from above and democratization from below differed in terms of their protagonists, aims, and timings, they both achieved their goals by successfully mobilizing nationalist desire. The acute pains of poverty and dictatorship were shared by almost all members of Korean society, allowing the eradication of both to acquire a sanctity no less than that of national independence itself. The substantial if not fully satisfactory achievement of the goals of economic development and democratization by the 1990s, however, greatly weakened the sanctity of nationalism in these areas. Meanwhile, the fact that half a century has passed since national division means that most Koreans have grown used to the situation and even regard it as natural.[15] As a result, national unification appears to have effectively lost its urgency as an issue. Of course, the National Security Act and anticommunist ideology, which prevent political criticism including freedom of thought and expression, freedom of association and assembly, and freedom of political criticism and opposition, are still powerful, as shown by recent accusations of the so-called *jongbuk* activity against certain politicians and activists. Nonetheless, today their effects are not felt so acutely by the general public in comparison with other pressing everyday issues such as widespread unemployment, unlike in the days of dictatorship. And, although the assertion that national division poses a decisive obstacle to economic development and democratization may once have been persuasive, contributing to the diffusion of the belief that unification was urgently needed, the development and democratization achieved by South Korea while the nation was still divided have ultimately undermined this assertion. The fact that South Korea has overcome the adversity posed by national division, has achieved economic development and democratization, and is generally satisfied with these achievements means it is unlikely that its citizens will now welcome wholeheartedly the unification that is likely to be accompanied by political confusion and economic difficulty, even if a collapsed North Korea is "absorbed" by the South.

Various surveys of South Korean public opinion unanimously confirm the weakening of unification-oriented nationalism. Writing about the transformation in Korean nationalism since democratization, Jeon Jae-ho (2012) shows empirically how the views of South Koreans on unification have changed from being "emotional and "normative" to "realistic" and "lukewarm" (95–100). Jeon uses three points to make the argument that desire for unification in South Korea reached a peak with predictions of the imminent collapse of the North Korean regime in the mid-1990s but gradually cooled down after the adoption of an engagement policy vis-à-vis the North by the Kim Dae-jung government from the late 1990s: First, Jeon cites the statistic that 73.8 percent of South Koreans surveyed in 1994 expected unification within ten years, marking the sentiment's highest point, but states this figure had fallen to 30 percent by 1999 (96–97). In a 2002 survey, meanwhile, only 12.8 percent of respondents agreed with the statement that "unification must take place as soon as possible," whereas more than half (61.6 percent) expressed a desire for "gradual unification" and, furthermore, 24.8 percent actually responded that they would prefer South and North Korea to remain divided and coexist on good terms rather than be unified (97).[16]

Second, Jeon cites the result of a 2005 survey in which the overwhelming majority of South Korean respondents (88.2 percent) "demanded unification in which the South Korean system would be maintained at least," be it by maintaining both regimes on the peninsula (for example, in the form of a federal government) or by unification under the South Korean system (Jeon Jae-ho 2012, 98). In other words, with the establishment of democracy in the South, almost all South Koreans surveyed shared the view that unification no longer merited giving up the liberal democratic system, sending a strong signal that unification-oriented nationalism had to at least be based on liberal democratic ideology.[17] This serves as a good illustration of the practical attitude that thoroughly undermined the proclamations of Kim Gu and Kim Young-sam that ethnic nationhood was more important than any ideology.

Third, as another factor influencing lukewarm public attitudes toward unification Jeon identifies the widening economic gap and mutual heterogeneity between South and North Korea, which became apparent in the course of the ongoing contact and exchange between the two states from the 1990s onward. In addition, German reunification served to create the concern among South Koreans that unification, even if led by the South, would impose heavy social burdens and demand hefty economic sacrifices. This can be seen as having dampened the enthusiasm of many South Koreans for unification. Consequently, in the latter half of the 2000s, under the Lee Myung-bak administration, several survey questions on why unification was necessary saw practical answers ("to remove the threat of war" or "so that Korea can become more advanced") gradually catching up with answers based on national homogeneity ("because Koreans are part of the same nation"), despite a general preponderance of the latter, with the balance even slightly reversed (44.8 percent to 43 percent) in one 2010 survey (Jeon Jae-ho 2012, 98–99). The fact that most South Koreans today are gradually placing more emphasis on practical, realistic grounds for unification than on notions of shared blood and nationhood is another indication that the sanctification of unification-oriented nationalism has been fading.[18]

Finally, there is one further reason South Korean attitudes on unification have shifted toward realism and half-heartedness. Though it overlaps to some extent with the three reasons outlined previously, it is nonetheless worth mentioning in its own right. Peaceful unification requires negotiation and agreement between the two Koreas, but the South Korean general public perceives the North Korean regime—under both Kim Jong-il and Kim Jong-un—as unwilling to offer such cooperation. Unless some fundamental regime change takes place, and given that the North has continued to develop nuclear weapons and missile technology for the sake of its own survival and national security despite the best efforts of previous South Korean governments and has pulled off a second hereditary leadership succession to perpetuate one of the worst dictatorships in history, few South Koreans expect the regime in the North to earnestly reciprocate South Korean efforts at peaceful unification in the near future. It therefore appears that South Koreans favor either gradual unification or peaceful coexistence. Unlike modernization or democratization, which the South Korean people achieved through their own efforts and struggles, unification is a much more difficult task that requires not only good nationalist intentions on the part of the South Korean government but also earnest cooperation from its counterpart in the North. In other words, "it takes two to tango," or "it takes two hands to clap."

In sum, the attitude of the South Korean people has now changed in alignment with the following three orientations: gradual rather than fast, on the basis of liberal democracy rather than to transcend ideological differences, and desired in order to remove the threat of war or to become an advanced country rather than because Koreans all belong to the same nation. This shift combined with the experience and prospect that it has not been and will not be easy to expect active cooperation from North Korea has led to a decline in nationalist passion for unification in the three decades since democratization.

Before democratization, when various political forces clashed over whether anticommunism (national security), modernization, democratization, or unification was the most urgent national task, advocates of each task justified their respective stance by claiming their choice to be a necessary precondition for reunification.[19] In this way, the ultimate importance of unification was never denied; instead it was strengthened, albeit deferred. Once the nationalist tasks of modernization and democratization had been achieved, however, they no longer had to compete with the unification task. Moreover, the success of modernization and democratization was accompanied by the effective political victory of the South Korean regime in its struggle with the North, decreasing the power of anticommunist nationalism to the extent that anticommunism is no longer claimed to be the state doctrine in South Korea.[20] This has led, in turn, to a decline in the influence of the claim that the North Korean communists are "not part of the same nation." Consequently, it can be said that other tasks of nationalism no longer compete with unification over which is more urgent or more important. Now leaving only unification to be achieved, however, Koreans find themselves in a baffling paradox in which the desire for unification has been dampened unexpectedly.

So far we have pointed to the weakening of the sanctification of unification-oriented nationalism while examining it with regard to the dynamics of internal change in South Korean society and inter-Korean relations. Finally we explore the weakening of both unification-oriented nationalism and nationalism in general due to the huge changes brought by modernization, democratization, and the more recent transformation of globalization and informationization. First, there is strong persistence of various types of collectivism based on family and school ties and regionalism as well as nationalism and statism; yet industrialization, urbanization, and rationalization accompanied by economic development and modernization have resulted in the slow but continuous growth of individualism and weakening of nationalism and other kinds of collectivism in Korean society. It is important to remember that even before democratization the problem of growing individualism almost always cropped up when discussing intergenerational conflict, although Korean society was characterized in cultural terms by a generally strong collectivism based on familism. Morever the huge changes brought to Korean society by globalization and informationization in the three decades since democratization in 1987 have further reinforced and diffused individualism, weakening nationalism. The globalization that accompanied the opening of the country with such major events as the 1988 Olympics and the 2002 World Cup, as well as the liberalization of overseas travel, has offered Koreans a variety of international experiences. This has led, in turn, to the recession of the type of closed, inferiority complex–infused nationalism rooted in the country's history. Koreans are now experimenting with a transition to a more open and civic nationalism on the basis of positive national pride (Kim Su-ja 2005).

As Korean society has been rapidly undergoing globalization, an increasing number of migrant workers, North Korean defectors, ethnic Korean workers of Chinese nationality, immigrant foreign spouses, and foreign individuals and overseas Koreans working for transnational companies has come to live and settle in Korea, an unprecedented phenomenon meaning that more postnationalist tolerance and respect for cultural diversity are demanded of Koreans than ever before. This pressure, combined with the long-term trend of a gradually growing number of foreigners acquiring Korean nationality or the right to long-term residence, looks set to dissolve the previously stable fusion of the state and nation based on the myth of a single and pure nation, thereby reinforcing concepts of citizenship based on individualism.

Korea's graduation to an information-based society and the expansion of gender equality based on active women's movements have also proved to be powerful mechanisms in the weakening of nationalism. Netizens relying on the anonymity of cyberspace to express their unencumbered selves transcend temporal and spatial barriers to effectively individualize in its most extreme form: atomization. Experienced this way in virtual space, individualism can clearly go beyond virtual space and be transferred and expanded into the physical realm. Women's movements, too, are playing a leading role in dissolving the patriarchal family, the cradle of collectivism, through various activities, including the successful abolition of the traditional family-registry system. The exposure and resulting accusations of sexual harassment, abuse, and discrimination suffered by women as they increasingly enter and become active in social realms such as company life, education, and even the military are not only serving to improve women's rights but are also securing more breathing space for individualism by contributing decisively to the dissolution of Korea's male-centered, collectivist-organization culture. Of course the neoliberal employment practices—the destruction of seniority-based systems and lifetime employment, the general spread of irregular contract-based employment, the increased use of dispatched workers, and the higher number of Koreans working for foreign companies—introduced in earnest after the financial crisis of 1997 are turning Korea's collectivist corporate culture toward individualism (Kang Jung In 2008b, 142–43). In sum, this increase in individualism is set to weaken nationalism, the most potent hotbed of collectivism, and its sanctification while at the same time mitigating the overdetermining of liberalism by nationalism.

Some theoretical discussions and actual trends differ from the picture I have painted here, however. The debate about how globalization affects nationalism (or the nation-state), for example, is fraught with controversy. The growth of transworld space due to globalization has blurred the differences between nations, whereas the close contact between various nations as a result of global markets and media sometimes serves to strengthen national identity. Moreover, by removing the protective barrier once provided by territorial distance and borders, globalization sometimes provokes nationalists into taking reactionary measures. Nonetheless, globalization is eating away at the view of the nation as the primary framework of the community and is creating a new framework of multiple, alternative bonds. In the process the building of collective identity inevitably takes on a multidimensional, fluid, and unclear appearance. It is commonly pointed out that this leads to a greater diversity in forms of nationalism and modes of their existence, which also are no longer as stable as in the past (Scholte 2000). This implies that nationalism in Korea, too, can only continue to exist in a different form and diverse mode of existence and that the sanctification of nationalism of past years is inevitably set to fade.

Neither can we ignore the currently deepening nationalist conflict among South Korea, China, and Japan over territorial and historical disputes, including the issue of coping with past evils. As is well illustrated by media reports in each country, externally directed nationalist conflict naturally increases internal nationalism. Recent research illustrates persuasively the fact that the Internet, the leading mechanism of informationization, is actually exacerbating this conflict (Lew Seok-jin, Cho Hui-jeong, and Park Seol-a 2013). This recent phenomenon and its study remind us that the relationship between globalization/informationization and nationalism is far more complex than it appears at first glance and requires serious examination. But my intention here is, via the concept of the sanctification of nationalism, to note the collective sentiment that had formed originally as a reflexive response to a pent-up national inferiority complex brought on by experiences such as colonialization and has grown stronger within the Korean nation in the processes of modernizing as a latecomer in order to overcome nonsimultaneity. Then nationalism that arises with the development of new circumstances after the successful accomplishment of the tasks of modernization, and the consequent considerable reduction of the national inferiority complex, is not likely to enjoy the same powerful sanctification as before.

In accordance with these changing realities, the academic discourse on nationalism tends to raise increasingly vociferous criticism of its sanctification. This is symbolically demonstrated by the titles of several recently published books about nationalism. In 1999, when Lim Ji-hyeon published the provocatively titled *Minjokjuuineun Banyeogida: Sinhwawa Heomuui Minjokjuui Damnoneul Neomeoseo* (Nationalism Is Treason: Beyond the Myth and Emptiness of Nationalist Discourse), nationalism held a high enough profile to make it the target of such a powerful attack. But, although criticism of nationalism among Korean academics continued to rise for some time after this, titles of works published from 2000 onward—such as Lee Seon-min's (2008) *Minjokjuui, Ijeneun Beoryeoya Hana* (Is Now the Time to Abandon Nationalism?), Kwon Hyeok-beom's (2009) *Minjokjuuineun Joeaginga* (Is Nationalism a Sin?), and *Jaesaengui Damnon: 21 Segi Minjokjuui* (Regenerative Discourse: Twenty-First Century Nationalism) by Jeong Su-il and others (2010)—hint at a defensive stance toward nationalism.[21]

From 1994 on, the government of Kim Young-sam made *segyehwa* (globalization) a national priority and introduced a series of policies in line with the global neoliberal trend, such as national openness and concessions to free-market forces. At the same time, from the late 1990s onward, scholars of various theoretical backgrounds began positing a strain of "postnationalism" critical of the sanctification and infallibility of nationalism (Jeon Sang-bong 2010, 294–95).[22] Here I want to briefly examine criticism of nationalism by both the New Right and some progressives.

Some New Right intellectuals, such as Kim Young-hwan, Park Ji-hyang, and Lee Young-hun, brand progressive unification-oriented nationalism "left-wing," equating it with "national supremacism" and "exclusivist nationalism" and fiercely criticize its harmful effects (Kim Chi-gwan, 2010, 239–41). Kim Young-hwan—who once advocated direct struggle against American imperialists in the mid-1980s (as examined in chapter 3) before changing his ideological color to become a campaigner for human rights for North Korea in the late 1990s—claims that Korean nationalist tendencies are even stronger than world-famous Arab nationalism, criticizing their excesses. "For the last fifty-five years," says Kim, "Korean nationalism has steadily grown stronger in the complete absence of obstacles, a near-total lack of restraining forces. At times, it has even been encouraged, supported, and protected by strongly nationalist presidents such as Rhee Syngman and Park Chung-hee" (Kim Young-hwan 1999; quoted in Kim Chi-gwan 2010, 242). As this quotation illustrates, it is a baffling paradox to observe the tone of the New Right argument that lumps together two deadly contending political forces—unification-oriented progressive nationalists who were branded "communist sympathizers" by the ruling elite on the one hand and the division-maintaining nationalists such as Rhee Syngman and Park Chung-hee who were attacked as "antination" by the progressive nationalists on the other—and slams them as excesses of nationalism and "national supremacism."

Haebang Jeonhusaui Jaeinsik (A New Understanding of History before and after the Liberation; Park Ji-hyang et al. eds.) was published in two volumes in 2006 by various New Right scholars in order to criticize the doctrine of the necessity for popular (*minjung*) revolution and national supremacism contained in the *Haebang Jeonhusaui Insik* (Understanding History before and after the Liberation) series,[23] a major source of ideological inspiration for radical activists and progressive intellectuals in the 1980s. Park Ji-hyang

(2006), who wrote the preface to the book as one of the four editors, branded nationalism as "originally an exclusive and violent ideology" before slamming its sanctification: "It seems that national supremacism is only satisfied when the nation has overwhelmed all other values and occupied the highest position of all" (Park Ji-hyang 2006, 13–14). Lee Young-hun (2007), too, criticizes sanctified nationalism in view of the danger of its abuse. "Why, then," Lee writes, "do we need to speak out in condemnation of nationalism? Because no other ideology, be it democracy, liberalism, or anything else, has yet become a match for the excessive power of nationalism. Were the huge mobilizing power of nationalism to be misused for political ends, I think, it would be very hard to control the result" (45). Thus New Right scholars such as Lee Young-hun claim that Korea can only enter a group of truly advanced nations once it escapes "the trap of nationalism" as understood according to a "fundamentalist" viewpoint. They suggest liberalism as an alternative to nationalism in the age of globalization (ibid., 32; Bae Jin-young 2006, 219; Kim Il-young 2006a).

Attacks on sanctification are not limited to the New Right but have also emerged in strong form from some progressive circles. In 2007, when the Jajupa (Autonomy Faction) gained control of the Democratic Labor Party, the Pyeongdeungpa (Equality Faction) broke away in protest and published a book under the author name Jinbojeongchiyeonguso (Institute for Progressive Politics; 2007) titled *Sahoe Gukga, Hanguk Sahoe Jaeseolgyedo* (The Social State: A New Design for Korean Society), seeking to justify its decision. Though acknowledging the positive role played by nationalism in the twentieth century, the book identified "the nationalist tradition firmly rooted among progressives and social activists" as an outmoded legacy that had to be swept away resolutely for the sake of a new, twenty-first-century progressivism. "It is clear that nationalism was among the progressive, liberation-oriented projects of the twentieth century," they wrote. "Many oppressed peoples armed themselves with it in the fight against imperialism, winning nation-states as their trophies as a result. But having won a victory—having secured nation-states—nationalism has been transformed from an instrument of progress and liberation to a source of oppression and contradiction. The revenge-based nationalisms that solidify in each nation-state end up falling into endless tension and conflicting with one another. Is this not exactly what is currently happening in East Asia?" (289).[24] The Jinbojeongchiyeonguso goes on to claim that "we must accept whole-heartedly" the twenty-first century's progressive trends such as "ecology, pacifism, and feminism . . . no matter how unfamiliar they may seem" (309).

In a keynote speech at an academic conference in 2010, while acidly attacking the failure of party politics as witnessed in Korea since democratization, Choi Jang-jip, a recent advocate of progressive liberalism, identified the "phenomenon in Korean society whereby political conflicts and issues driven by the radicalism of movements leaned more toward nationalist issues, where passions and ideologies collided head-on, than toward socioeconomic issues that could have been handled rationally, thus wasting progressive energy in the process"; he called this phenomenon one of the fundamental causes of the failure to address issues of labor and everyday life. In other words, Choi was criticizing excessive nationalism by asserting that "nationalism or statism that emphasized the collectivist sacrifice for the sake of the state and the community" was incapable of addressing the political issues considered important in today's representative democracy—namely, "issues of daily life" that accord importance to "the dignity and value of the individual" (Choi Jang-jip 2010).

As I have described so far, we are witnessing a phenomenon, three decades after the advent of democracy, whereby the sanctification has been weakened considerably both in practical terms and in academic discourse. The overdetermination of other ideologies by nationalism—the phenomenon whereby ideologies such as liberalism, radicalism, and conservatism are overdetermined by nationalism after invoking it in order to secure greater legitimacy for themselves—is now fading. And, as discussed previously, the diminished passion for unification-oriented nationalism, the final stage of the nationalist project, has also greatly reduced the overpowering presence of the unification task in nationalism.[25]

THE LEGACY OF PARK CHUNG-HEE'S POLITICAL THOUGHT

I now conclude this book by discussing how the political thought represented by Park Chung-hee, which has functioned as a comprehensive version of right-wing conservatism in Korea, has undergone a change as a source of continuity and renewal for conservatism in Korea over the last three decades and then explore the prospect for how it will endure in the future.

As of 2017, almost forty years have passed since the end of Park's eighteen-year rule. When it comes to discussion of the positive and negative aspects of his legacy, however, the fact that much more time has passed since his demise than the time during which he actually held power should by no means be used to undermine its ongoing significance with some sort of complacency. Even after Park's death the military rule of Korea continued, in effect, more than thirteen years, until the installation of the Kim Young-sam government in 1993. The Chun Doo-hwan regime that held power from 1980 to 1987 is often referred to as "the Park Chung-hee regime without Park Chung-hee." Although the government of Roh Tae-woo, which followed it, was launched by a democratic election, Roh was another key figure in the surprise mini coup d'état in December 1979 that followed Park's death the same year. Moreover, under the Roh government, large numbers of civilians such as bureaucratic, legal, and big-business groups who supported the Park and Chun regimes as well as members of Chun's "Hanahoe" military faction remained intact, constituting the overwhelming majority of the ruling elite. Meanwhile, oppressive instruments of state control such as the Agency for National Security Planning and the Defense Security Command survived in strong form. In this respect, as Koh Jong-seok (2005) insightfully points out, "the Chun Doo-hwan and Roh Tae-woo regimes were substantially filled by members of the 'Park Chung-Hee tribe,' so that Park effectively ruled Korea, even after his physical death in October 1979, until February 1993 as a kind of posthumous ruler."

Seen from this angle, the Park Chung-hee regime lasted in a broad sense for thirty-two years, whereas proper democracy has existed in Korea for only twenty-four years as of this writing. Furthermore, Lee Myung-bak—winner of the 2007 presidential election with a manifesto promising to raise Korea to the ranks of advanced nations through high economic growth, relying on his background as an executive at one of the chaebol conglomerates, cultivated by intensive support during the years of Park Chung-hee's developmental dictatorship—and Park Geun-hye—current president and daughter of Park Chung-hee—who reached power while defending the "inevitability" of her father's regime—illustrate how Park Chung-hee's posthumous rule has appeared intermittently in various guises even after democratization. By contrast, democratic governments showing a strong will for reform and the thorough elimination of the vestiges of authoritarianism have held power for a surprisingly short period of time, fifteen years at most, even including the rule of the Kim Young-sam government.

In the same vein, Park Myeong-lim (2006) makes lucid comments in the beginning of his article dealing with Park Chung-hee's rule. "If the most influential event in Korean contemporary history, in the memory of the Korean people, is the Korean (June 25) War," writes Park Myeong-lim, "the most influential individual is Park Chung-hee. . . . None of the major changes in Korean society, in any field, can be understood if Park and his era are bypassed. . . . The magnetic field of influence covered by him and his era is indeed a large and wide one" (32). For this reason, conservative commentators discussing contemporary politics describe Park Chung-hee as a hero responsible for all the positive achievements of Korean politics, whereas progressive ones criticize him as the villain behind all of the country's political ills. When it comes to the merits and demerits of economic development, for example, Park is sometimes praised as the star of the "Miracle on the Han River" narrative but is also attacked as the originator of the economic structure that led to Korea's so-called trusteeship at the hands of the IMF after the foreign-exchange crisis of 1997. When it comes to democratization, too, there is disagreement between those who believe the economic development achieved under Park Chung-hee became a sustainable economic basis for Korean democratization and those who claim that the authoritarian legacies left by his rule, such as regionalism, a serious rich-poor divide as symbolized by the chaebol-dominated economy, abuse of human rights, and excessive state power, are decisively obstructing the consolidation of democracy (ibid.). But these polarized assessments tacitly share the assumption that Park, for better or worse, was a kind of omniscient and omnipotent Übermensch.

Of course, such thinking is ahistorical or antihistorical; what is needed is a more academic approach whereby the rule of Park Chung-hee, as a politician with both admirers and detractors, is assessed according to the kind of "Park Chung-hee–style developmental-dictatorship paradigm"[26] that his regime built. This paradigm begins with politician Park Chung-hee, endowed with strong leadership skills and charisma, who sets a national goal of rapid economic growth through export-led industrialization in order to drive modernization and secure a superior position in the struggle between South and North Korea. In order to push economic development strongly ahead, he builds a social system, achieving political stability, establishing social order, and creating a complete system of education, while maintaining a powerful national administration including an efficient bureaucracy. He then establishes and implements a strategy to maximize the mobilization of human and material resources in order to undertake his national goal. He makes efficient use of both sticks and carrots in the process of establishing and implementing such goals. In other words, he tries to induce a voluntary popular consensus as far as possible using material incentives, but he creates physical organs of coercion in order to suppress opponents when necessary and does not flinch at using them to exercise highly efficient (read: merciless) coercive power. Of course, the respective proportions of spontaneous consensus and physical coercion varied according to the political situation at any given time. This paradigm understands the strong leadership and consequent authoritarian rule as being indispensable in establishing and implementing national goals; the combination of goal establishment and implementation and strong leadership (authoritarian rule) is, in broad terms, coalesced into an economic-development strategy through strong initiative and intervention on the part of the state.

If the Park Chung-hee–style developmental-dictatorship paradigm is understood as outlined here, then Park's political thought can be regarded as a political discourse produced in order to justify the establishment and implementation of national goals and the exercising of powerful leadership in the process of realizing the paradigm. According to this view, Park produced discourses of anticommunism, democracy, antiliberal conservatism, and nationalism in the process of establishing national goals of national security and economic development (modernization) and justifying the resolute, efficient pursuit of these goals; the entirety of these discourses can be understood as constituting Park's political thought. In the process of producing his political discourses, Park concocted appropriate mixtures of the filial piety and collectivism of Confucian culture, the traditional patriarchal authoritarianism, the fascist legacy of Japanese rule, and the "eternal state of emergency" created by security crises such as the June 25 War, North Korean military provocations, the fall of Vietnam, and the withdrawal of US troops from South Korea (Jeon In-gwon 2006, 254–57).

It is not easy to ascertain just how much of the political thought extracted from these discourses is actually the personal thought of Park Chung-hee. In some ways his thought is an overall expression of historical hardships suffered by the Korean nation since the late nineteenth century: the aggression of foreign powers, the failure of autonomous modernization, loss of sovereignty and colonial exploitation at the hands of Japan, the Japanese fascist system, the division and occupation of the Korean Peninsula by the US and Soviet militaries and ensuing national division, the June 25 War, the dictatorship of Syngman Rhee, the student-led April Revolution, the chaos of the Second Republic, extreme poverty and corruption, and so on. It is also a product of a cultural heritage that he used in order to justify his own rule in the process of producing political discourses. In this respect Park's thought, a coalescence of various political discourses, was a product of its times. On the other hand, however, it was spread widely and became deeply embedded among conservatives, the general public, and even his opponents during his long rule, via various ideological media and mechanisms including education, propaganda, films, military life and discipline, and the Saemaeul Movement, and can therefore be regarded as having exerted a powerful formative influence on political thought and ideas in general during the era of his rule. In other words, Park's political thought both represented intensively the conservative right-wing thought that had coalesced in Korean politics since national liberation, led by anticommunism and modernization, and was instilled continuously and systematically into the people throughout Park's long rule. In this sense, it was the ruling ideology of its time.

Seen from this perspective, the antidemocratic, antiliberal, and right-wing nationalist thought inherent in Park's developmental-dictatorship paradigm cannot be viewed merely as his own personal ideas. Rather, it is a representation and enhancement of the political culture formed primarily by right-wing conservatives since the late nineteenth century with the addition of Park's particular style of leadership—policies implemented like military strategies, rampant intelligence politics using the KCIA and public-security apparatuses, excessive use of emergency measures to suppress political opposition, and so on. Here, bearing this in mind, we take a brief look at the legacy and future of Park Chung-hee's political thought in light of the political changes in the three decades since democratization, nonsimultaneity, and sanctification. We do this in order of Park's discourses of democracy, antiliberal conservatism for modernization, and nationalism, as discussed in part 2.

First, Park never fully denied the desirability of Western liberal democracy in the discourse on democracy he produced, in a situation where authoritarianism and liberal democracy existed in parallel. But he quibbled that the proper implementation of liberal democracy was hard to achieve, sometimes due to the need to prioritize anticommunism (national security) and economic development (or modernization), sometimes due to Korea's unique history and cultural traditions, and sometimes because factors such as Korea's lack of political experience would produce chaos and a lot of other undesirable side effects. Instead he promoted the "'Koreanization of democracy,' grafted onto the subjectivity of the history of Korean political thought," advocating "Korean-style democracy" as its final, complete version that emasculated political democracy altogether (Park Chung-hee 1962, 130–31).

But in Korean politics today, with the progress made since 1987, despite the strong residual presence of the obsession with anticommunism (opposition to North Korea) and economic development (developmentalism)—albeit in different forms—the democratic discourse put forward by Park Chung-hee with regard to the Koreanization of democracy can be seen to have all but collapsed. In other words, the political goals of modernization and democratization have been reached, the Cold War order has ended with the fall of socialist regimes, and South Korea has secured a position of overwhelming superiority vis-à-vis the North. As a result, the overlap of two political orders has also come to an end. It has now become impossible to justify authoritarianism or "Korean-style democracy" in the name of anticommunism and economic development. In this sense, Park's discourse on democracy has lost its efficacy with the disappearance of nonsimultaneity as a result of successful modernization and democratization.

This point is confirmed once again by the fact that conservative groups such as the Grand National Party and the New Right, who found themselves out of power with the emergence of the Kim Dae-jung and Roh Moo-hyun governments for a ten-year period starting in 1998, attacked these relatively reformist and progressive governments by labeling them "populists" or "pro-North leftists." The term *populist* was a criticism aimed at the way the Kim and Roh governments allegedly gained popular support using so-called demagogic discourses and "adulatory discourses" that appealed directly to the masses while bypassing parliament, which was dominated by the opposition party at the time, using the according support to put pressure on the opposition while implementing their own reformist policies. The "pro-North leftist" label contained criticism of the way the same two governments pursued policies of engagement aimed at reconciliation and cooperation with North Korea and allegedly sucked vitality out of the free market and the economy by implementing redistributionist and welfare-oriented policies on the domestic front (Kang Jung In 2009b, 92–116). The fact that conservatives criticized the Kim Dae-jung and Roh Moo-hyun governments, calling them leftists hostile to market economy and liberalism, on the pretext of defending the market economy and representative democracy, shows paradoxically that Park Chung-hee–style criticism of liberal democracy no longer carries any weight.

Second, in his discourses on conservatism Park Chung-hee emphasized anticommunism and economic development based on a state-centered view of politics, developing a form of antiliberal conservatism for modernization. Though much of the antiliberal aspect of his thought has diminished since the advent of democracy, it still wields considerable influence in Korean politics. In chapter 1 I point out that liberalism consists of individualism, political liberalism, and economic liberalism, naming the guarantee of human rights, a limited state, and division between public and private realms, constitutionalism, the principle of the separation of powers, and representative systems of democracy as core elements of political liberalism. It appears, however, that almost all of these elements still are lacking or have suffered from stunted growth in Korea since democratization. Indeed, in the several governments that have held office since democratization, power has often been concentrated in the president, the president's family or close associates from informal networks in the Blue House (*Cheongwadae*), and public-security organs such as the Supreme Prosecutors' Office and the National Intelligence Service, with no systematic control over the exercising of this power. It still appears, moreover, that despite Korea's adoption of a presidential system the National Assembly and the judiciary are still not playing the proper roles necessary to achieve checks and balances in accordance with the separation of powers as stipulated by the constitution. Under a government where, rather than a weak ruling party suffering from legislative gridlock at the hands of a powerful opposition, a strong ruling party and weak opposition have created a unified government, the authority of parliament, whose role is to supervise government and debate bills, is considerably weakened. More serious than this, political parties are still unable to properly mediate and aggregate the opinions and interests of the people even after democratization. In particular, the mentality of the life-or-death confrontation between dictatorial regimes, which maintained power through heavy oppression while torturing and incarcerating their citizens, and their opponents, who often responded with self-immolations and death leaps, hunger strikes, and fierce demonstrations, has survived since democratization in the form of an ingrained political culture of deeply rooted mistrust and extreme confrontation, a negative legacy of dictatorial rule. As a result, the formation and maturing of a democratic culture of dialogue, compromise through mutual concession and respect, and political consensus and decision-making through negotiation has been retarded in Korean politics in and outside parliament, in political parties, and in labor-management relations.

Reasons for this lack of progress in political liberalism include, at close hand, the legacy of the Park Chung-hee–style developmental-dictatorial paradigm, linked to the coercion and ruthless suppression of opponents by the Park and Chun governments. But in more far-reaching terms it must be noted that, despite the industrialization, urbanization, and rationalization achieved through the rapid economic development since the 1960s, the growth of individualism in Korean society has been severely delayed. Individualism as a worldview puts reasonable, independent individuals before society or the state and regards the protection of individual life, freedom, and property as paramount. This type of thought holds that the state is merely an artificial mechanism created to safeguard such individual rights. Collectivism, by contrast, regards the group as more important than the individuals who constitute it, prioritizing the goals and order of the group as of primary importance. Koreans often ascribe the delayed growth of individualism to a collectivist mindset based on the Confucian culture that survives from the Joseon period as well as on the nationalist and statist traditions that formed from the late nineteenth century onward and still highly influential. But the long continuation of the Park Chung-hee–style developmental dictatorship that emphasized state nationalism contemptuous of individual liberties and rights also exerted a decisive influence on the stunted growth of political liberalism and individualism in Korean society even after the advent of democracy.[27] One study of the individualist tendencies of Koreans in the 1990s, after democratization, found that "Korea scores 18 points in terms of individualism, showing a strong tendency for collectivism along with Hong Kong (25 points), Singapore (20 points), and Taiwan (17 points)," but "countries with the highest scores for individualism are the United States (91), the United Kingdom (89), Canada (80), and the Netherlands (80)" (Cho Geung-ho 2006, 34–35).[28]

In this way, the tendency for weak individualism is closely linked to the nationalism strongly propagated to the general public throughout Park Chung-hee's rule. In chapter 6 I suggest that Park's nationalism was characterized by anticommunism and modernization based on a powerful fusion of nation and state and that statist elements held the highest status of all with Park's brand of nationalism. Park himself asserted that "the right of the nation to survival" was "an absolutely inviolable, natural right" (October 1, 1973, 5:136), regarding "the survival of the nation" and "the integrity of the state" as indivisible and placing them before individual freedom or democracy. "Individual freedom," Park said, "can only be firmly guaranteed and Korean democracy expanded and developed only if Korea is defended. . . . The survival of thirty-five million people is the ultimate form of human rights guarantee when it comes to Korea" (February 4, 1977; quoted in Park Myeong-lim 2006, 54).

Defense of the state as the guardian of the nation, then, was both an indispensable element and a priority task in order to guarantee not only the survival of the nation but also the freedom of the individual and the expansion of democracy. And since the gravest physical threat to the survival of the nation was North Korea, and economic development and modernization provided the foundations for the nation's physical survival, Park Chung-hee's nationalism was one of anticommunism, branding North Korea antinationalist, and one of modernization. The integral agent in achieving these tasks was the state, whereas the state doctrine of the Republic of Korea that protects the nation was anticommunism.

But, as was pointed out earlier when discussing the fading sanctification of nationalism, South Korea's attainment of a superior position vis-à-vis the North and achievement of modernization meant that the fading of nationalism and statism as engines of anticommunism and modernization became inevitable after democratization. We can therefore expect that under the influence of democratization and industrialization, not to mention globalization and informationization, liberalism will grow more powerful, leading in turn to a weakening of statism and nationalism and a gradual dissolution of the powerful fusion of the two.

Of course, we have also witnessed how calls for Park Chung-hee–style leadership return when Korean society faces a sudden crisis and desires a powerful leader to command the state and lead the nation through the storm. For example, when the foreign-exchange crisis struck in late 1997, under the Kim Young-sam government, popular demand for a powerful and charismatic leader led to an eruption of nostalgia for Park, a phenomenon that was known among Koreans for quite some time as "Park Chung-hee syndrome." At this time, as dissatisfaction with the misrule of the Kim Young-sam government reached a peak, a succession of conservative newspapers and figures began calling for Park Chung-hee. From April 1997, *JoongAng Ilbo* (the Joongang Daily) serialized the memoirs of Kim Jeong-ryeom, Park Chung-hee's former chief presidential secretary. A biography of Park Chung-hee, titled *Nae Mudeome Chimeul Baeteora* (Spit on My Grave; 1998) was written by Cho Gab-je and serialized in *Chosun Ilbo* (Joseon Daily), whereas novelist Lee In-hwa published *Inganui Gil* (The Human Way; 1997), which portrayed Park as a hero.

Various interpretations of Park Chung-hee syndrome, which was produced and magnified by endless conservative-led attempts to create a Park Chung-hee myth, were put forward. Positive interpretations included those by conservatives who claimed that Park had belatedly been properly appreciated, whereas progressives took an approach of ascribing "the phenomenon to the interests of or a conspiracy by reactionary conservatives" dissatisfied with democratization. Others interpreted the syndrome as benefiting reflexively from either the misrule of the Kim Young-sam government or a popular sense of dependence, part of the structure of popular consciousness that sought charismatic authority to rely on (Jeong Hae-gu 1998, 62–66). There is no denying that each of these interpretations is persuasive in its own way.

Nonetheless, seen as part of a contemporary reillumination of Park Chung-hee's political thought, it is certain that the syndrome and the various interpretations of it were not due to any positive appraisal of Park's political thought as such. In other words, Park Chung-hee syndrome originated not with his thought but with nostalgia for his leadership, on the basis of his powerful charisma and decisiveness. The general public, unhappy with the corruption, impotence, and economic failure under the Kim Young-sam government, then the most democratic ever in Korean history, were reacting against it and longed for the powerful leadership style of Park Chung-hee, which, they hoped, could overcome the crises they faced. It is wrong, however, to think that the general public at the time had begun newly supporting antiliberal ideology that ignored people's basic human rights or antidemocratic thought that disregarded majority opinions and governed the country unilaterally. In this sense, Park Chung-hee syndrome, as Kang Jun-man shrewdly pointed out in a book analyzing the phenomenon, managed to capture and magnify a moment of nostalgia similar to the way Korean men who have completed military service at certain moments look back with nostalgia to the exhausting trials and tribulations of military life but would never actually want to return to it (Kang Jun-man 1999, 42).

As mentioned previously while discussing the Korean public's attitude toward unification, since most South Koreans want any future unification to be based on liberal democratic order at least, they will no longer support or tolerate authoritarian or totalitarian thought that denies democracy unless national security faces some desperate predicament, such as the outbreak of war (with North Korea, Japan, or China), or some dire emergency, such as all-out economic disaster. Rather, we may interpret Park Chung-hee syndrome as an expression of the antidemocratic tendencies or dissatisfactions of some members of Korean society who enjoyed particular privilege during Park Chung-hee's rule or faithfully dedicated part of their lives to the Park regime.[29] As can always be witnessed in long-established Western democracies, some segments of the population even in democratic states are deeply dissatisfied with democracy and thus desire the return of authoritarianism or totalitarian government.

NOTES

1. Since 2005, conservative New Right scholars and progressive-nationalist historians have been engaged in a fierce debate over the writing of modern and contemporary Korean history in high school textbooks. The subject related to the sanctification of nationalism constitutes one of the most heated issues in the debate. For more details on this point, see Jeon Jae-ho 2010, Lee Jun-sik 2013, and Hong Seok-ryul 2013.

2. Most of the content addressed here has already been examined in chapter 2. To avoid repetition, only some important points are highlighted.

3. The phenomena that exemplify the progressive overwhelming of local Korean historical time by world historical time are not confined to the past. The import and diffusion of (radical) feminism, ecological thought, and lesbian, gay, bisexual, and transgender movements in contemporary Korean society can also be attributed to this progressive challenge.

4. This doctrine insists on the equality of the people in three realms: politics, the economy, and education (Jo So-ang 1992).

5. See Seo Hui-kyeong 2012 for an excellent study of the process of drafting and enacting the founding constitution of South Korea.

6. As is well known, neoliberalism is opposed to state intervention in the market and stresses the free market, deregulation, and private property. Accordingly, it is also opposed to the social-welfare system, which reduces workers' motivation to work and increases fiscal spending of the government. Thus it advocates the reduction of governmental intervention, vitalization of the market, privatization of the public corporations, and flexibility of the labor market.

7. According to T. H. Marshall's (1965) schematic thesis that extracted and distilled mainly from the English historical experience in the evolution of democracy, England had developed democracy in terms of citizenship, from civil citizenship (civil liberties) in the eighteenth century through political citizenship (universal suffrage) in the nineteenth century to social citizenship (social welfare) in the twentieth century. Then the introduction of neoliberalism in the late twentieth century may well be interpreted to mean the partial withdrawal of social citizenship in Western nations. In contrast, the premature introduction of neoliberalism in Korea immediately after democratization means a delay of the introduction of social citizenship from the beginning.

8. For the interpretation suggested here, I am indebted to Kim Dong-chun (1996b, 1997b).

9. However, if the perpetuation of the North Korean regime—once driven nearly to collapse in the mid-1990s—had been made possible substantially by political support and economic aid from China, and thus the national division as the legacy of the past Cold War had been renewed and prolonged, then it would be possible to interpret the persistence of the national division in the Korean Peninsula as corresponding prefiguratively to the bipolar order now being formed in East Asia between the United States and China. In this case the perpetuation of the national division might not be out of sync with global historical time but rather synchronized with it in advance. In this regard it is important to remember that the division and occupation of South and

North Korea by US–Soviet armed forces at the end of World War II did not follow but preceded the formation of the Cold War.

10. Observing such phenomena of synchronization, Cho Hui-yeon (2004) interprets them as the transition from the state of "abnormality" to "normality" or "normal state."

11. In this sense, *segyehwa* has a unique Korean implication distinct from "globalization."

12. The general election of April 2016, however, witnessed a significant shift in the party system of Korean politics. Just before the election, the opposition Tonghapmin-judang (United Democratic Party) was divided into the Deobureo Minjudang (Democratic Party) and the Gungminuidang (Gungmin's Party). Despite the pessimistic prospects resulting from the division of opposition parties, the opposition Deobureo Minjudang won a stunning victory, emerging as the largest party in the election by gaining 123 seats, narrowly defeating the ruling Saenuridang, which gained 122 seats, whereas the opposition Gungminuidang secured the status of a stable third party by gaining no fewer than thirty-eight seats, while the progressive Jeonguidang obtained six. The Saenuridang regained status of the largest party by recruiting seven assemblypersons after the election, but the opposition parties still held the majority, controlling the National Assembly. It is evident, therefore, that the current party system is not a two-party but a multiparty one. Nevertheless, the 2017 presidential election will confirm whether the current multiparty system turns out to be enduring and stable.

13. In this regard Sandra Halperin (1997) has also reminded us of the uneven development of capitalism and democracy in Western history and the subsequent dialectic of nonsimultaneity in her excellent work.

14. As examined in chapter 3, thus, both the forces for modernization and those for democratization had to assert that the achievement of their respective task was a necessary stage in preparing for the ultimate task of unification.

15. Of course, this phenomenon is attributable to the fact that the generations born after the division have become the overwhelming majority of the population in South Korea.

16. Inter-Korean relations reached their worst point under the Lee Myung-bak administration when the *Cheonanham*, a South Korean naval ship, was sunk in March 2010, allegedly due to North Korean attack. According to a survey of South Koreans conducted at the time, 43.1 percent of respondents agreed with either the statement "We don't have to be in a hurry for unification" (23.5 percent) or the statement "We'd rather not achieve unification" (19.6 percent). The figure was a 15.9–percentage point increase from 27.2 percent in 2005. In contrast, the number of respondents who agreed with the statement "We have to achieve unification as soon as possible" decreased from 17.4 percent to 10.4 percent during the same period (Jeon Jae-ho 2012, 99).

17. Of course, the statement that the overwhelming majority of South Koreans are not willing to give up liberal democracy for the sake of unification should be understood to mean that they do not exclude a more progressive democracy such as social democracy, welfare democracy, or participatory democracy as a proper form of government in a unified Korea.

18. Tracing the shift in South Koreans' perception of North Korea after democratization, Jeon notes that "the emotional and blind hostility toward North Korea during the authoritarian period" has been transformed into "confident anticommunism based on economic superiority" (Jeon Jae-ho 2012, 101–2). Of course, this shift is worth welcoming as a positive change. But, granted that "the emotional and blind hostility toward North Korea" originated invertedly from a love-hate relationship based on national homogeneity and a blood-based single-ethnic mentality, this shift would certainly reflect the weakening national homogeneity. Therefore it is a phenomenon in line with the decrease of the refrain "national homogeneity" for the necessity for unification.

19. Of course, unification-oriented nationalists advocate that unification take precedence over any other tasks, as examined in chapter 3.

20. Objection to this interpretation might be raised in that the conservative governments of Lee Myung-bak and Park Geun-hye and other conservative right-wing elements in South Korea have taken advantage of the so-called *jongbuk* controversy, labeling their political opponents *jongbuk* and oppressing them effectively. One cannot deny that anticommunism underlies the *jongbuk* controversy. It should be noted, however, that being (called) *jongbuk* cannot be a good cause for legal punishment or expulsion from the political realm, not to mention social banishment, unless one explicitly violates the positive law, whereas in the past being called a communist or a communist sympathizer was sufficient cause to become a social outcast, not to mention being legally prosecuted.

21. There is some great variation in the tone of defense among these authors. In particular, Jeong Su-il's (2010) argument merits special attention, revealing his nationalist fundamentalism without any disguise. Defining "nationalism as a universal value of history, universal progressivism, and the ideology of perfect logic and coherent structure," Jeong declares that "nationalism as a historical and progressive universal value would not admit such negative and unproductive evils as conservativeness, exclusiveness, and treacherousness," thereby advocating strongly the infallibility and sanctity of nationalism (62, 49). Naturally Jeong refutes the so-called fallacies of nationalism: "Such expression as negative aspects of nationalism is inappropriate. For nationalism as such, the universal value of history, cannot have negative aspects. If any, they are only negative aspects immature nationalists may reveal in acting out nationalism" (63). This shows clearly that nationalist fundamentalists exist in the conservative camp of Korea as well as in the progressive one.

22. See Lee Seon-min 2008 (15–26) for a succinct but systematic survey of diverse controversies over nationalism since 2000.

23. These books are reviewed briefly in chapter 3 when the sanctification of nationalism is discussed.

24. Kim Young-hwan (2005) also points to "excessively exclusive nationalism," "excessive attachment to leveling," and "lack of tolerance" as three notable problems Korean society has to cope with. Kim estimates nationalism positively as a dynamic that has made a great contribution to rapid economic development in the last four decades, and at the same time he criticizes the exclusive nationalism in the age of globalization for aggravating unnecessary conflicts with neighboring nations as well

as engendering excessive divisions within Korean society. In this respect Kim shares the concern about the evils of excessive nationalism with the Equality Faction in the Democratic Labor Party.

25. However, the frantic *jongbuk* controversy raging over the trial of Lee Seog-gi—National Assembly member from the Tonghapjinbodang (United Progressive Party), who was found guilty in early 2015 on charges of sedition and violation of the National Security Act by the Supreme Court of Korea under the Park Geun-hye government—is a reminder of the urgent need for unification to upgrade Korean democracy to a more sophisticated level. In addition, President Park Geun-hye boosted the *gungmin*'s desire for unification by stating in her 2014 New Year's press conference that, "in a word, unification is a bonanza. . . . I think that unification of the Korean Peninsula is a great opportunity for our economy to make another leap forward" (Choi 2014). In this way she seemed to have reignited unification-oriented nationalism, which was in a stagnant, dampened state for a while.

26. I have borrowed this concept from Jeong Hae-gu (1998, 64–65) and elaborated on it for the purpose of examination here.

27. It appears to be contradictory to previously note and diagnose the gradual decline in the influence of nationalism on the one hand and to stress the persisting influence of statism and nationalism on the other. However, it could be understood as, on the one hand, previously saying that the water in a glass has been diminishing gradually and, on the other, now stressing that a considerable portion of water is still left.

28. Even though Korea, Hong Kong, Singapore, and Taiwan shared the Confucian culture as a staunch pillar of collectivism, the fact that the scores for individualism in Korea and Taiwan are lower than those in Hong Kong and Singapore could be interpreted, should the difference be meaningful, as coming from factors common to both Korea and Taiwan: strong nationalism, a national division, and historical legacies from antiliberal dictatorships.

29. This latter group might have found the meaning of their lives betrayed upon hearing the Park regime, to which they had earnestly devoted their lives, so severely criticized for its dictatorial oppression and upon seeing their involvement in it also become a target of subsequent criticism. So they seem to have an inherent tendency to defend the regime to keep the meaning of their lives intact, deriving a sense of relief from Park Chung-hee syndrome. In this way they have become its active supporters.

References

ENGLISH

Althusser, Louis. 1979. *For Marx*. Translated by Ben Brewster. London: Verso.

Anderson, Benedict. 1985. *Imagined Communities: Reflections on the Origin and Spread of Nationalism*. London: Verso.

Ball, Terence, and Richard Dagger. 2004. *Political Ideologies and the Democratic Ideal*. 5th ed. New York: Longman.

Bloch, Ernst. 1991. *Heritage of Our Times*. Berkeley: University of California Press.

Burke, Edmund. 1978. *Reflections on the Revolution in France*. Edited with an introduction by Conor Cruise O'Brien. Harmondsworth, UK: Penguin.

Chatterjee, Partha. 1986. *Nationalist Thought and the Colonial World: A Derivative Discourse?* London: Zed Books.

Durst, David C. 2002. "Ernst Bloch's Theory of Nonsimultaneity." *The German Review* 77 (3): 171–94.

Eckert, Carter J. 1999. "Epilogue: Exorcising Hegel's Ghosts: Toward a Postnationalist Historiography of Korea." In *Colonial Modernity in Korea*, edited by Gi-Wook Shin and Michael Robinson, 363–78. Cambridge, MA: Harvard University Press.

Fichte, Johann Gottlieb. 1922. *Addresses to the German Nation*. Translated by R. F. Jones and G. H. Turnbull. Chicago: Open Court.

———. 1999. "The Characteristics of the Present Age." In *The Popular Works of Johann Gottlieb Fichte*, vol. 2, translated by W. Smith, with new introduction by D. Breazeale, 1–288. London: Thoemmes Press.

———. 2000. *Foundations of Natural Right*. Translated by Michael Baur. Cambridge: Cambridge University Press.

Foucault, Michel. 1980. *Power/Knowledge*. New York: Pantheon.

Gellner, Ernest. 1983. *Nations and Nationalism*. Oxford: Basil Blackwell.

Halperin, Sandra. 1997. *In the Mirror of the Third World*. Ithaca, NY: Cornell University Press.

Hirschman, Albert O. 1991. *The Rhetoric of Reaction*. Cambridge, MA: Belknap Press of Harvard University Press.

Hobbes, Thomas. 1962. *Leviathan*. Edited by Michael Oakeshott. New York: Macmillan.

Hobsbawm, Eric. 1990. *Nations and Nationalism since 1780*. Cambridge: Cambridge University Press.

Jameson, Fredric. 1991. *Postmodernism, or, the Cultural Logic of Late Capitalism*. Durham: Duke University Press.

Klemperer, Klemens von. 1972. "Conservatism." In *Marxism, Communism, and Western Society: A Comparative Encyclopedia*, vol. 2, edited by C. D. Kernig, 164–69. New York: Herder and Herder.

Langewiesche, Dieter. 2000. *Liberalism in Germany*. Houndmills, UK: Macmillan Press.

Lerner, Max. 1971. "Liberalism." In *Encyclopaedia Britannica*, rev. 14th ed., vol. 13, 1017–20. Chicago: Encyclopaedia Britannica.

Lummis, Douglas. 1996. *Radical Democracy*. Ithaca, NY: Cornell University Press.

Machiavelli, Niccolò. 1965. *Discourses in Machiavelli: The Chief Works and Others*. Vol. 1. Translated by Allan Gilbert. Durham, NC: Duke University Press.

Marshall, T. H. 1965. *Class, Citizenship, and Social Development*. New York: Doubleday.

Meinecke, Friedrich. 1970. *Cosmopolitanism and the National State*. Translated by Robert B. Kimber, with an introduction by Felix Gilbert. Princeton, NJ: Princeton University Press.

Nisbet, Robert. 1986. *Conservatism*. Minneapolis: University of Minnesota Press.

Rossiter, Clinton. 1968. "Conservatism." In *International Encyclopedia of the Social Sciences*, vol. 3, edited by Robert King Merton and David L. Sills, 290–95. New York: Macmillan.

Rousseau, Jean-Jacques. 1967. *"The Social Contract" and "Discourses on the Origin of Inequality."* Edited and with an introduction by Lester G. Crocker. New York: Washington Square Press.

Schmid, Andre. 2002. *Korea between Empires, 1895–1919*. New York: Columbia University Press.

Scholte, Jan Aart. 2000. *Globalization: A Critical Introduction*. New York: St. Martin's Press.

Schwartz, Benjamin I. 1964. *In Search of Wealth and Power: Yen Fu and the West*. Cambridge, MA: Belknap Press of Harvard University Press.

Schwartz, Frederic J. 2001. "Ernst Bloch and Wilhelm Pinder: Out of Sync." *Grey Room* 3 (Spring): 54–89.

Shohat, Ella, and Robert Stam. 1994. *Unthinking Eurocentrism*. London: Routledge.

Smith, Anthony D. 1999. *Myths and Memories of the Nation*. Oxford: Oxford University Press.

———. 2000. "Theories of Nationalism: Alternative Models of Nation Formation." In *Asian Nationalism*, edited by Michael Leifer, 1–20. London: Routledge.

Tuck, Richard. 1989. *Hobbes*. Oxford: Oxford University Press.

Wolin, Sheldon S. 2004. *Politics and Vision*. Expanded edition. Princeton, NJ: Princeton University Press.

KOREAN

Ahn, Byeong-uk. 1968. "Changjowa Hondonui Jang: Sajoui Byeoncheon" [The site of creation and chaos: Change in the ideological trend]. *Sasanggye* (August): 131–40.

Bae, Jin-young. 2006. "Nyuraiteu Yeonswae Inteobyu, Lee Young-hun Nakseong-daegyeongjeyeongusojang: Minjokjuuironeun Seonjinhwa Mot Irwo, Jayujuuiga Minjokjuuiui Daean" [A series of "New Right" interviews: Lee Young-hun—It is hard to reach the status of an advanced nation by nationalism; liberalism is the alternative]. *Wolganjoseon* (August): 208–19.

Cha, Gi-byeok. 1965. "Oyongdoen Minjokjuui: Minjokjuuineun Gyeolko Seon-geoguhoe Geuchil Su Eopda" [Abused nationalism: Nationalism can never remain only an election slogan]. *Sasanggye* (May): 101–7.

———. 1978. *Hanguk Minjokjuuiui Inyeomgwa Siltae* [Ideas and realities of Korean nationalism]. Seoul: Kkachi.

Chang, Chun-ha. 1956a. "Gwondueon: Minjujuuiui Jaehwagin" [Foreword: Reconfirming democracy]. *Sasanggye* (May): 12–13.

———. 1956b. "Gwondueon: Ttatteutan Jeongchireul Baranda" [Foreword: Hope for warm politics]. *Sasanggye* (June): 12–13.

———. 1958. "Gwondueon: Jasingwa Huimangeul Gatgehara" [Foreword: Let people have confidence and hope]. *Sasanggye* (May): 16–17.

———. 1961. "Gwondueon: 5·16hyeongmyeonggwa Minjogui Jillo" [Foreword: 5/16 revolution and the proper course for the nation]. *Sasanggye* (June): 34–35.

———. 1985. *Jangjunhamunjip: Je1gwon Minjokjuuijaui Gil* [The collected writings of Chang Chun-ha. Vol. 1, The way of the nationalist]. Seoul: Sasang.

Cheon, Gwan-u. 1976. "Hanguk Minjokjuuiui Yeoksajeok Gujo: Jaebalgyeon" [Reexamining the historical structure of Korean nationalism]. In Deok-gyu Jin 1976a, 75–102.

Cho, Gab-je. 1998. *Hyeongmyeong Jeonya* [On the eve of revolution]. Vol. 3 of *Nae Mudeome Chimeul Baeteora* [Spit on my grave]. Seoul: Chosunilbosa.

———. 1999. *Gimjongpirui Pungun* [Great vicissitudes of Kim Jong-pil]. Vol. 5 of *Nae Mudeome Chimeul Baeteora* [Spit on my grave]. Seoul: Chosunilbosa.

Cho, Geung-ho. 2006. *Isangjeok Inganhyeongnonui Dong-Seo Bigyo* [The comparison of the ideal man in the East and the West]. Seoul: Jisiksaneopsa.

Cho, Gwang. 1989. "Minjubyeonhyeok (CNP) Nonjaenge Daehayeo" [On the controversy over democratic revolution (CNP)]. In Hyeon-chae Park and Hui-yeon Cho 1989, 180–89.

Cho, Hui-yeon. 1989. "80nyeondae Sahoeundonggwa Sahoeguseongchenonjaeng" [The social movement and controversies over the social formation in the 1980s]. In Hyeon-chae Park and Hui-yeon Cho 1989, 11–36.

———. 1992. "80nyeondae Minjuhwaundonggwa Chejenonjaeng" [The democratization movement and the controversy over the character of the regimes in the 1980s]. In *Hyeondae Hangukchejenonjaengsa Yeongu* [A study of the history of controversies over contemporary Korean regimes], edited by Gwang-sik Kang, 217–58. Seongnam, KOR: Hangukjeongsinmunhwayeonguwon.

————, ed. 2003a. *Hangugui Jeongchisahoejeok Jibaedamnongwa Minjujuui Dong-hak* [The dominant political and social discourses in Korea and the dynamic of democracy]. Seoul: Hamkkeingneunchaek.

————. 2003b. "Jeongchisahoejeok Damnonui Gujobyeonhwawa Minjujuui Dong-hak: Hanguk Hyeondaesa Sogeseo Jibaedamnongwa Jeohangdamnonui Sang-hojagyongeul Jungsimeuro" [Structural change in political and social discourses and the dynamic of democracy: Focusing on interactions between dominant and opposing discourses]. In Hui-yeon Cho 2003a, 33–120.

————. 2004. *Bijeongsangseonge Daehan Jeohangeseo Jeongsangseonge Daehan Jeohangeuro* [From resistance to abnormality to resistance to normality]. Seoul: Arche.

Cho, Hyeon-yeon. 2003. "'Jayuminjujuui' Jibaedamnonui Yeoksajeok Gwejeokgwa Jibaehyogwa" [Historical trajectory of liberal democracy as dominant discourse and its ruling effect]. In Hui-yeon Cho 2003a, 293–361.

Choi, Hyeong-ik. 2008. "Ipeondokjaeron: Kal Syumiteuui Jugwonjeok Dokjaewa Hangugui Yusinheonbeop" [On the theory of constitutional dictatorship: Carl Schmitt's sovereign dictatorship and the Korean Yusin Constitution]. *Hangukjeongchiyeongu* 17 (1): 241–69.

Choi, Jae-hyuk. 2014. "'Seol Isan Sangbongi Cheot Danchu' . . . Buge Sonnaemilda" ["Meeting of Divided Families on Lunar New Year's Day Is the First Step" . . . Holding out Hand to Pyongyang]. *Chosun Ilbo*, January 7. http://news.chosun.com/site/data/html_dir/2014/01/07/2014010700180.html.

Choi, Jang-jip. 1996. *Hangungminjujuuiui Jogeongwa Jeonmang* [Conditions and prospects for Korean democracy]. Seoul: Nanamchulpan.

————. 2010. "Minju-Banminju Gudo Neomeo 'Salmeul Wihan Jeongchi'ro" ["Politics for everyday life" beyond the dichotomy of democracy vs. anti-democracy]. *Hankyoreh*, April 14. http://www.hani.co.kr/arti/society/society_general/416132.html.

Choi, Jang-jip, and Seong-hyeong Lee. 1991. "Hanguksahoeui Jeongchiideollogi" [Political ideologies of Korean society]. In Hanguksaneopsahoeyeonguhoe 1991, 211–25.

Chun, Doo-hwan. 1981. "Je12dae Daetongnyeong Chwiimsa" [The inaugural address of the twelfth president]. Daetongnyeonggirokgwan, Daetongnyeonggirogyeon-gusil [Research Center for Presidential Records, Presidential Archives of Korea]. March 3. http://www.pa.go.kr/research/contents/speech/index04_result.jsp.

Cumings, Bruce. 2007. "Minjokjuuiui Iyulbaeban" [The antinomy of nationalism]. In *Minjokjuui, Pyeonghwa, Jungyong* [Nationalism, peace, and the golden mean], edited by Sang-yong Choi, 63–92. Seoul: Kkachisa.

Daetongnyeongbiseosil [The Presidential Secretariat]. 1973. *Park Chung-hee Dae-tongnyeongyeonseolmunjip, Choegohoeuipyeon* [The collected speeches of President Park Chung-hee]. 4 vols. Seoul: Daetongnyeongbiseosil.

————. 1976. *Park Chung-hee Daetongnyeongyeonseolmunjip* [The collected speeches of President Park Chung-hee]. Vol. 5. Seoul: Daetongnyeongbiseosil.

————. 1979. *Park Chung-hee Daetongnyeongyeonseolmunjip* [The collected speeches of President Park Chung-hee]. Vol. 6, *jip* (booklet) 16. Seoul: Daetongnyeongbiseosil.

Gellner, Ernest. 1995. "Geundaehwawa Minjokjuui" [Modernization and nationalism]. In *Minjokjuuiran Mueosinga* [What is nationalism?], edited by Nak-cheong Paik, 127–65. Seoul: Changjakgwa Bipyeongsa. Originally published as "Nationalism," in *Thought and Change*, edited by Ernest Gellner, 147–78. London: Weidenfeld and Nicolson, 1964.

Gong, Je-uk, ed. 2008. *Gukgawa Ilsang: Park Chung-hee Sidae* [The state and daily life: The Park Chung-hee era]. Paju, KOR: Hanul.

Gongbocheo [Public Information Office]. 1953. *Daetongnyeong Rhee Syngman Baksadamhwajip* [The collected speeches of President and Dr. Rhee Syngman]. Seoul: Gongbocheo.

Ha, Sang-bok, and Su-ja Kim. 2009. "Minjokjuui" [Nationalism]. In Jung In Kang. 2009a, 202–58.

Ham, Seok-heon. 1984. *Hamseokeonjeonjip: Minjoktongirui Gil* [The complete works of Ham Seok-heon: The road to national unification]. Vol. 17. Seoul: Hangilsa.

Han, Bae-ho. 1994. *Hangukjeongchibyeondongnon* [Theory of Korean political change]. Seoul: Beommunsa.

Hanguksaneopsahoeyeonguhoe, ed. 1991. *Hanguksahoewa Jibaeideollogi* [Dominant ideologies in Korean society]. Seoul: Nokdu.

Hong, Seok-ryul. 2001. *Tongilmunjewa Jeongchi·Sahoejeok Galdeung, 1953–1961* [The unification problem and sociopolitical conflicts, 1953–1961]. Seoul: Seouldaehakgyochulpanbu.

———. 2002. "1960nyeondae Hanguk Minjokjuuiui Du Heureum" [Two currents of Korean nationalism in the 1960s]. *Sahoewayeoksa* 62: 169–203.

———. 2013. "Naengjeonjeok Yeoksa Seosulgwa Sangcheobadeun Jayujuui: Gyohaksa Hanguksa Gyogwaseo Hyeondaesa Seosul Bipan" [Cold War–centered historiography and injured liberalism: A critique of contemporary history in the Kyohaksa history textbook]. *Yeoksabipyeong* 105: 82–103.

Hong, Seong-tae. 2008. "Jumindeungnokjedowa Chongchejeok Gamsisahoeui Hyeongseong" [Residents' registration system and the formation of a surveillance society]. In Je-uk Gong 2008, 85–111.

Hong, Seung-jik. 1962. "Daehaksaengeun Mueoseul Saenggakago Inna? Gachigwanui Yebijosae Uigeohayeo" [What are university students thinking about? A study based on a preliminary survey of value orientations]. *Sasanggye* (April): 118–28.

Hong, Tai-young. 2010. "Feurangseu: Hyeongmyeonggwa Gonghwagugui Jeongchihak" [France: The revolution and the politics of the republic]. In Jung In Kang 2010, 129–210.

Hwang, Seong-mo. 1976. "Mnjokjuuiwa Gongsanjuui: Gongsanjuuieneun Mnjokgwani Eopda" [Nationalism and communism: The nationalist outlook is absent from communism]. In Deok-gyu Jin 1976a, 30–43.

Im, Hyeok-baek. 2012. "Park Chung-hee-e Daehan Jeongchihakjeok Pyeongga" [A political evaluation of Park Chung-hee]. *Pyeonghwayeongu* 20 (2): 51–84.

Jang, Young-min. 2008. "Guksagyoyugui Ganghwawa Gukgajuui" [The strengthening of Korean history education and the consequent statism]. In Je-uk Gong 2008, 399–469.

Jeon, Bok-hui. 1996. Sahoejinhwarongwa Gukgasasang [Social Darwinism and the idea of the state]. Seoul: Hanul.

Jeon, In-gwon. 2002. "Park Chung-hee Minjujuuigwan: Yeonseolmuneul Jungsimeuro" [Park Chung-hee's view of democracy: Focusing on his speeches]. *Hangukjeongchiyeongu* 11 (2): 139–55.

———. 2006. *Park Chung-hee Pyeongjeon* [A critical biography of Park Chunghee]. Seoul: Ihaksa.

Jeon, Jae-ho. 1997. "Park Chung-hee Chejeui Minjokjuui Yeongu: Damnongwa Jeongchaegeul Jungsimeuro" [A study of nationalism in the Park Chung-hee regime: Focusing on discourses and policies]. PhD diss., Sogang University.

———. 2000. *Bandongjeok Geundaejuuija Park Chung-hee* [The reactionary modernizer Park Chung-hee]. Seoul: Chaeksesang.

———. 2010. "Hanguk Geun·Hyeondaesa Yeoksagyogwaseoreul Dulleossan Yeoksainsik Galdeung Yeongu: Hanguk Minjokjuuiui 'Gyunyeol'eul Jungsimeuro" [A study of the conflict over historical understandings in textbooks of modern and contemporary Korean history: Focusing on cleavages in Korean nationalism]. *Hangukgwa Gukjejeongchi* 26 (3): 159–91.

———. 2012. "Minjuhwa Ihu Hanguk Minjokjuuiui Byeonhwa" [The change in Korean nationalism after democratization]. *Hyeondaejeongchiyeongu* 5 (1): 91–121.

Jeon, Sang-bong. 2010. "Hanguksahoeui Byeonhwawa 21segi Minjokjuui" [The change in Korean society and twenty-first century nationalism]. In Su-il Jeong 2010, 288–310.

Jeong, Hae-gu. 1998. "Park Chung-hee Sindeuromui Yangsanggwa Seonggyeok" [The complexion and nature of Park Chung-hee syndrome]. In *Park Chung-heereul Neomeoseo* [Beyond Park Chung-hee], edited by Hangukjeongchiyeonguhoe, 51–71. Seoul: Pureun Sup.

Jeong, Seung-hyeon. 2009. "Geupjinjuui" [Radicalism]. In Jung In Kang 2009a, 260–335.

Jeong, Su-il, ed. 2010a. *Jaesaengui Damnon: 21 Segi Minjokjuui* [Regenerative discourse: Twenty-first century nationalism]. Seoul: Tongillyuseu.

———. 2010b. "Minjokgwa Minjokjuui, Geu Jaesaengjeok Damnon" [Nation, nationalism and their regenerative discourses]. In Su-il Jeong 2010a, 14–82.

Jin, Deok-gyu, ed. 1976a. *Hangugui Minjokjuui* [Nationalism in Korea]. Seoul: Hyeondaesasangsa.

———. 1976b. "Minjokjuuiui Jeongaewa Hangye" [The development and limitation of nationalism]. In Deok-gyu Jin 1976a, 44–68.

———. 1992. "Hyeondae Hangukjeongchi Byeondonggwa Minjokjuuiui Byeonyonge Daehan Yeonguseoseol" [A research note on the change in contemporary Korean politics and the transformation of nationalism]. In *Hangungmunhwayeonguwon Nonchong* [The collected writings of the Academy of Korean Culture] 60 (2): 131–64. Seoul: Ewha Womans University Press.

Jinbojeongchiyeonguso. 2007. *Sahoe Gukga, Hanguk Sahoe Jaeseolgyedo* [The social state: A new design for Korean society]. Seoul: Humanitas.

Jo, So-ang. 1992. *Jo So-ang* [Jo So-ang], edited by Man-gil Kang. Seoul: Hangilsa.

Jungangilboteukbyeolchwijaetim. 1998. *(Sillok) Park Chung-hee: Han Gwoneuro Ingneun Je3gonghwaguk* [(True stories) Park Chung-hee: The Third Republic read through one book]. Seoul: Jungang M & B.

Kal, Bong-geun. 1976. *Yusinheonbeomnon* [A treatise on the Yusin Constitution]. Seoul: Hangukheonbeopakoechulpanbu.

Kang, Cheol. 1985. "Haebangseosi" [A prologue for liberation]. In Shindonga Pyeon-jipsil 1990, 127–34.

Kang, Jung In. 2004. *Seogujungsimjuuireul Neomeoseo* [Beyond the shadow of Western-centrism]. Seoul: Acanet.

———. 2007. "Edmund Burke: Geundae Bosujuuiui Wonjo" [Edmund Burke: The founder of modern conservatism]. In *Seoyang Geundae Jeongchisasangsa* [The history of modern Western political thought], edited by Jung In Kang, Yong-min Kim, and Tae-yeon Hwang, 474–506. Seoul: Chaeksesang.

———. 2008a. "Minjuhwa Ihu Hangukjeongchieseo Jayuminjujuuiwa Beopchijuuiui Chungdol" [The clash of liberal democracy and the rule of law in Korean politics after democratization]. *Seouldaehakgyo Beophak* 49 (3): 40–75.

———. 2008b. "Minjuhwa Ijeon Hanguk Jayujuuiui Inyeomjeok Teukseonggwa Balhyeonyangsange Daehan Gochal" [A consideration of Korean liberalism before democratization: Focusing on its ideational attributes and configuration]. *Asean Yeongu* 51 (4): 115–47.

———, ed. 2009a. *Hangukjeongchiui Inyeomgwa Sasang* [Political ideas and ideologies in Korean politics]. Seoul: Humanitas.

———. 2009b. "Bosujuui" [Conservatism]. In Jung In Kang 2009a, 36–119.

———, ed. 2010. *Yureop Minjuhwaui Inyeomgwa Yeoksa* [The ideas and history of democratization in Europe]. Seoul: Humanitas.

———. 2011. "Park Chung-hee Daetongnyeongui Minjujuui Damnon Bunseok: 'Haengjeongjeok'·'Minjokjeok'·'Hangukjeok' Minjujuuireul Jungsimeuro" [An analysis of Park Chung-hee's discourses on democracy: Focusing on "administrative," "national," "Korean-style" democracy]. *Cheolhangnonjip* 28: 287–321.

Kang, Jung In, and Hui-kyeong Seo. 2013. "Gimseongsuwa Hangungminjudang Yeongu: Hanguk Bosujuui Jeongchiinyeomui Giwongwa Yeonsokseongeul jung-simeuro" [A study of Kim Seong-su and the Korea Democratic Party: Focusing on the origin and continuity of contemporary Korean conservatism]. *Hangukjeongchi-hakoebo* 47 (1): 103–26.

Kang, Jun-man. 1999. "Park Chung-hee Sindeuromeul Haebuhanda" [Anatomizing Park Chung-hee syndrome]. *Inmulgwa Sasang* 10 (February): 28–43.

———. 2002. *Hanguk Hyeondaesa Sanchaek: 1970nyeondaepyeon* [A stroll through contemporary Korean history: The 1970s]. Vol. 2 of 3. Seoul: Inmulgwa Sasangsa.

———. 2004a. *Hanguk Hyeondaesa Sanchaek: 1960nyeondaepyeon* [A stroll through contemporary Korean history: The 1960s]. Vol. 2 of 3. Seoul: Inmulgwa Sasangsa.

———. 2004b. *Hanguk Hyeondaesa Sanchaek: 1960nyeondaepyeon* [A stroll through contemporary Korean history: The 1960s]. Vol. 3 of 3. Seoul: Inmulgwa Sasangsa.

————. 2013. *Kapgwa Eurui Nara* [The country of the dominant and the dominated]. Seoul: Inmulgwa Sasangsa.

Kang, Man-gil. 1978. *Bundansidaeui Yeoksainsik* [The proper historical perspective in the era of division]. Seoul: Changjakgwa Bipyeongsa.

————, ed. 1985a. *Haebang Jeonhusaui Insik* [Understanding history before and after the liberation]. Vol. 2. Seoul: Hangilsa.

————. 1985b. "Haebangjeonhusa Insigui Banghyang" [The proper direction for understanding history before and after the liberation]. In Man-gil Kang. 1985a, 9–15.

————. 1987. "Hanguk Minjokjuuironui Ihae" [Understanding theories of Korean nationalism]. In *Hangugui Minjokjuuiundonggwa Minjung* [The nationalist movement and the people in Korea], edited by Young-hui Lee and Man-gil Kang, 17–32. Seoul: Dure.

Kim, Bo-hyeon. 2003. "Sasanggye-ui Gyeongjegaeballon, Park Chung-hee Jeong gwongwa Eolmana Dallanna? Gaebaljuuie Jeohanghan Gaebaljuui" [How different was *Sasanggye*'s theory of economic development from that of the Park Chung-hee regime? Developmentalism resisting developmentalism]. *Jeongchibipyeong* 10: 345–80.

————. 2006. *Park Chung-hee Jeonggwongi Gyeongjegaebal: Minjokjuuiwa Baljeon* [Economic development in the Park Chung-hee regime: Nationalism and development]. Seoul: Galmuri.

Kim, Chi-gwan. 2010. "Nyuraiteuui Minjokgwan Bipan" [A critique of the New Right's view of the nation]. In Su-il Jeong 2010a, 233–62.

Kim, Dong-chun. 1994. "1960·70nyeondae Minjuhwaundongseryeogui Daehangide-ollogi" [Counterideologies of democratization movement forces in the 1960s and 1970s]. In *Hangukjeongchiui Jibaeideollogiwa Daehangideollogi* [Dominant and resistant ideologies of Korean politics], edited by Yeoksamunjeyeonguso, 209–49. Seoul: Yeoksabipyeongsa.

————. 1996a. "Sasangui Jeongaereul Tonghae Bon Hangugui Geundae Moseup" [Complexion of Korean modernity seen in light of the evolution of political ideas]. In Yeoksamunjeyeonguso 1996, 273–309.

————. 1996b. "1980nyeondae Hangugui Minjokjuui: Godosaneopwa Sidaeui Ttae-neujeun Minjokjuui" [Korean nationalism in the 1980s: Delayed nationalism in the high industrial age]. *Geunhyeondaesagangjwa* [Lectures on modern and contemporary history] 8: 159–84.

————. 1997a. "1980nyeondae Minjubyeonhyeogundongui Seongjanggwa Geu Seonggyeok" [The rise and characteristics of the democratic-revolutionary movement in the 1980s]. In *6wolminjuhangjaenggwa Hanguksahoe 10nyeon* [Korean society ten years after the June struggle for democracy], edited by Haksuldanche-hyeobuihoe, 65–103. Seoul: Dangdae.

————. 1997b. "80nyeondae Huban Ihu Hanguk Makseujuui Ironui Seonggyeok Byeonhwawa Hanguk Sahoegwahak" [The change in Korean Marxist theory and Korean social sciences since the late 1980s]. In *Hanguk Sahoegwahagui Saeroun Mosaek* [A new search for Korean social science], edited by Dong-chun Kim, 296–313. Seoul: Changjakgwa Bipyeongsa.

————. 2000. *Geundaeui Geuneul: Hangugui Geundaeseonggwa Minjokjuui* [The shadow of modernity: Korean modernity and nationalism]. Seoul: Dangdae.

————. 2006a. *(1997nyeon Ihu) Hanguksahoeui Seongchal: Gieopsahoeroui Byeon-hwangwa Gwaje* [A reflection on Korean society (since 1997): Tasks to counter with the transformation into a corporate society]. Seoul: Gil.

————. 2006b. *Jeonjaenggwa Sahoe* [War and society]. Seoul: Dolbegae.

Kim, Dong-taek. 1992. "Hanguksahoewa Minjubyeonhyeongnon: 1950nyeondaeeseo 1980nyeondaekkaji" [Theories of democratic-revolutionary change in Korean society: From the 1950s to the 1980s]. In *Hyeondaeminjujuuiron* [Theories of contemporary democracy], vol. 2, edited by Hangukjeongchiyeonguhoe Sasangbungwa, 477–503. Seoul: Changjakgwa Bipyeongsa.

Kim, Gu. 1973. *Baekbeomeorok* [Quotations from Baekbeom]. Seoul: Sasangsa.

————. 1997. *Baekbeomilji* [Baekbeom's journal]. Seoul: Hangminsa.

Kim, Hye-su. 1995. "Jeongbusurip Jikhu Iseungman Jeonggwonui Tongchiinyeom Jeongnipgwajeong" [The process of establishing ruling ideology in the Rhee Syngman regime immediately after the foundation of the Republic of Korea]. *Idaesawon* 28: 317–52.

Kim, Il-young. 2006a. "Hangukjeongchiui Saeroun Inyeomjeok Jwapyoreul Chajaseo: 'Nyurait'wa 'Nyurept' Geurigo Gongtongdoen Jipyeongeuroseoui Jayujuui" [A search for a new ideological direction for Korean politics: Liberalism as the common horizon for "New Right" and "New Left"]. *Hangukjeongchioegyosanonchong* 27 (2): 373–401.

————. 2006b. "Park Chung-hee Sidaewa Minjokjuuiui Ne Eolgul" [Four faces of nationalism in the Park Chung-hee era]. *Hangukjeongchioegyosanonchong* 28 (1): 223–56.

————. 2008. "Chotbulsiwiui Heemanggwa Buran" [The hope and anxiety of candlelight protests]. *Cheolhakgwa Hyeonsil* 79: 46–56.

Kim, Jeong-hun. 2000. "Bundanchejewa Minjokjuui: Nambukan Jibaedamnonui Minjokjuuiui Yeoksajeok Jeongaewa Dongjirihyeongseong" [The division system and nationalism: The historical evolution of nationalism as two Koreas' dominant discourses and their allotropism]. *Donghyanggwa Jeonmang* 44 (Spring): 166–91.

————. 2004. "Jinagan Geoseun Jinagan Geosida" [What is gone is gone]. *Hankyoreh*, December 8. http://legacy.www.hani.co.kr/section-001038000/2004/12/001038000200412081826155.html.

Kim, Jeong-hun, and Hui-yeon Cho. 2003. "Jibaedamnoneuroseoui Bangongjuuiwa Geu Byeonhwa" [Anticommunism as dominant discourse and its change]. In Hui-yeon Cho 2003a, 123–99.

Kim, Kap-sik. 2007. "Park Chung-hee Sidae Yeongugyeonghyanggwa Jaejomyeong" [Reexamining the Park Chung-hee era with a critical review of research trends]. *Hangukjeongchiyeongu* 16 (1): 81–110.

Kim, Nam-sik. 1985. "Bakeonyeonggwa 8wolteje" [Park Heon-young and the August thesis]. In Man-gil Kang 1985a, 104–42.

Kim, Sam-ung. 1984. *Minjok·Minju·Minjung Seoneon* [Manifestos for nation, democracy, and people]. Seoul: Irwolseogak.

————. 1994. *Tongillon Sunansa* [The history of indictment for advocacies on unification discourse]. Seoul: Hankyoreh Shinmun.

————. 1997. *Saryoro Boneun 20segi Hanguksa* [Twentieth-century Korean history seen through historical materials]. Seoul: Garamgihoek.

Kim, Su-ja. 2005. "Hyeondae Hanguk Minjokjuuiui Jeongae Yangsang: Woldeuk eopgwa 'Yeollinminjokjuui'ui Ganeungseongeul Jungsimeuro" [The evolution of nationalism in contemporary Korea: Focusing on prospects of "open nationalism" by way of the World Cup game]. *Hangukdongyangjeongchisasangsayeongu* 4 (2): 231–46.

Kim, Young-hwan. 1999. "Jaeballon—Minjokjuuiwa Uri Eoneoui Mirae" [Surrebuttal—Nationalism and the future of our language]. *Sidaejeongsin* 3. http://www.zeitgeist.co.kr/2005html/sub/popup/303.htm.

————. 2005. "Tonggwon 30ho Ginyeom Inteobyu-Minjokjuuiwa Pyeonggyunjuuireul Neomeo Segyero Naagaja" [An interview on the celebration of serial number 30: Let's move into a world beyond nationalism and leveling egalitarianism]. *Sidaejeongsin* 30. http://www.zeitgeist.co.kr/2005html/sub/popup/30/3001.htm.

Kim, Young-sam. 1993. "Je14dae Daetongnyeong Chwiimsa" [Inaugural address of the fourteenth president]. Daetongnyeonggirokgwan, Daetongnyeonggirogyeongusil [Research Center for Presidential Records, Presidential Archives of Korea]. February 25. http://www.pa.go.kr/research/contents/speech/index04_result.jsp.

Kim, Young-su. 2001. "Park Chung-hee-ui Jeongchirideosip" [Political leadership of Park Chung-hee]. In *Changmyon·Yunposun·Park Chung-hee: 1960nyeondae Cho Juyo Jeongchijidoja Yeongu* [Chang Myon, Yun Posun, and Park Chung-hee: A study of major political leaders in the early 1960s], edited by Hangukjeongsinmunhwayeonguwon, 165–281. Seoul: Baeksanseodang.

Koh, Jeong-hun. 1966. "Okjungdansang" [Fragmented Thoughts in the Prison]. In *Myeonginokjunggi* [Memories of famous figures regarding their imprisonment], edited by Jeong-hun Koh et al., 34–36. Seoul: Heemangchulpansa.

Koh, Jong-seok. 2005. "Daetongnyeong Danimjeneun Olta" [The single-term system for the presidency is correct]. *Hangugilbo*, February 16. http://news.naver.com/main/read.nhn?mode=LSD&mid=sec&sid1=110&oid=038&aid=0000269840.

Koh, Won. 2008. "Saemaeurundongui Nongmindongwongwa 'Gungmin Mandeulgi'" [Peasant mobilization by the Saemaeul Movement and "making Gungmin"]. In Je-uk Gong 2008, 27–54.

Kwon, Hyeok-beom. 2009. *Minjokjuuineun Joeaginga* [Is nationalism a sin?]. Seoul: Saenggagui Namu.

Kyungnamdaehakkyo Geukdongmunjeyeonguso, ed. 2004. *Namnamgaldeung: Jindan Mit Haesobangan* [South-South conflicts: Diagnosis and solution]. Seoul: Kyungnamdaehakkyo Geukdongmunjeyeonguso.

Lee, Chang-ryeol. 1963. "Gyeongjeanjeonggwa Seongjangeul Wihayeo: Gyeongjeseongjangeun Anjeongdoen Gibanwieseo" [For economic stability and growth: Economic growth should be based on stability]. *Sasanggye* 11 (8): 108–13.

Lee, Geuk-chan. 1976. "Sinsaengguk Minjokjuuiui Ilbannon" [General theory of nationalism in newly independent states]. In Deok-gyu Jin 1976a, 13–29.

Lee, Geun-sik. 2001. "Jayujuuiwa Hanguksahoe" [Liberalism and Korean society]. In *Jayujuuiran Mueosinga* [What is liberalism?], edited by Geun-sik Lee and Gyeong-sik Hwang, 13–75. Seoul: Samseonggyeongjeyeonguso.

Lee, Hae-young. 2004. "Kal Syumiteuui Jeongchisasang: 'Jeongchijeogin Geot'ui Gaenyeomeul Jungsimeuro" [Political thought of Carl Schmitt: Focusing on the concept of the "political"]. *21segi Jeongchihakoebo* 14 (2): 1–25.

Lee, Hong-gu. 1976. "Hanguk Minjokjuuiui Bonjilgwa Banghyang" [The nature and direction of Korean nationalism]. In Deok-gyu Jin 1976a, 171–86.

Lee, Hwa-yong. 2010. "Yeongguk: Minjujuuiui Sinhwawa Yeoksa (1832–1928nyeon)" [England: The myth and the real history of democracy, 1832–1928]. In Jung In Kang 2010, 53–128.

Lee, In-hwa. 1997. *Inganui Gil* [The human way]. 3 vols. Seoul: Sallim.

Lee, Jae-hwa. 1990. "NL-PD Nonjaeng" [Controversy over National Liberation vs. People's Democracy]. In *80nyeondae Hanguksahoe Daenonjaengjip* [Great debates on Korean society in the 1980s], edited by Wolganjungang, 253–57. Seoul: Jungangilbosa.

Lee, Jun-gu. 2013. "Imyeongbak Jeongbuui Gyeongjejeongchaek: '747gongyak'e Balmogi Japyeo Bonaen 5nyeon" [Economic policy of the Lee Myeong-bak administration: Five years trapped in the "7-4-7 election pledge"]. *Hangukgyeongjeporeom* 5 (4): 59–75.

Lee, Jun-sik. 2013. "Hanguk Yeoksa Gyogwaseoinga, Animyeon Ilbon Yeoksa Gyogwaseoinga? Gyohaksa Hanguksa Gyogwaseo Iljegangjeomgi Seosul Bipan" [Korean history textbook or Japanese history textbook? Critique of the description of Japanese colonial rule in Kyohaksa's history textbook]. *Yeoksabipyeong* 105: 54–81.

Lee, Kwang-il. 1997. "'Park Chung-hee Chejeron' Bipan" [Critique of discourses on the Park Chung-hee regime]. *Jeongchibipyeong* 3: 121–40.

———. 1998. "Park Chung-hee Jeonggwone Gwanhan Yeonguhyeonhwanggwa Gwaje" [The current status of research on the Park Chung-hee regime and future tasks]. *Yeoksawa Hyeonsil* 29: 275–96.

———. 2003. "Seongjang·Baljeonjuui Jibaedamnonui Sinhwawa Dillema" [The myth and dilemma of growth-developmentalism as dominant discourses]. In Hui-yeon Cho 2003a, 201–36.

Lee, Kyeong-nam. 1981. *Seolsan Changdeoksoo* [Seolsan Chang Deok-Soo]. Seoul: Dongailbo.

Lee, Myung-bak. 2009. "Je64junyeon Gwangbokjeol Gyeongchuksa" [Congratulatory speech on the 64th anniversary of Liberation Day]. Daetongnyeonggirokgwan, Daetongnyeonggirogyeongusil [Research Center for Presidential Records, Presidential Archives of Korea]. August 15. http://www.pa.go.kr/research/contents/speech/index04_result.jsp.

Lee, Seon-min. 2008. *Minjokjuui, Ijeneun Beoryeoya Hana* [Is now the time to abandon nationalism?]. Seoul: Samseonggyeongjeyeonguso.

Lee, Young-hun. 2007. *Daehanminguk Iyagi* [A story of the Republic of Korea]. Seoul: Giparang.

Lew, Seok-jin, Hui-jeong Cho, and Seol-a Park. 2013. "Ollain Sinminjokjuuiui Jeongchihwa Ganeungseong: Hanjungil Ollain Galdeung Yuhyeonggwa Hwaksan Saryeoeul Jungsimeuro" [On the possible politicization of "online neonationalism": Focusing on types and diffusion of online conflicts among Korea, China, and Japan]. *Hangukjeongchiyeongu* 22 (3): 153–86.

Lim, Ji-hyeon. 1994. "Minjokjuui" [Nationalism]. In *Seoyangui Jijeok Undong* [Intellectual movement in the West], edited by Young-han Kim and Ji-hyeon Lim, 537–66. Seoul: Jisiksaneopsa.

———. 1999. *Minjokjuuineun Banyeogida: Sinhwawa Heomuui Minjokjuui Damnoneul Neomeoseo* [Nationalism is treason: Beyond the myth and emptiness of nationalist discourses]. Seoul: Sonamu.

Lim, Young-il. 1991. "Hanguksahoeui Jibaeideollogi" [The dominant ideologies of Korean society]. In Hanguksaneopsahoeyeonguhoe 1991, 67–87.

Ma, Sang-yun. 2003. "Anbowa Minjujuui, Geurigo Park Chung-hee-ui Gil: Yusincheje Suribwonin Jaego" [Security, democracy, and Park Chung-hee's road: The origin of the Yusin system revisited]. *Gukjejeongchinonchong* 43 (4): 171–95.

Maruyama, Masao. 1997. *Hyeondaejeongchiui Sasanggwa Haengdong* [Thought and behavior in contemporary Japanese politics]. Translated by Seok-geun Kim. Seoul: Hangilsa.

———. 1998. *Ilbonui Sasang* [Political thoughts in Japan]. Translated by Seok-geun Kim. Seoul: Hangilsa.

Minjuhwaui Gil. 1989. "80nyeondae Hanguksahoewa Minjokminjuundongui Jeongae" [The development of a national-democratic movement in Korean society of the 1980s]. In Hyeon-chae Park and Hui-yeon Cho 1989, 41–114.

Moon, Ik-hwan. 1985. "Ganhaengsa" [Foreword]. In Chun-ha Chang 1985, 3–4.

Moon, Ji-young. 2009. "Jayujuui" [Liberalism]. In Jung In Kang 2009a, 122–99.

Paik, Nak-cheong. 1994. *Bundancheje Byeonhyeogui Gongbugil* [The road to learn how to transform the division system]. Seoul: Changjakgwa Bipyeongsa.

Park, Chan-pyo. 2007a. *Hangugui Gukga Hyeongseonggwa Minjujuui* [State building and democracy in Korea]. Seoul: Humanitas.

———. 2007b. "Beopchi Minjujuui Dae Jeongchijeok Minjujuui" [Democracy by rule of law vs. political democracy]. In *Eotteon Minjujuuiinga* [What kind of democracy?], edited by Jang-jip Choi, Chan-pyo Park, and Sang-hun Park, 197–229. Seoul: Humanitas.

Park, Chan-seung. 2010. *Minjok·Minjokjuui* [Nation and nationalism]. Seoul: Sohwa.

Park, Chung-hee. 1962. *Uri Minjogui Nagal Gil* [The path for our nation to take]. 5th ed. Seoul: Dongachulpansa.

———. 1963. *Gukgawa Hyeongmyeonggwa Na* [The state, the revolution, and I]. Seoul: Hyangmunsa.

Park, Dong-cheon. 2008. "Minjogui Silcheseonge Gwanhan Cheolhakjeok Geomto" [A philosophical investigation into the true nature of nation]. *Hangukjeongchihakoebo* 42 (3): 29–49.

Park, Ho-seong. 1997. *Nambukan Minjokjuui Bigyoyeongu: "Hanbando Minjokjuui" reul Wihayeo* [The comparative study of two Koreas' nationalism: For the "nationalism of the Korean Peninsula"]. Seoul: Dangdae.

Park, Hyeon-chae, and Hui-yeon Cho, eds. 1989. *Hanguksahoeguseongchenonjaeng* [Great controversies over the social formation of Korea]. Vol. 1. Seoul: Juksan.

Park, Hyeon-mo. 2007. "Park Chung-heeui 'Minjugonghwajuuigwan Byeonhwa Yeongu: Park Chung-hee Daetongnyeongyeonseolmunjip-eul Jungsimeuro"

[A study of the change in Park Chung-hee's view of "democratic republicanism": Focusing on the analysis of the collected speeches of President Park Chung-hee]. *Hangukdongyangjeongchisasangsa* 6 (2): 71–93.

Park, Il-gyeong. 1972. *Yusinheonbeop* [The Yusin Constitution]. Seoul: Bagyeongsa.

Park, Ji-hyang. 2006. "Meorimal" [Preface]. In *Haebang Jeonhusaui Jaeinsik* [A new understanding of history before and after the liberation], vol. 1, edited by Ji-hyang Park, Cheol Kim, Il-young Kim, and Young-hun Lee, 11–21. Seoul: Chaeksesang.

Park, Myeong-lim. 1996a. "Geundaehwa Peurojekteuwa Hangungminjokjuui" [The modernization project and Korean nationalism]. In Yeoksamunjeyeonguso 1996, 311–48.

———. 1996b. "Bundansidae Hanguk Minjokjuuiui Ihae" [Understanding Korean nationalism in the division era]. *Segyeui Munhak* (Summer): 48–75.

———. 2006. "Hanguk Hyeondaesawa Park Chung-hee·Park Chung-hee Sidae: Tongchicheolhakgwa Sasang, Gukgajeollyak, Geurigo Minjujuui Munje" [Park Chung-hee and the Park Chung-hee era in contemporary Korean history: Governing philosophy and ideas, national strategy, and the problem of democracy]. In *Park Chung-hee Sidaewa Hanguk Hyeondaesa* [The Park Chung-hee era and contemporary Korean history], edited by Jeong Seong-hwa, 31–79. Seoul: Seonin.

Rhee, Syngman. 1948. "Cheongnyeondeureun Gwolgihayeo Banyeokbunja Tadohara" [Stand up, young people, and overthrow national traitors]. Daetongnyeonggirokgwan, Daetongnyeonggirogyeongusil [Research Center for Presidential Records, Presidential Archives of Korea]. November 29. http://www.pa.go.kr/research/contents/speech/index04_result.jsp.

———. 1954. "Haeoechuljeong Jaehyanggunindeure Daehan Yeonseol" [Speech to soldiers dispatched abroad]. Daetongnyeonggirokgwan, Daetongnyeonggirogyeongusil [Research Center for Presidential Records, Presidential Archives of Korea]. August 1. http://www.pa.go.kr/research/contents/speech/index04_result.jsp.

———. 1955. "'Migunui Nal'eul Gyeongchukam" [Celebrating the Day of US Soldiers]. Daetongnyeonggirokgwan, Daetongnyeonggirogyeongusil [Research Center for Presidential Records, Presidential Archives of Korea]. May 21. http://www.pa.go.kr/research/contents/speech/index04_result.jsp.

Schmitt, Carl. 1996. *Dokjaeron* [The dictatorship]. Translated by Kim Hyo-jeon. Seoul: Beobwonsa. Originally published in 1920. Korean version translated from Carl Schmitt, *Die Dictatur*, 6th ed. (Berlin: Duncker and Humblot, 1994).

Segyeilbo [The World Daily]. 2011. "Yeokdae Daetongnyeong Lideosip: Park Chung-hee, Roh Moo-hyun Sun" [Leadership of past presidents: Park Chung-hee and Roh Moo-hyun top the list]. June 23. http://www.segye.com/content/html/2011/06/22/20110622005080.html.

Seo, Hui-kyeong. 2005. "Hangukjeheongukoeui Jeongchiseryeok Hyeongseonge Gwanhan Yeongu: Ilje Singminji Sigiui Sahoeseryeokgwaui yeongwanseongeul jungsimeuro" [A study of the formation of political forces in the Korean Constitutional Assembly: Focusing on their interrelationship with social forces in the Japanese colonial period]. *Hangukjeongchioegyosanonchong* 26 (1): 351–88.

———. 2012. *Daehanminguk Heonbeobui Tansaeng: Hanguk Heonjeongsa, Manmingongdonghoeeseo Jeheonkkaji* [The birth of the constitution in the Republic of

Korea: The constitutional history of Korea from the All People's Assembly in the late Joseon to the making of the constitution]. Paju, KOR: Changbi.

Seo, Jung-seok. 1983. "Iseungman Daetongnyeonggwa Hanguk Minjokjuui" [President Rhee Syngman and Korean nationalism]. In *Hangungminjokjuuiron 2* [Discourses on Korean nationalism 2], edited by Geon-ho Song and Man-gil Kang, 222–71. Seoul: Changjakgwa Bipyeongsa.

———. 1991. *Hangukyeondaeminjogundongyeongu* [A study of the contemporary Korean nationalist movement]. Vol. 1. Seoul: Yeoksabipyeongsa.

———. 1992. "Chobongam·Jibodangui Jinboseonggwa Jeongchijeok Giban" [Progressivism and the political base of Cho Bong-am and the Progressive Party]. *Yeoksabipyeong* 20: 16–32.

———. 1995a. "Hangukjeonjaeng Hu Tongilsasangui Jeongaewa Minjokgongdongcheui Mosaek" [The development of unification thought and the search for national community after the Korean War]. In *Bundan 50nyeongwa Tongilsidaeui Gwaje* [The fifty years after division and the task for the unification era], edited by Yeoksamunjeyeonguso, 309–62. Seoul: Yeoksabipyeongsa.

———. 1995b. "Hangugeseoui Minjongmunjewa Gukga: Bureujuacheung Ttoneun Jibaecheungeul Jungsimeuro" [The national problem and the state in Korea: Focusing on the bourgeoisie or the ruling class]. In *Geundae Gungmingukgawa Minjongmunje* [Modern nation-state and the national problem], edited by Hanguksayeonguhoe, 111–50. Seoul: Jisiksaneopsa.

———. 1996. *Hangukyeondaeminjogundongyeongu* [A study of the contemporary Korean nationalist movement]. Vol. 2. Seoul: Yeoksabipyeongsa.

———. 2002. *Bigeugui Hyeondaejidoja: Geudeureun Minjokjuuijainga Banminjokjuuijainga* [Tragic contemporary leaders: Are they nationalist or antinationalist?]. Seoul: Sungkyunkwandaehakgyo Chulpanbu.

———. 2004. *Baebandanghan Hangungminjokjuui* [Korean nationalism betrayed]. Seoul: Sungkyunkwandaehakgyo Chulpanbu.

———. 2005. *Iseungmanui Jeongchiideollogi* [political ideologies of Rhee Syngman]. Seoul: Yeoksabipyeongsa.

———. 2009. *Jobongamgwa 1950nyeondae (sang): Jobongamui Sahoeminjujuuiwa Pyeonghwatongillon* [Cho Bong-am and the 1950s: Social democracy and the peaceful unification doctrine of Cho Bong-am]. Vol. 1. Seoul: Yeoksabipyeongsa,.

Seo, Sang-il. 1957. "Heomnanhalmangjeong Yeonggwangseureon Meon Gil" [Long road, rugged but glorious]. In *Naega Georeoon Gil, Naega Georeogal Gil* [The road I have followed and the road I will follow], edited by Sintaeyangsa, 47–58. Seoul: Sintaeyangsa.

Shim, Ji-yeon. 1982. *Hangugminjudangyeongu* [A study of the Korea Democratic Party]. Vol. 1. Seoul: Pulbit.

Shin, Gi-Wook. 2009. *Hanguk Minjokjuuiui Gyebowa Jeongchi* [The lineage and politics of Korean nationalism]. Translated by Lee Jin-jun. Seoul: Changbi.

Shindonga Pyeonjipsil [Shindonga Editorial Board], ed. 1990. *Seoneoneuro Bon 80nyeondae Minjok·Minjuundong* [National democratic movements in the 1980s seen through manifestos]. Seoul: Shindonga.

Song, Geon-ho, ed. 1979. *Haebang Jeonhusaui Insik* [Understanding history before and after the liberation]. Seoul: Hangilsa.

Song, Geon-ho. 1986. *Minjoktongireul Wihayeo* [For national unification]. Seoul: Hangilsa.

Sonn, Ho-cheol. 2011. *Hyeondae Hangukjeongchi: Iron, Yeoksa, Hyeonsil, 1945–2011* [Contemporary Korean politics: Theory, history, and reality, 1945–2011]. Seoul: Imaejin.

Yang, Ho-min. 1961. "Minjujuuiwa Judoseryeok" [Democracy and its leading forces]. *Sasanggye* (November): 45–53.

———. 1976. "Hanguk Minjokjuuiui Hoegowa Jeonmang" [Retrospect and prospects for Korean nationalism]. In Deok-gyu Jin 1976a, 250–68.

Yeo, Hyeon-deok. 1987. "8·15 Jikhu Minjujuui Nonjaeng" [Controversy over democracy after 8/15]. In *Haebang Jeonhusaui Insik* [Understanding history before and after the liberation], vol. 3, edited by Hyeon-chae Park, 23–75. Seoul: Hangilsa.

Yeoksamunjeyeonguso, ed. 1996. *Hangugui Geundaewa Geundaeseong Bipan* [A critique of modern times and modernity in Korea]. Seoul: Yeoksamunjeyeonguso.

Yeon, Jeong-eun. 2003. "Anhosangui Ilminjuuiwa Jeongchi·Gyoyukwaldong" [Ahn Ho-sang's doctrine of the unitary nation and his political and educational activities]. *Yeoksayeongu* 12: 7–38.

Yun, Seok-in. 1989. "1986nyeon Sangbangi Haksaengundong Naebunonjaeng Gaegwan: Jamintu·Minmintuui Deungjanggwa Geu Non-ri" [An overview of internal debates within the student movement in the first half of 1986: The emergence of Jamintu and Minmintu and their arguments]. In Hyeon-chae Park and Hui-yeon Cho 1989, 338–52.

Index

absolute monarchy, 150, 172
absolutism, 47, 77, 150
American boundary line, 115–16
American (US) imperialism/imperialist, 17, 22, 55, 69, 70, 74, 75, 94, 212
anti-Americanism, 21, 85; anti-American (anti-US), 17, 20, 38, 74, 101n26, 104–5n46; anti-American (anti-US) consciousness/sentiment(s), 71–73, 94, 102n29, 102n31. *See also* anti-imperial(ism)
anticommunism, xxi, xxv, 5, 7–17, 21, 23, 26, 29, 32n5, 33n13, 34n18, 42, 50, 53–55, 64, 66–68, 70, 77–78, 83–85, 87–88, 91, 94, 97–98, 101n15, 102n36, 105n53, 112–15, 118, 134n8, 137, 140–45, 147, 150–51, 156n3, 157nn15–16, 161–63, 176–78, 182–83, 194, 199, 202, 209, 216, 217–21, 225n18, 225n20; anticommunism for the sake of anticommunism (for its own sake), xxi, 53, 151; anticommunism supremacy, 87; liberal anticommunism, 53; as state doctrine, 13, 67, 86, 101n25, 107n60, 116, 118, 140, 209, 221
anticommunist liberalism, 53–54, 77–78, 102n35; nationalism, 67–68,

92, 101n19, 104n45, 105n46, 177, 209
antiliberal (illiberal), 13, 80, 103, 137, 149, 155, 158n27, 217, 219, 222, 226; conservatism 137, 140, 155, 156n1, 216, 218–19
antination (nonnation), 67–69, 87–88, 94, 105n48, 166, 176–78, 186n20, 212; antinational(ism) 8–9, 13–14, 17, 20, 22, 33n12, 56, 60n25, 63, 67–68, 72, 78, 83, 86–87, 90, 92, 94–98, 105n48, 107n63, 141, 161, 166, 170, 177, 179, 182–83, 187nn24–25, 188n33, 206, 221
anti-US. *See* anti-American
April (Student) Revolution, 5, 9, 11, 15, 72, 86, 96, 159n37, 179, 217
authenticity controversy, 36, 52–56, 99n9
authoritarian conservatism (conservatives), 17, 21, 24, 26, 76, 104, 112
authoritarian government/regime/rule, xviii, xxii–xxv, 3–5, 7–8, 17, 24, 26, 30, 42–44, 50, 60, 83–84, 88, 105, 111–12, 115–17, 142, 145, 147, 216
authoritarianism, xiii, xxv, 7, 34n18, 35, 50, 133n1, 143, 157n19, 176, 198, 215, 217–18, 222; dressed up as democracy, 111, 112–17, 122, 126

About the Author

Jung In Kang is professor of political theory in the Department of Political Science at Sogang University. He has published numerous books and articles both in Korean and in English. His recent publications in English include *Western-Centrism and Contemporary Korean Political Thought* (Lexington, 2015) and "Reexamining Political Participation in Rousseau's Political Thought: Does Citizens' Political Participation Include Public Discussions and Debates?" *Interpretation* 39, no. 2 (Spring/Summer 2012). He is also editor of *Contemporary Korean Political Thought in Search of a Post-Eurocentric Approach* (Lexington, 2014). He was the Korean National Research Foundation's first nominee for the distinguished scholarship grants in political science, from 2009 to 2014.